An Assumption of Sovereignty

HARRY A. KERSEY JR.

An Assumption
of
Sovereignty

Social and Political
Transformation among the
Florida Seminoles,

1953–1979

UNIVERSITY OF NEBRASKA PRESS

LINCOLN & LONDON

Library of Congress Cataloging-in-Publication Data
Kersey, Harry A., 1935–
An assumption of sovereignty : social and political
transformation among the
Florida Seminoles, 1953–1979 / Harry A. Kersey Jr.
p. cm. – (Indians of the Southeast)
Includes bibliographical references and index.
ISBN 0-8032-2728-0 (cloth : alk. paper)
ISBN 978-0-8032-2249-6 (paper : alk. paper)
1. Seminole Indians – Politics and government.
2. Seminole Indians – Government
relations. 3. Seminole Indians – Land tenure.
I. Title   II. Series
E99.S28K46   1996   323.1'1973–DC20
95-36382   CIP

This book is dedicated to

my keepers of the matrilineage

Ruth, Karen, and Laura

CONTENTS

Series Editors' Foreword

In this contribution to the series Indians of the Southeast, Harry Kersey addresses two of the most important political issues for Native people, sovereignty and polity. For a people to assert sovereignty, much less exercise it, a polity must lay claim to that prerogative. In many ways, the Seminoles had sovereignty before they developed a polity to pursue the kinds of rights and privileges that sovereignty implies.

In the 1950s, the Seminoles moved beyond the clans and bands that had formed the basis of their social organization to develop a tribal government. This move was fraught with difficulties. The people called Seminole spoke two distinct languages and diverged on fundamental issues that did not necessarily correlate to linguistic divisions. They had three separate reservations, and many Seminoles, preferring public land deep in the Everglades, did not even live on one of those. Furthermore, traditional leadership came from medicine men, but these individuals generally lacked the language skills or inclination to create a unified Seminole people. Consequently, new leaders arose from a younger generation that had received some English education, converted to Christianity, or developed managerial skills in the Seminole cattle industry.

This departure from traditional leadership, as well as traditional values, placed enormous strains on Seminole society. Perhaps a third of the Seminoles wanted nothing to do with tribal organization or federal recognition and services. After this group failed to thwart Seminole recognition in 1957, they organized the separate Miccosukee tribe that received recognition in 1962.

Kersey also focuses on the Seminoles' exercise of sovereignty (including a chapter on what happened to the Miccosukees), in particular, the Seminoles' establishment of tax free smoke shops and high-stakes bingo parlors, the settlement of their land-claims cases, and the resolution of their water rights and use of conservation areas. Kersey's work is an important contribution to our understanding of Native southerners in the late twentieth century and to the issues involved in the exercise of Native sovereignty.

Theda Perdue / Michael D. Green

Preface

The early 1950s might have become the worst of times for the Florida Seminoles, for their very existence as a tribe appeared to be in jeopardy. Although most were safely ensconced in federal reservations by the end of the Great Depression, the Seminole people remained mired in poverty, poorly educated, and underemployed; federal housing and healthcare programs were marginal at best, and they had developed no tribal government. At this nadir of their social and economic life, Seminoles also confronted the threat that Congress might terminate all services to the tribe. Fortunately, the tribe averted a disastrous loss of reservation lands and its situation began to improve. When the secretary of the interior approved a constitution and corporate charter for the Seminole Tribe of Florida in 1957, it signaled the official resumption of tribal sovereignty after more than a century of political disarray. Not since the treaties of Payne's Landing (1832) and Fort Gibson (1833) — both coerced documents committing the tribe to removal — had the federal government recognized Florida Seminoles as a sovereign nation.

Nevertheless, significant questions remained concerning the nature of this sovereignty. During the Indian New Deal of the 1930s, Commissioner of Indian Affairs John Collier adopted the position that tribes possessed inherent powers of limited self-government. By this Collier only meant to free Indian tribes from direct congressional control; he never intended them to exercise unrestricted sovereignty. An overly paternalistic Bureau of Indian Affairs allowed the tribes limited authority, and they could do little to redefine their legal status. In fact, during the 1950s Congress attempted to end the government's historic trust relationship with various tribes. This "termination policy" galvanized resistance from Indians and their allies, and the ensuing decades would see a struggle to redefine the nature and extent of tribal sovereignty.

This work places Florida's Indians in the context of federal policy shifts during the volatile decades following World War II and examines the tribe's social, economic, and political structures which transformed to meet the challenges. The Seminole tribe began the era by surviving termination, struggled through some lean years under government supervision, and ultimately emerged as a beneficiary of the self-determination movement. All the while, a progression of court decisions and federal statutes established the parameters of Seminole sovereignty.

This is the concluding volume in a trilogy begun some two decades ago to highlight the defining eras of Florida Seminole history over the century between the 1870s and 1970s. The initial study, *Pelts, Plumes and Hides: White Traders among the Seminole Indians, 1870–1930*, explored a critical period of postremoval contact between whites and Indians on the Florida frontier. The profitable economic interaction established a rough social parity and paved the way for Seminole acceptance in communities which grew up around the trading posts by the end of the nineteenth century. This initiated a unique Indian-white relationship in Florida that persists in many respects to this day. By the early twentieth century, the lucrative trade had ended, a victim of Everglades drainage and the loss of markets due to World War I; also, Indians were being displaced from their lands by an influx of settlers into the lower peninsula. While some traditionalists retreated to their camps in the Everglades, most of the Seminoles were forced into a marginal economic existence. The efforts to gather a destitute and dispirited Indian population into federal reservations while establishing programs to meet their employment, health, and education needs during the Great Depression was the subject of *The Florida Seminoles and the New Deal, 1933–1942*. Each of these three works stands alone, but taken together they recount a remarkable Seminole cultural evolution.

I owe personal and intellectual debts too numerous to be adequately acknowledged in a brief statement, but a few must be noted. This research has been supported in part by grants from the Florida Atlantic University's Division of Sponsored Research, the Florida

Humanities Council, and the Schmidt College of Arts and Humanities Endowment. My conceptualization of tribal sovereignty was extended and refined as a participant in the 1991 National Endowment for the Humanities Summer Seminar "The Ethnohistory of Southeastern Indians," at the University of Kentucky, as well as the 1992 NEH Summer Institute "American Encounters: New Societies in a New World," at the University of North Carolina, Chapel Hill, and the 1993 NEH Summer Institute "Beyond Texts: Teaching Religion and Material Culture," at the University of Hawaii. These programs provided an opportunity for interaction with those who approached sovereignty issues from a variety of disciplinary perspectives.

Members of the Seminole tribe rendered invaluable support and cooperation, particularly Chairman James Billie, General Counsel Jim Shore, and Billy Cypress, Director of the Ah-Tha-Thi-Ki Seminole Tribal Museum, on the Big Cypress Reservation. This study relies heavily on oral narratives, and tribal elders who were members of the 1957 Seminole constitutional committee graciously consented to taped interviews, as did several retired members of the Florida congressional delegation. Of particular value were the accounts of George Smathers, a key member of the Senate Subcommittee on Indian Affairs during the termination era, and longtime congressman Paul Rogers. Former Seminole chairman Howard Tommie provided insights into Indian self-determination from a tribal leader's perspective. To them and the others who participated in the research go my sincere thanks.

This book would never have appeared without the assistance of archivists, librarians, government officials, attorneys, and friends who contributed in innumerable ways. In Washington DC, remarkable assistance was rendered by staff at the National Archives, the Washington National Records Center, and the Bureau of Indian Affairs, while attorneys Jerry Straus and S. Bobo Dean unselfishly shared their vast knowledge of American Indian law. The resources of the University of Florida Oral History Archives were always accessible through the good offices of Samuel Proctor, perhaps the prime instigator and most constant supporter of this project over the years. Two chapters first appeared as articles in the *Florida Historical Quarterly* during his editorship and are reprinted by permission. Librarians are always indispensable, especially Elizabeth Alexander of the P. K. Yonge Library of Florida History, in Gainesville, and Margaret Walker of the Florida Atlantic University Library; both were always able to provide the missing documentary links. The manuscript was assiduously critiqued by Donald Curl and Helen Bannan, my colleagues in the Department of History at Florida Atlantic University; their incisive comments and suggestions have vastly improved the prose. With the usual caveat that I alone assume final responsibility for its content, the book is much richer for having passed through their hands. Finally, my wife, Ruth Dyer Kersey, provided that ineffable mix of focused critique tempered by loving encouragement which every author and husband needs to survive.

An Assumption of Sovereignty

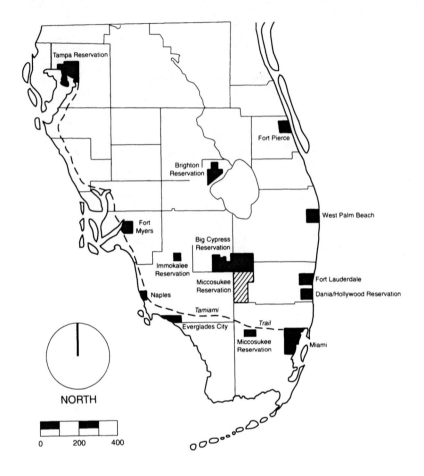

1. Florida's Seminole Reservations

CHAPTER I

Why the Seminoles?

To outward appearances, life in "Indian Country" remained relatively serene during the late 1940s, as tribes seemed to be enjoying a brief respite between the waning Indian New Deal and the onset of congressional termination. However, while the reservations slumbered, politicians and bureaucrats in Washington were quietly planning their legal demise.

The years of World War II and the immediate postwar period have frequently been portrayed as a vacuous era in American Indian affairs, devoid of significant federal activity impacting the tribes. Nevertheless, recent scholarship has revealed it to be an interval that incubated far-reaching and significant changes in federal Indian policy. Virtually all of the efforts toward limited tribal political and economic self-determination, which Commissioner of Indian Affairs John Collier and his fellow New Deal progressives implemented following passage of the 1934 Indian Reorganization Act (IRA), would be challenged, and in many cases reversed, by a conservative coalition in the Congress. Most federally funded reservation programs initiated by the Bureau of Indian Affairs (BIA) during the Depression years were either halted or greatly attenuated after the nation's entry into a global conflict.

Indeed, Indian issues rapidly receded from the national agenda during the war years. Perhaps the most telling manifestation of this could be found in the summary relocation of the bureau's headquarters to Chicago in 1942, thereby providing office space in Washington for other federal agencies deemed more crucial to the war effort.

Throughout his tenure in office, John Collier was subjected to criticism from those in the Congress, as well as from dissident Indian groups who both economically and philosophically opposed his vision of the Indians' role in American life. Collier's position represented a revolutionary break with the paternalistic tradition which viewed Indians as wards of the government.

For the better part of sixty years prior to Franklin Roosevelt's administration, prevailing governmental policy promoted extinction of tribalism and assimilation of Indians into the American mainstream. Influential private national Indian welfare groups such as the Indian Rights Association, Women's National Indian Association, and the annual Lake Mohonk Conferences also supported this position. But the policies advocated by both bureaucrats and reformers not only failed to "civilize" the Indian, but also initiated a backlash calling for the protection of tribal cultures.[1]

As head of the American Indian Defense Association during the 1920s, the charismatic and often abrasive Collier led a progressive reform movement committed to reversing the assimilationist bent of Indian policy; as commissioner he translated this reform agenda into federal policy. Essentially, the new commissioner pursued three goals: restoration of Indian cultural and religious liberty, rebuilding of the Indian land base, and development of limited self-government for the tribes.

First, though, Collier moved to meet the immediate needs of Indians who were suffering greatly from the economic malaise that gripped the nation. He succeeded in securing funds from various New Deal agencies to initiate relief programs on the reservations. These included the Indian Emergency Relief Work (later called Civilian Conservation Corps–Indian Division), Works Progress Administration (WPA), and Civil Works Administration (CWA) employment schemes. Indian health and education programs were also upgraded with federal funds. Next the commissioner proposed a comprehensive piece of legislation which would provide a framework for implementing his Indian agenda. From an economic perspective Collier's plans for rebuilding the Indian land base, as well as providing a wide range of services that had been promised by treaties and other political arrangements, were expensive. The commissioner held, and certainly the Citizenship Act of 1924 affirmed, that as U.S. citizens, Indians had rights to the same programs and services available to other citizens. However, bureau programs became unpopular with congressional appropriations committees struggling to stretch the budget during the Depression and early war years, so they were perennially underfunded. Moreover, the special legal status afforded Indian tribes perpetuated their existence as separate governmental entities, which also implied continuation of a legal relationship requiring long-term economic support from the U.S. government.

The assimilationist element in Congress remained philosophically opposed to Collier's position that American Indians should be allowed to survive as separate cultural and political groups. Their opposition was rooted primarily in the nineteenth-century Christian reform imperative, which held that Indians should be converted from their heathen ways to save their souls and made individually responsible for achieving social and economic success or failure in American society.[2] The Dawes General Allotment Act of 1887 articulated this position by stating that the Indians' future would be best served by abandoning tribalism, taking up individual land allotments, and becoming productive farmers and citizens. Probably not coincidentally, this position predominated among senators and representatives from western states in which large Indian populations had vast amounts of land and natural resources protected in federal trust status as reservations. Their posture can be directly related to two key political issues in western states: the control of Indian resources and jurisdiction over Indian land. Many private cattle and timber interests resented the fact that they were prevented from using or acquiring Indian lands and resources, while state legislatures opposed the idea of independent tribal governments within their territories.

Initially Commissioner Collier received strong support from influential western congressmen who had long been at odds with Bureau of Indian Affairs policies. Yet when it became known that Collier's proposals would grant tribes a voice in the disposition of Indian lands and resources, he ran into bitter opposition. This first surfaced in the struggle to pass the Indian Reorganization Act. Senator Burton Wheeler, of Montana, had his Indian Affairs Committee redraft the legislation and eliminated some key provisions from Collier's original bill, such as Indian courts and a large revolving credit fund for new tribal governments. However, some of Wheeler's changes actually strengthened the act and made it easier to form tribal governments.[3] Despite this opposition, Collier employed provisions of the act to halt the dismantling of Indian reservations and the forced assimilation process; as a result, several congressional leaders never relented in their opposition to the commissioner and his programs. Later, when most members of Congress were too engrossed with wartime issues to pay much attention to Indian policy, control of the Indian Affairs Committees in both houses gravitated into the hands of those forces most dedicated to reversing the trends of the previous decade.

When Congress voted to discontinue funding for the Civilian Conservation Corps–Indian Division in July 1942, it signaled an unofficial end to the Indian New Deal.[4] The residential ccc–id camps on Indian reservations rapidly closed, medical and educational services were reduced or suspended, and heavy equipment used in reclamation and road building programs was transferred to the military services for use in the war effort. The government also appropriated large portions of several reservations for military bombing ranges and for other uses; for example, the War Relocation Authority utilized reservation lands in Arizona for internment camps housing Japanese Americans "relocated" from the West Coast.

The war years also saw a massive exodus of Indians from the reservations. Many tribal people who depended on the government-subsidized projects for income were left to either find off-reservation employment or to remain on the land and subsist by their own devices. This initiated such a great out-migration that "by war's end 40,000 persons—perhaps one half of the able bodied men who had not entered the military and one fifth of the women—had left Indian lands for war related work."[5] Many left because they were disillusioned with bia or tribal government policies, as well as the lack of economic opportunity. Another 25,000 Indians would serve in the armed forces during the war years.[6]

This exodus dealt a severe blow to tribal government and to reservation life in general. Commenting on the period of social disruption, a scholar has observed that

> the reservations were rapidly depopulated of the age groups that would have been most involved in tribal government, leaving elders and children ... with their grandparents while their parents sought work. Many tribal enterprises stopped functioning

for lack of any trained people to operate them. Tribal lands were again leased to white farmers and cattlemen who had the capital to expand their operations rapidly and take advantage of the wartime rise in agricultural and beef prices. When the war ended, many Indians remained in the cities where they had jobs; many Indian veterans returned home briefly, realized they would not be happy in what now seemed too restrictive an environment, and after visiting relatives left to find work outside the reservation.[7]

This appraisal appears to confirm the validity of Collier's concern about the impact of World War II on the American Indian. While he approved of the tribes supporting the war effort, he feared that the more Indians participated in war-related activities, especially work in defense industries, the more they would become like other Americans. This would inevitably lead to a disruption of traditional culture which he had fought so long and hard to protect from judicial and bureaucratic interference. Although thousands of acres of Indian land taken for military use were never returned to the tribes, conservatives believed it would be inconsequential since reservation populations were in decline. The fact that a large segment of the Indian population had made a seemingly successful transition from the reservations to urban life appeared to support those who contended that social and economic assimilation was the Indians' future.

Beginning in 1937, as part of the political fallout from President Roosevelt's failed court-packing scheme, which Collier openly supported, congressional conservatives started to reject the Indian New Deal. Ironically, Senator Wheeler, who coauthored the Indian Reorganization Act, broke with Collier and led this attack. By 1943, congressional opposition to federal Indian programs in general, and to Commissioner Collier's cultural preservation and political self-determination policies in particular, had reached a flash point. Senator Elmer Thomas, from Oklahoma, an implacable Collier adversary, introduced a report calling for abolition of the BIA.[8] In the House, the committee concerned with Indian affairs held public hearings on the subject, which gave Collier an opportunity to defend his policies, and he eloquently rebutted critics such as Senator Thomas and Joseph Bruner, who headed a militant anti-IRA group known as the American Indian Federation. Even so, by the following year opposition had become so intense that the Senate Committee on Indian Affairs approved a measure recommending repeal of the Indian Reorganization Act, but never brought it to a floor vote.[9] These attacks on the administration's Indian policy were beaten back only after a vigorous defense by Collier and Secretary of the Interior Harold Ickes. Yet it became increasingly obvious that the commissioner's political effectiveness had reached an end. Professing a desire to work with Native peoples on an international scale, John Collier resigned as Commissioner of Indian Affairs in February 1945.

Without Collier, Ickes, or the recently deceased President Roosevelt to act as a protective buffer, the Congress that convened in the fall of 1945 initiated a systematic assault on the last vestiges of the Indian Reorganization Act. In general, the legislators were abetted by a succession of Indian commissioners who shared their goal of assimilating Indians as quickly as possible. Within a short time, the new Congress reorganized itself and reduced the Indian affairs committees of both houses from full standing-committee status to subcommittees of the powerful Committee on Interior and Insular Affairs. This sent a clear signal that in the future, Indian policy would receive little priority in national deliberations. Next the assimilationists on Capitol Hill instituted a number of measures specifically designed to undermine tribal political integrity and to wreck the Bureau of Indian Affairs. In an effort to break the Washington central office's "monopoly" in the field of Indian policy, Congress authorized a reorganization of BIA administrative functions. President Truman signed a bill authorizing the Commissioner of Indian Affairs to simplify budgeting procedures and to disperse control to area offices in five geographic regions. This ostensibly placed day-to-day decision making closer to the Indian population.

Most significantly, Congress approved the Indian Claims Commission Act in 1946.[10] Up to that time, tribes with claims for fair compensation for aboriginal lands signed away by treaty had to press their cases in the U.S. Court of Claims. Congress responded to demands by Indians and reformers alike that a more efficient and fair mechanism was needed for settling Indian claims. The establishment

6

of an Indian Claims Commission could be interpreted as an honest congressional effort to provide tribes with a special forum to expedite their legitimate historical claims to fair compensation for lands taken. On the other hand, it could also be construed as a requisite legal step to clear away lingering legal claims against the federal government which, when settled, would set the stage for termination of any further federal obligation to the tribes. Even though the establishment of yet another government bureaucracy to deal with Indians appeared to be inconsistent with the direction taken by federal policy of the day, fiscal conservatives believed that spending millions to settle tribal claims would save even greater expenditures in the long run. To the extent that the Indian Claims Commission made settlements in money and not in land, it did not advance the concept of tribes as independent entities empowered to increase their own land base. Over $800 million would be awarded to tribes during the life of the commission which, after several congressional extensions, expired in 1978.

Early in 1947, following an election in which Republicans took firm control of the Congress, the postwar conservative fervor to reduce federal expenses accelerated rapidly. The Senate Committee on the Post Office and Civil Service focused on the Bureau of Indian Affairs as an agency with an inflated budget and an excess of employees that could be cut back drastically. Equally important, it had no powerful constituency to be placated. William Brophy, the commissioner who replaced Collier, became seriously ill and was unable to testify at the hearings. Attorneys for the Department of the Interior also advised the assistant commissioner, William Zimmerman, not to appear before the hostile committee; nevertheless, he was ultimately subpoenaed by the committee and compelled to respond. Zimmerman testified that there were only two ways to reduce the number of BIA employees: either cut back the extent of services offered to Indians or reduce the size of the client population by terminating federal services altogether for some tribes. Zimmerman articulated four criteria to be used in determining a tribe's readiness for the latter: the tribal members' degree of acculturation, overall economic condition, willingness to end the special relationship with the federal government, and willingness and ability of the states to assume responsibility for tribal welfare. He then identified tribes within three categories: those

7

that could succeed without federal assistance immediately, those that would be ready for withdrawal of federal services within a decade, and those that for the foreseeable future would need federal assistance.[11]

This was the infamous Zimmerman Plan for termination. However, Zimmerman would later complain bitterly that the Senate committee focused only on that aspect of the testimony which presented termination of services to tribes as an option and paid scant attention to the criteria that he offered for determining readiness.[12] The bureau's leadership evidently accepted termination as the inevitable long-term thrust of federal policy; in retrospect, John Collier had only taken a unique approach to preparing the tribes for that eventuality. Under the IRA, tribes were allowed to set their own agenda for assimilation; now the timetable had been set, and accelerated, by the Congress. As acting commissioner, Zimmerman instructed the bureau's field units to gather data from previous surveys of reservation resources in anticipation of major social and economic development programs that would enable the government to discontinue its supervision and control as soon as possible. The acting commissioner could also report that some reservation populations had already been selected to begin the development effort.

The attack on the bureau continued in October 1948, when the Project Committee on Indian Affairs of the Commission on Organization of the Executive Branch of the Government—popularly known as the Hoover Commission—issued a highly critical report. It found that under bureau stewardship the Indians had not gained the education and experience necessary to run their own affairs, and called for assimilation of the Indian as a major goal of federal policy. The Hoover Commission, which had been charged with recommending means by which the federal government could reduce expenditures, suggested that states should begin to assume responsibility for most services provided for Indians. In 1949 Dr. John Nichols, a professional educator and member of the Hoover Commission, was named Commissioner of Indian Affairs. He became committed to withdrawing the federal government from involvement with the tribes as rapidly as Indians could be prepared to take over. During Nichols's short eleven-month administration, Congress

8

transferred civil and criminal jurisdiction over a California tribe from federal to state authorities—a sign of things to come.

Dillon Myer, who held the post of commissioner from 1950 to 1953, has been called "the father of real termination."[13] During World War II he headed the controversial War Relocation Authority (WRA), which interned approximately 120,000 Japanese Americans and later supervised the relocation of thousands of internees from the camps to eastern urban areas.[14] Two of the camps were situated on Indian reservations, and Collier often clashed with Myer over policy issues; the latter considered reservations little more than permanent internment camps for Indians. Despite the dire predictions of WRA staff anthropologists, many of whom were on loan from the BIA, many Japanese Americans made a successful transition to new cities, even during wartime. By the war's end some 50,000 internees had left the camps for resettlement. This experience convinced Myer that Indians could be assimilated in a similar manner through a process of bureau-sponsored out-migration from the reservations. He followed this principle in initiating an Indian relocation policy, completely overlooking or ignoring the vast differences that existed between the repatriated Japanese Americans and reservation Indians.

Throughout the 1950s the underfunded bureau sponsored thousands of Indians on what some have called a one-way bus ride from rural to urban poverty. They arrived in cities such as Denver, Los Angeles, Minneapolis, Salt Lake City, and Chicago with inadequate funds, limited job training or skills, and virtually no social support system to ease the transition. In some of these cities, Indian neighborhoods that developed during the war years were still intact; in others, they had virtually dissolved when defense industries closed. Despite such obstacles, many of the newcomers persevered and formed the nucleus of today's urban Indian communities; over time, though, large numbers of unemployed and dispirited Indians also gravitated back to the reservations.

Under Commissioner Myer the bureau was restructured to advance termination on a variety of fronts. A new program division was created to plan the withdrawal of services from the reservations and prepare the Indians to stand on their own. In 1952, Congress authorized compilation of the "Domesday Report"—reminiscent of

William the Conqueror's compilation of English land wealth for re-distribution in the eleventh century—to gain a complete picture of Indian resources, and the bureau was required to provide an estimate of each tribe's readiness to be relieved of federal support. The broad plan called for placing Indian children in public schools and turning tribal healthcare over to appropriate local authorities. The BIA also proceeded to draft legislation calling for termination of services to a number of specific tribes.

The end of a decade during which congressional conservatives had attempted to dismantle the Indian Reorganization Act on a piece-meal basis came in 1953. That summer the Eighty-third Congress took action that severely undermined the federal trust relationship with the tribes, which had been a cornerstone of federal Indian law since 1831. Perhaps most significant was passage of Public Law 280.[15] This transferred civil and criminal jurisdiction over Indians to five states and opened the way for others to assume similar jurisdiction if they wished. Twelve states eventually elected to assume legal control over their Indian inhabitants. Nonetheless, the adoption of House Concurrent Resolution 108, which expressed the "sense of Congress" that elimination of services should become the fundamental principle of federal Indian policy, represented the most dramatic and potentially devastating congressional action.[16] Interestingly, this resolution drew support from political liberals who desired to free tribes from what they perceived as abusive federal paternalism, as well as from conservative assimilationists who would have them brought into the mainstream of American life. As former Assistant Commissioner James Officer pointed out, "nowhere in the resolution do we find the word *termination* that has come to carry such ominous portent in more recent times. Rather, the tone of the document is one of emancipation and equalization 'to end the wardship status of the Indians and to grant them their rights and prerogatives pertaining to American citizenship.'"[17]

In one sense, supporters of the Indian Reorganization Act were *too* effective in promoting the view that Indians were fully capable of conducting their own affairs. Analyzing the rapidly declining political fortunes of the American Indians during the 1950s, Vine Deloria concludes that "at least part of the blame for the state of affairs could be attributed to John Collier. His optimistic characterization of self-government had led some members of Congress to believe that Indians were making considerably more progress than was actually occurring on the reservations."[18] Of course, the idealistic Collier had been premature in his assessment; tribal governments were slow in developing, and the war years had such a negative impact on the reservations that Indian communities remained almost totally dependent on governmental health, education, and land operations programs for the next three decades.

Moreover, few realized how much traditional tribal culture and values inhibited Indian entry into middle-class American society. Although there were numerous instances of successful social and economic integration, primarily by mixed-bloods, termination advocates overlooked the fact that most Indians who moved from the reservations to urban areas during and after the war encountered great difficulty assimilating, and there was a high rate of return. This inevitably led to conflict within the Indian communities. "Actually," as Donald Fixico has confirmed, "the Indian view on trust removal was divided. Primarily, mixed-bloods concurred with federal officials on removal of trust restrictions, while traditional full-bloods believed that their people still differed considerably from white Americans in their values and their outlook on life."[19] Despite misgivings voiced by Indians themselves, most members of Congress on both sides of the aisle opted to terminate the federal trust relationship with certain tribes.

The task of implementing tribal termination fell to Glenn Emmons, the recently appointed Commissioner of Indian Affairs. President Eisenhower selected Emmons, a banker and Republican politician from New Mexico, for the post partly on the strength of a recommendation from the business-oriented Navajo Tribal Council, although traditional Navajos, some smaller tribes, and the National Congress of American Indians initially opposed his nomination. Following a brief but stormy confirmation hearing, the Senate approved his appointment only ten days prior to passage of HCR 108 in the Eighty-third Congress. The new commissioner was a determined proponent of termination, although he preferred the euphemistic *readjustment program* to either *termination* or *withdrawal*. However, he opposed any "wholesale termination" policy applied to all tribes, and expressed concern that Indians might be exploited or squander their funds. Consequently, Emmons became committed to allowing tribes to retain their lands in group ownership even after dissolving federal trusteeship. Because he attempted to implement the federal withdrawal as humanely as possible, the commissioner gained the respect of many Native Americans despite their disagreement with the overall policy.[20]

No organized Indian resistance to termination existed on the national level during the 1950s. The National Congress of American Indians (NCAI), founded in Denver in 1944, had not yet established an effective lobbying effort in Washington. Meanwhile, those tribes most directly affected by termination legislation, lacking both funds and political skills, could take only limited defensive action. When they were able to raise a strong objection to the federal policy and rally non-Indian allies to their side, particularly members of the state congressional delegations and Indian rights organizations, they were often successful in avoiding termination.

HCR 108 designated certain tribes to be "freed from federal supervision and control and from all disabilities and limitations applicable to Indians," including the Flathead of Montana, Klamath of Oregon, Menominee in Wisconsin, Potowatomi of Kansas and Nebraska, the Turtle Mountain Chippewa in North Dakota, and all the Indian tribes "and members thereof" located in the states of California, New York, Texas, and Florida. Although this list was considerably shorter than previous compilations of tribes considered ready for termination that the bureau had presented to Congress, it contained at least one group that had never appeared before: the Seminoles of Florida.

In the decade immediately following World War II, the Florida Seminoles were best known as a colorfully garbed tribe living in Everglades villages and wrestling alligators for the amusement of tourists. Some historically literate citizens might recall tales of Seminole resistance to removal from the Florida Territory before the Civil War, the heroism of Osceola, and the tribe's dramatic claim to be an "unconquered people." Fewer still were aware of the extensive reservation lands and other federal programs available to the Florida Indians — even though most of this assistance had been severely reduced during the war years. In truth, the Seminoles appeared to have made essentially no progress in their economic development and political organization since the years of the Great Depression. Between 1946 and 1950 the superintendent of the Seminole agency beseeched the bureau for additional funds to meet welfare needs, including food for families, burials, and improvements to the water supply and sanitation systems in the Indian camps; however, the annual expenditure approved for all programs did not exceed $3,600 by 1952.[21] While the superintendent requested allocations for specific reservation projects, some Washington bureaucrats assumed that the funds benefited the entire Florida Indian population. They made no distinction between Seminoles who lived on the reservations and those who did not. That was a mistake, for while the two tribal elements displayed numerous cultural similarities, significant issues divided them.

Following the nineteenth century Seminole wars, most tribal members were removed to the Indian Territory west of the Mississippi River. From midcentury onward, the remnant group in Florida survived in extended family camps. By the 1880s Seminole multicamp settlements could be found in five regions of the state: the Big Cypress Swamp, on Catfish Lake near Lake Wales, at Fisheating Creek and Cow Creek (both flowing into Lake Okeechobee), and in the Everglades west of Miami. These were not even bands in the strict sense of the term because they lacked a recognized chief or leader. In the early 1900s these settlements dispersed, and Seminoles established widely scattered family camps throughout the lower peninsula.

Although the Florida Indians had historically been divided between those who spoke Miccosukee, a Hitchiti language, and a minority of Muskogee (Creek) speakers, both elements shared a common Southeastern Indian cultural tradition based on a clan and kinship system, as well as an annual busk (fasting) ritual known as the Green Corn Dance. Seminoles belonged to one of several busk groups, each headed by a medicine man and council of elders, which functioned as the basic unit of social and political organization. But significant cleavages began to appear within the Seminole polity during the New Deal era. Major divisions existed between those who lived on the federal reservations and those who retained traditional camps in the pine woods north of Lake Okeechobee or deep in the Everglades;

between those who had converted to Christianity and those who retained traditional religious and cultural beliefs; and between those who had become acculturated in their modes of dress, housing, or occupation and their more traditional kin.

Throughout the Indian New Deal, between 1933 and 1942, many landless and displaced Seminoles gravitated to three federal reservations—Dania, Brighton, and Big Cypress—that the bureau had established in Florida. There they made permanent homes, cultivated family gardens, and tended hogs or cattle while the Seminole agency staff attempted to provide for their basic public health, education, and employment needs. Special BIA funding assured that a number of Seminole adults, as well as the children, were able to attend reservation day schools for the first time. The small Dania Reservation, located west of Fort Lauderdale on the lower east coast of Florida, opened in the late 1920s as a refuge for sick and indigent Indians, but it soon became the bureau's field headquarters as well as home to the Indian agent. All of the New Deal economic programs for Seminoles were first introduced there, and they attracted many Indians from the outlying areas; however, the CCC–ID and other projects were soon shifted to the larger rural reservations. In 1942, due primarily to transportation problems associated with the war, the BIA moved its field headquarters to Fort Myers, on the Gulf Coast, which had the additional advantage of being geographically closer to most of the Florida Indian population.

Economically, the reservation Seminoles enjoyed a significant advantage over their relatives who maintained independent camps. The days of a thriving Seminole hunting and trapping economy had long since disappeared, and most families living in the traditional way eked out a meager subsistence at isolated Everglades campsites. There they built the open-sided and thatched roof homes called chikees, planted small gardens on fertile hammocks or tree islands, and supplemented their diet by hunting and fishing. They had few sources of cash income. Men occasionally served as hunting or fishing guides for sportsmen who came to Florida, or sold a few animal pelts to local merchants; women made patchwork and other handicrafts which they sold to visitors at roadside stands or in commercial villages, principally during the winter tourist season. By contrast, most adult

Seminole males who came to the federal reservations found employment with New Deal programs such as WPA, CWA, and CCC–ID. During the Depression these federal rehabilitation programs became the Seminoles' primary source of cash income, although they provided virtually no employment opportunities for Indian women. Most jobs entailed heavy labor; moreover, contrary to tribal tradition, government regulations did not accept women as heads of households and thus they were ineligible for relief jobs. As an alternative, many of the Indian women, and also a few men, found employment as agricultural day laborers on nearby farms and ranches.

In the late 1930s, federal authorities added a significant amount of grazing land to the Brighton Reservation, near Lake Okeechobee, and introduced a starter herd of 1,200 beef cattle acquired from drought-stricken regions in the western states. The Seminoles adapted quickly to raising livestock and, under the tutelage of a dedicated agricultural agent, laid the groundwork for a tribal beef cattle program. This communal cattle enterprise expanded to the larger Big Cypress Reservation in the late 1940s. The bureau's emphasis on assimilating Indians into the economic and social mainstream of American life ultimately led to the dissolution of the communal cattle enterprise, and a number of Seminole families became individual cattle owners—even though they continued to graze their herds on communal lands. This created an economic stratification within the tribe that, over time, led to substantial political friction. For most Indian families at Brighton and Big Cypress, including those who were cattle owners, life was difficult at best. The community lacked adequate housing and sanitation; electricity and running water were virtually nonexistent, while public health services provided by the government were marginal; roads ranged from poor to impassable during inclement weather, isolating the reservations. Conditions were not much improved at the urban Dania Reservation, so when the federal employment programs were withdrawn during the war years, some families became destitute and dependent on government relief.

Unlike Indians on the larger western reservations, Seminoles never migrated to urban centers seeking employment during the war. The small, tightly knit reservation populations effectively precluded such migration. Furthermore, despite the claims of administrators that

CCC–ID was a training ground for developing skills which Indians could use in the outside world, few Seminoles acquired proficiencies for employment in industry.[22] Most were employed as unskilled laborers in the reservation projects, and only a limited number learned to operate sophisticated heavy equipment.[23] A very small group of Seminoles reported taking war-related jobs away from the reservations, but even they remained within Florida. Similarly, when the bureau initiated its subsidized employment relocation program in the 1950s, it generated little interest among the Florida tribes. Social isolation made the Seminoles indifferent to the war effort. They initially resisted the registration required by the Selective Service Act but ultimately agreed to participate; however, none were called for military service by local draft boards.[24] Only three young men from the tribe are known to have volunteered for the armed forces during the war years, and they served with distinction.

The lack of a tribal government became the most significant problem confronting Florida's Indians as termination loomed. Without a formal structure to deal with the bureau or convey their wishes directly to Florida's political leaders, the Seminoles were vulnerable to political manipulation. Yet the Florida Indians had long been eligible to form a government and business corporation as authorized by the Indian Reorganization Act. When the Wheeler-Howard bill became law in 1934, each tribe had a onetime opportunity to signify its acceptance or rejection of the legislation. Early in 1935 Commissioner Collier, accompanied by Secretary of the Interior Harold Ickes, visited several Florida Indian communities promoting acceptance of the act. When the BIA conducted an election in April 1935, only twenty-one Seminoles cast ballots—all in favor of the Indian Reorganization Act.[25] While this fell significantly short of the thirty percent tribal participation required by Congress, the Bureau of Indian Affairs solicitor ruled that Florida's Seminoles had legally accepted the act and thus qualified for its benefits. It would take two decades before the reservation Seminoles could bring themselves together to adopt a constitution establishing their own tribal government.

Nevertheless, there were precursors of tribal organization. In 1939 the Seminoles received bureau approval to select three trustees for their cattle program on the Brighton Reservation. It became their first, albeit limited, experience with the elective process. Following the war the bureau reorganized the livestock enterprises at both the Brighton and Big Cypress reservations. The cattle owners were still empowered to select three cattle trustees with the approval of the agency superintendent. Also, business affairs at the Dania Reservation were placed in the hands of an appointed business committee. An additional three persons, one elected from each of the large rural reservations (Brighton and Big Cypress plus another chosen at large by the superintendent), constituted a body known as the tribal trustees who were presumed to represent the entire tribe on all matters. However, this structure for tribal governance had little power, and the Seminoles were skeptical of its role, perhaps because it was perceived by many as an instrument of the government agent. One Indian woman recalled that the "Superintendent, who was about to retire tried to help us, by dealing with people who really didn't have the authority to speak for the whole tribe but [he] had to deal with someone. He formed the Business Committee on all three reservations, by appointing them himself."[26]

The rapid spread of Christianity by the end of World War II represented another dynamic force among reservation Seminoles. Beginning in 1907, the Indian Baptist churches of Oklahoma periodically dispatched missionaries to Florida, and the first resident minister, Willie King, was a Creek Indian.[27] Under his direction a small Baptist church opened at the Dania Reservation in 1936 with a congregation composed mainly of women and children. The Southern Baptist Convention assumed responsibility for Seminole mission work two years later, but there were few converts. This mission effort languished until a dynamic young Oklahoma Indian pastor, Stanley Smith, arrived to assist King in 1943.[28] His fervent preaching had a great effect among both men and women, and church membership grew rapidly. During 1946 five Seminole men attended the Florida Bible Institute in Lakeland and returned to the reservations as lay ministers. Smith proved to be mercurial and domineering, and alienated many tribal members; a church schism ensued. In the early 1950s the Southern Baptist Convention sent a new missionary to reorganize the First Seminole Baptist Church at the Dania Reservation, while those who followed Smith formed the Independent Mekusukey

Baptist Church. These two Indian congregations would vie for new members on the reservations, and their presence lent an important dimension to future social and political development of the tribe.

The religious factionalism further complicated life for an already divided people. Seminole reservation populations were comprised of closely related matrilineal clan lineages with their own social and political leadership. Each reservation considered itself an independent entity, and the people had a limited sense of common tribal identity. For example, the small Dania Reservation contained a mixture of Miccosukee- and Muskogee-speaking families, many of whom had gravitated there to take advantage of federal programs offered during the New Deal era. A bureau day school operated on the reservation with limited success from 1927 through 1935, but when it closed during the Depression, Seminole children were forced to attend a federal Indian Boarding School at Cherokee, North Carolina, to complete their education. In 1945 two Seminole girls from Dania became the first members of their tribe to complete a secondary education when they graduated from Cherokee. But only a few Indian families remained at Dania after the removal of the Seminole agency headquarters to Fort Myers in 1942, where it remained for the duration of the war. Dania residents subsisted on government aid and found employment as casual laborers in the nearby communities, but Florida's segregation laws kept their children from attending public schools. In 1950 the Seminole Agency headquarters returned to the Dania Reservation, and the population began to increase. To more accurately reflect its location in metropolitan south Florida, the tribe later renamed this community the Hollywood Reservation.

The Brighton Reservation was occupied almost exclusively by Muskogee-speaking families, most of whom engaged in the thriving beef cattle enterprise. It remained a socially conservative, self-contained community which followed the political directives of a council of elders and the medicine man who conducted their Green Corn Dance. Despite the best efforts of the Southern Baptists who maintained an active missionary effort among the Seminoles, there was no significant number of conversions among the Muskogee Seminoles until the 1950s. Even so, the Brighton people experienced frequent contacts with non-Indians in a variety of situations, so there were indications of growing acculturation. They were the first to elect trustees to oversee the cattle program and to request a government day school on the reservation.

The Big Cypress Reservation, on the western side of the Everglades and south of Lake Okeechobee, became an enclave of Miccosukee speakers who had broken with their kinsmen in the lower Everglades and moved to federal land in the late 1930s. A number of factors may have precipitated this move. One observer has speculated that many of these Indians were from clans which could not inherit official positions or status within the traditional structure.[29] Another explanation was that they followed their acknowledged leader, a medicine man who had fallen from favor with the traditional Miccosukee elders and later accepted Christianity.[30] Whatever their motivation, once they made the transition, Miccosukees on Big Cypress developed their own identity, particularly in religious and economic matters. Most families accepted both a new religion and a new way of life based on cattle herding and the development of agricultural lands. But even though they were no longer part of the traditional Miccosukee lifestyle, the Big Cypress people did not feel any particular unity with the other reservations.

At the southern tip of the peninsula a group of traditional Miccosukee-speaking families maintained their camps in the vicinity of the Tamiami Trail, a federal highway which crossed the Everglades between Miami and Naples. These so-called Trail Indians formed the least acculturated and most economically depressed element within the tribe.[31] They continued to live in chikee camps, dress in the traditional manner, and shun outside government and religion. Their own medicine men conducted a separate Green Corn Dance ceremony while a council of elders governed and spoke for the group, but even here there were political factions. All remained united, however, in adamant opposition to dealings with the federal government that would compromise their lifestyle. They wanted land, not money, and thus bitterly opposed the $50 million claim filed with the Indian Claims Commission by a group of Seminoles living on the reservations. This claim sought additional compensation for lands seized when the Seminoles were removed from Florida in the nineteenth century. Furthermore, the Trail Indians believed that the Indian agent had encouraged reservation Seminoles to file suit, and that further exacerbated the split between the two groups.

Federal policy also inadvertently played a role in fostering these divisions. Since the early 1940s there had been a propensity within the bureau, advocated initially by John Collier, to deal with the Florida Seminoles as two separate entities. Collier once briefly considered allowing the acculturated reservation families to organize under the IRA, while leaving the traditional Trail Indians to their own ways.[32] Laudable as this recognition of intratribal cultural diversity might have been, it also accentuated a social and religious bifurcation that left the Florida Indian polity divided and politically weakened.

Unquestionably, in the early 1950s there were few Indian tribes in the United States less prepared to assume control of their own affairs. Why then did Congress include this small, geographically isolated, relatively unacculturated, and virtually impoverished group, with barely 900 members, on the federal termination list along with much larger and more economically developed tribes? One clue has been provided by James Officer, who recalled that "while the Seminoles of Florida were a congressional 'add-on,' the legislators omitted a number of others perhaps—I might suggest cynically—because of the reluctance of particular congressmen to have their constituents singled out in this fashion."[33] A disturbing implication might be drawn from Officer's statement that Florida's congressional delegation either actively sought to have the Seminoles included in House Concurrent Resolution 108 or at least acquiesced in their inclusion.

None of the bureau's previous listings of Indian tribes that were candidates for termination included the Florida Seminoles. Indeed, it was just the opposite: in 1947 testimony before the Senate Post Office and Civil Service Committee investigating ways to cut governmental expenses, Acting Commissioner Zimmerman had placed the Seminoles of Florida in the category of those tribes which would need federal assistance for the foreseeable future.[34] Again in 1952, as a result of House Resolution 698, passed by the Eighty-second Congress, the commissioner had to provide a list of tribes, bands, or groups of Indians then qualified for full management of their own affairs. The BIA circulated a questionnaire to all agencies, and the results appeared in House Report 2680, of the Eighty-third Congress, in 1954. An annotated list of the tribes indicated the readiness of each to be relieved of federal support; a No signaled that, in the opinion of local bureau officials, the group was not yet qualified to handle its own affairs. The report which Congress ultimately received included the entry, "Seminole of Florida: No."[35]

No congressional reports, administrative findings, or other evidence justified a termination of federal services to the Florida Seminoles. Nor was there a public outcry for termination from state and local officials in Florida such as some tribes in western states had encountered. A parade of Seminole leaders, Indian rights activists, tribal attorneys, anthropologists, and ordinary citizens were prepared to appear before congressional committees and speak against immediate termination of the Florida tribe. It is possible that by vigorously pursuing their case before the Indian Claims Commission, Seminoles had sent a message to Congress that they were capable and ready to manage their own affairs following termination. Certainly the prospect of a multimillion-dollar land claim award by the commission might be taken as an indication that the government no longer owed the tribe any support; but the commission had not delivered its decision, and there could be no assurance that it would uphold the Seminole claim. Therefore we must seek an answer to why the Florida Seminoles were included on the list of tribes marked for termination by House Concurrent Resolution 108—yet were ultimately spared from its drastic mandates—through examining the internal dynamics of the Indian Affairs subcommittees in the Eighty-third and Eighty-fourth Congresses, as well as by profiling those political figures who dominated congressional deliberations during the height of the termination frenzy.

Termination and Turmoil

T he Eighty-third Congress, which convened in January 1953, became notorious to those in Indian affairs as the "termination Congress" for its initiation of legislation directly threatening the existence of tribal communities. In general, its members reflected a sentiment building since the end of World War II that American Indians were ready to stand on their own without support or supervision from Washington. Thus they assumed that federal expenditures could be radically reduced by eliminating services to the tribes, while at the same time allowing Indians freedom from government restrictions in order to pursue their own economic interests. To that end, over two hundred bills and resolutions pertaining to Indians were introduced and forty-six became law, including House Concurrent Resolution 108.

Although the 1946 elections had returned Republican majorities in both houses, the determination to force assimilation of the American Indian crossed party lines. As a rule, Indian affairs held little interest for most members, so conservatives of both parties were able to secure their program with little opposition. An unusual level of agreement existed between Democrats and Republicans on the issue of termination, although generally for different reasons. Liberal Democrats subscribed to the position that a paternalistic Bureau of Indian Affairs oppressed Indians by keeping them in a status that restricted their social and economic progress. They sought to ensure Indian civil liberties, end social segregation, and promote economic self-development. For example, when Representative Henry Jackson of Washington introduced legislation in 1945 to create an Indian Claims Commission, it was with the understanding that funds thus derived would enable tribes to improve economic opportunities for their people. Conservatives, on the other hand, viewed the bill as an opportunity to discharge federal obligations to the tribes and get out of the Indian business altogether. In 1953 Jackson, then a senator and still convinced that termination held the best hope for assuring Indian prosperity, sponsored HCR 108 in the Senate. He and other western Democrats, such as Clinton Anderson of New Mexico and Frank Church of Idaho, accepted the conservatives' interpretation of events when they became members of the Senate Interior Committee and remained strong supporters of termination.[1]

At the opposite end of the political spectrum was Senator Arthur Watkins, an archconservative Republican from Utah and the leading proponent of Indian termination. Watkins won election to the Senate in 1946 and served for two terms. A Mormon, he strongly believed in hard work and self-reliance and abhorred governmental assistance or interference with the free enterprise system. Far from considering that tribes were stifled on the reservations, Watkins believed the Indians had been coddled and given too much support for their own good; moreover, he thought the BIA services on the reservations were a fiscal burden which American taxpayers should not have to bear. He did not recognize the possibility that Indian cultural values and psychological conditioning might impede their assimilation and saw no reason to retain any of the reservations. As chairman of the Senate Subcommittee on Indian Affairs, Watkins took an aggressive role in the passage of termination bills for a number of tribes; he then exerted political pressure to overcome Indian resistance to the legislation. Conservatives were convinced that Indians who objected to termination were trying to avoid taxation and refusing to accept responsibility for their own future, and that the Indian rights organizations which protested termination did so to justify their own continued existence.

Each tribe had to approve its termination bill in some manner, and Watkins seized upon small assimilated minorities willing to leave the reservation as a sign that all Indians desired this course. Appealing to his liberal colleagues, the senator from Utah compared termination with the Emancipation Proclamation in its liberating impact on the Indian.[2] With support from Congressman E. Y. Berry of South Dakota, the staunchest proponent of termination in the House, Watkins coerced the Menominee tribe into accepting termination with about eight percent of the tribe voting on the issue. In other cases, merely the consent of the tribal council, often dominated by acculturated Indians, was taken as assent by an entire tribe. With such relentless antagonists leading the attack, it would be very difficult for a small, unsophisticated tribe like the Seminoles to resist being swept away by the rising tide of assimilationist sentiment.

Fortunately for the Seminoles, two influential congressional figures from Florida, both of whom became increasingly sympathetic to the tribe's position, served on the subcommittees which dealt with Indian affairs during the termination era. Senator George Smathers, a first-term Democrat, held one of five seats on the Senate Subcommittee on Indian Affairs. In 1950 Smathers, a Marine Corps veteran and popular congressman from Miami, unseated the incumbent New Deal liberal Claude Pepper by advocating fiscal conservatism and exploiting anti-Communist sentiment. As Florida's junior senator he sought appointment to the interior committee primarily because it dealt with national parks and other public lands, accepting a place on its Indian Affairs subcommittee almost as an afterthought.

Historians of Indian termination agree that Smathers had originally been a supporter of HCR 108 but later reversed his position. However, they disagree somewhat as to his motivation in breaking with Watkins. Donald Fixico holds that Smathers modified his position after he became familiar with the problems of termination and the poor living conditions in Indian communities. "Senator Smathers," he wrote, "sympathized with Native Americans for he believed they lacked the capability to take advantage of the federal government and did not yet have the capacity to live successfully among other Americans."[3] By contrast, Larry Burt links Smather's concern directly to the impact such a bill would have on the Seminoles: "Florida Senator George Smathers generally went along with Watkins's termination policy, but in this case he feared that unscrupulous outsiders would exploit the land and resources of these inexperienced people."[4] Smathers enjoyed good relations with the Seminoles dating from high school days in Florida when he played football with a member of the tribe, and after he became a congressman Indians often visited his Washington office. As a result, he claimed to have kept an open mind on the termination issue.[5]

Representative James Haley, Democrat of Florida, served as a member and later chairman of the House Subcommittee on Indian Affairs. Haley, an accountant who once managed the estate of circus magnate John Ringling, later married John's cousin, Aubrey Ringling, and became managing vice president of the Ringling Brothers Circus. In 1944 a number of circus officials were placed on trial in the aftermath of the tragic Hartford, Connecticut, circus fire in which 168 perished. Haley received the stiffest prison sentence, one year and a day. However, he was hailed as a local hero in Sarasota, winter home of the circus, and became president of the reorganized Ringling Brothers, Barnum and Bailey Circus.[6] In 1952, Haley won election to represent the seventh (later eighth) congressional district, one of the most conservative constituencies in Florida. He served in the House from the Eighty-third through the Ninety-fourth Congresses. His arrival in Washington coincided with the height of Republican control in the Congress; the conservative Haley received an assignment to the Committee on Interior and Insular Affairs and in 1954 became chairman of the Subcommittee on Indian Affairs. Rarely had an easterner held this position, which was usually reserved for representatives from western states with large Indian populations. Haley filled the position with distinction. Even Vine Deloria, a critic of federal Indian policy, praised the chairman's defense of Indian lands against outside development during the Kennedy and Johnson administrations.[7] However, Haley remained an ardent fiscal conservative who subscribed to the underlying philosophy of the terminationists, and it now appears likely that he engineered placement of the Seminoles on the list of tribes to be terminated. A former colleague in the Florida congressional delegation ventured an opinion that Haley subjected Seminoles to the same scrutiny which he demanded for other tribes, assuming that investigation would reveal they were not ready for termination.[8] If so, he took a gamble given the protermination tenor of the Congress.

Termination bills for the thirteen tribes identified in HCR 108 were to be introduced in both the House and Senate. Each tribe would have two options for disposing of its properties: it could organize into a corporation for continued management under a trustee of its choice, or it could sell all properties and assets and distribute the proceeds among tribal members.[9] Eventually, termination bills were approved for only six tribes—the Menominee in Wisconsin, Klamath and western Oregon bands, Utes of Utah, mixed-blood Paiutes in Nevada, and the Alabama-Coushattas in Texas—while other small, disorganized groups seemed headed for a similar fate. For the first time in history the two subcommittees sat in joint session to consider the bills that were drawn. This would prevent efforts to forestall legislation by assuring that the language in both versions was identical, eliminating the necessity for a conference to reconcile differences. Conference committees had traditionally been the place where compromises were struck and tribes were able to kill legislation.

On 18 January 1954, Rep. A. L. Miller of Nebraska, a member of the House Subcommittee on Indian Affairs, introduced a package of termination bills. One of the bills, HR7321, would "provide for the termination of Federal supervision over the property of the Seminole Tribe of Indians in the State of Florida and the individual members thereof, and for other purposes."[10] A companion measure, S2747, was introduced in the Senate. The bills had been drafted by the Bureau of Indian Affairs and were identical in content. They were submitted to the Speaker of the House and president of the Senate with a request for immediate action.[11]

The joint subcommittee hearings on Seminole termination convened in Washington on 1 March 1954, with Senator Watkins presiding.[12] Smathers was the only other member of the Senate subcommittee present for the session. Those representing the House subcommittee included Chairman E. Y. Berry of South Dakota, as well as Haley of Florida and George Shuford of North Carolina. Congressman Dwight Rogers also attended, and the subcommittee invited him to participate in its deliberations. Rogers, a Democrat, represented the sprawling eleven-county sixth district, which extended from the Atlantic Ocean to the Gulf of Mexico in southern Florida. All of the Seminole reservations were located in his district, and Rogers often intervened on their behalf with state and federal officials. After introductory remarks, the hearings focused on the termination bill's impact on the tribe. The key provision of the legislation authorized the secretary of the interior to transfer within three years all property of the tribe to a corporation established by the tribe or its elected trustees for liquidation or management. The proceeds of this liquidation or management were to be vested in those Seminoles whose names appeared on the official tribal roll. It authorized the secretary, after disposing of the lands, to publish a proclamation in the *Federal Register* declaring the federal trust relationship in affairs of the tribe had been terminated. However, the BIA report accompanying this legislation cautioned that "wide differences of opinion were expressed as to the length of time that Federal supervision should be continued."[13] Underscoring this concern, over twenty individuals testified or had statements entered into the record, and all but three opposed immediate or rapid termination of supervision for the Florida Seminoles.

The first to testify before the joint subcommittee were Associate Commissioner H. Rex Lee and Kenneth Marmon, superintendent of the Seminole agency. Marmon, who had served in Florida since 1942, provided an account of the Seminole reservations, resources, and people. Under questioning from Senator Smathers, who appeared intent on establishing whether the Seminoles were ready for termination, he confirmed that the tribal population was 918, sixty percent of whom lived on the federal reservations or had affiliations with them through owning cattle; an estimated 640 Indians, about seventy percent of the tribe, were non-English speaking and could neither read nor write; only ninety-six Seminoles were enrolled in public school while forty-seven attended reservation schools; the Seminoles were scattered throughout five south Florida counties, and since there was no tribal government it was necessary to work with leaders chosen by each of the Indian communities; although eighty-eight Indian families owned about fifty cattle each, most Seminoles were employed only seasonally. The annual federal appropriation for the tribe amounted to $137,000, and most of that went to building roads; it provided nothing for unemployed Seminoles.

When Smathers inquired what would happen to the non-English-speaking Indians if the bill was adopted, Marmon admitted that even though contacts with the white world had improved, it would be a good many years before the Seminoles were ready or able to assimilate into the larger community. Smathers then asked, "If there were a referendum, if all of the Indians were permitted to vote on what they wanted insofar as ending Federal control, what do you think the result would be?"[14] The superintendent offered that over seventy-five percent would vote against it, primarily because they would be afraid of losing their land to property taxes if they became independent. Rogers also stressed the Seminole readiness issue, asking Marmon directly, "in your experience with the Indians from 1942 until now, do you think they are prepared for the termination of Federal supervision?" Marmon replied, "No; I do not. I think there should be additional time given them in order that they may progress as they are going at the present time."[15]

Representative Berry, intent on establishing that the Seminoles were self-sufficient, asked Rex Lee if the government had done much for these Indians in the past or had they pretty much taken care of themselves; also, if the government intervened wouldn't that just make them more dependent?[16] When Lee, the bureau's leading termination advocate, answered that possibly the Seminoles could become more dependent, Senator Smathers launched into a long discourse by asking Lee if he had heard of the Point Four program and the Marshall Plan which the federal government initiated in countries around the world to help people become strong and independent. He suggested that it had been the goal of federal policy to move the Seminoles toward self-sufficiency and protect them; with three-fourths of the Indians unable to speak English, the possibility of exploitation was great unless the government set up a corporation that would guarantee title to Indian lands. Lee replied that tribes had the responsibility to set up such a legal entity and, under the bill, the secretary of the interior had the right to approve or disapprove it and appoint trustees to liquidate the land. "But," he noted, "I have more faith in the Secretary than that. I don't think he is looking toward liquidation. He is trying to put these people on their feet and to give them the type of organization and the type of protection that they want."[17]

Watkins interjected that under the Marshall Plan aid had not gone directly to individuals but to their government, and as for the Point Four program, he was not sure it had been all that successful. He stated, "I wanted to call your attention to that because my good friend from Florida rather bore down on that just a bit. It doesn't get to the individual people. I would be just as much against giving the Europeans a dole direct to individuals as I would be to giving the Indians that sort of thing."[18] Smathers countered that nothing in the bill would give the Seminoles a direct dole; what they were talking about was federal supervision over Indian lands and health and education programs. He disagreed with Watkins about the effectiveness of Point Four and Marshall Plans in making people independent, noting that is what federal supervision over Indians was supposed to do, but had failed. This exchange between Watkins and Smathers set the tone for the remainder of the session; the assimilationists exploited every point that would signal Seminole readiness for termination, while Smathers, Rogers, and to a lesser degree Haley took the opposite tack.

Prominent among those scheduled to testify was a delegation of eight Seminoles chosen by their people. On 9 October 1953, the Seminole agency hosted a meeting in which government officials from the bureau's Muskogee Area Office—at that time Florida Seminole affairs were still administered from Oklahoma—discussed the implications of HCR 108 with a large number of reservation Seminoles, as well as a few from the Tamiami Trail. As a result, the Seminoles present decided that each Indian community would select two representatives to attend the upcoming Washington hearings on the Seminole termination bill. The delegates from Dania were Sam Tommie and Laura Mae Osceola; from the Brighton Reservation, Billy Osceola and Toby Johns; Joseph Billy and Jimmy Cypress were sent by the Big Cypress Reservation; Henry Cypress and Curtis Osceola represented an off-reservation group. This delegation spoke for approximately sixty percent of the Florida Indian population; most important, these were the people who would be directly affected by the withdrawal of federal services and protection. They entered a prepared statement into the record which made the plea, "We, the Seminole Indians of Florida, request that no action be taken on the termination of Federal supervision over the property of the Seminole Indians for a period of 25 years."[19]

The Seminole statement outlined a number of reasons why termination should not take place. A lack of formal education meant that the Seminoles needed time to develop a leadership cadre which could administer their property. They feared that their lands, particularly pasturage, were insufficiently developed to become income producing, and if they failed to meet tax obligations, the property would be lost. The general state of Seminole health was poor, and the delegation recognized that the people had much to learn about proper sanitation, infant care, disease prevention, and so on, which could come about only if public health services were continued. They needed better housing on the reservations, along with council houses to help develop community spirit in the Indian settlements. Rural reservations such as Big Cypress and Brighton had much acreage that needed to be drained before the land could be used for pasturage or other agriculture. The delegates thought this could best be achieved through federal cooperation with state drainage and conservation projects in Florida. In conclusion, the Indians stated that "during the past 20 years our advancement has been rapid, but we need guidance for a longer period and we look to the Federal Government for continuance of their supervision."[20]

Obviously the Seminoles feared losing their reservation lands; nor did they want them placed under the trusteeship of a bank or other nongovernmental institution. Billy Osceola, a Baptist lay minister and cattle owner from the Brighton Reservation, stated, "These Indians want more time to get better education in that period of 25 years. At that time the Indians want to take over; they don't want to turn it over to some other organization. They want to control it. They want to handle their own affairs."[21] An early spirit of Indian self-assurance could be sensed in a response by the Seminoles' highly respected interpreter, Laura Mae Osceola. She was the only woman in the delegation, and its youngest and best educated member. A twenty-two-year-old housewife with young children, she had worked diligently to ensure that Seminoles would be present at the Washington hearings, often appearing before church and civic groups in the Fort Lauderdale area to solicit funds for the trip. When Representative Berry challenged her on how far she thought the Seminole people could be expected to progress, her retort was spirited and optimistic: "In twenty-five years they won't need your help. We will be giving you help!"[22]

Concerned individuals supported the Seminole position. All agreed in principle that the Indians ultimately could become self-sufficient and stand on their own, but felt that it would take much longer than the three years proposed in the legislation. Ivy Stranahan, of

Fort Lauderdale, had many years' experience working with the Indians. She came to the little settlement on New River in 1899 as the schoolteacher, but soon married trading post operator Frank Stranahan, who did a thriving business with the Seminoles. The young woman befriended Indian families who camped on her husband's property during visits to the store, and championed their cause for nearly seven decades. Mrs. Stranahan became active in organized Indian reform early in the century; as Indian Affairs Chairman of the Florida Federation of Women's Clubs during the 1920s, she strongly supported John Collier's reform movement, and later founded the "Friends of the Seminoles," a state-chartered tribal support group based in Fort Lauderdale.[23] Mrs. Stranahan became well known in Washington through her extensive correspondence with the Bureau of Indian Affairs and the Florida congressional delegation. She favored having the Seminoles conduct their own affairs at the appropriate time, but believed that would be in the very distant future.

The Friends of the Seminoles sent a contingent to monitor the Washington proceedings, and Mrs. O. H. Abbey entered their statement opposing termination into the subcommittee record. Although Mrs. Stranahan could not attend the hearings due to illness, her friend Congressman Dwight Rogers entered her statement expressing concern that "this hard work of 50 years will lose all its meaning and morale building, if we permit our government to withdraw all their protection."[24] Stranahan had already pursued the issue with officials in Washington. As early as December 1953, Commissioner Emmons wrote to her affirming that termination was desirable—but conceded there were differing estimates on how long supervision should continue. At the same time Senator Smathers also promised her, "I am keeping in close touch with developments on this matter, and want to assure you that I shall continue to protect the welfare of the Indians on every hand."[25]

Congressman Rogers submitted his own statement in support of the federal trusteeship over the Seminole lands and people; he suggested: "It seems to me that when this bill was drawn up one essential point was forgotten—the Seminoles' ignorance of the ownership of real estate or its handling, or of mortgaging, or of foreclosure, or of taxes, or of its value. How can their property be handled properly when they do not have the knowledge to protect their own interests? . . . Since this legislation is so vital to so many Indians, there is no need for hasty, ill-considered action which will only serve to multiply the problems of our Seminoles, not to solve them."[26]

William Sturtevant, an anthropologist who later became curator of North American ethnology at the Smithsonian Institution, had conducted extensive fieldwork among the Florida Indians. His opinion would weigh heavily in subcommittee deliberations. He estimated that 625 were opposed to termination and 275 were in favor, but also cautioned, "The Seminoles are so divided into factions that it will be impossible to turn the tribal property over intact to a tribal organization. . . . I would say that for this tribe at least, termination of Federal supervision at this time would cause great hardships."[27]

Bertram Scott, executive secretary of the politically active Seminole Indian Association, based in the Orlando area, also spoke. He offered a brief review of the Seminole cattle industry which developed in the 1930s after the government provided the starter herd. The business had originally operated as a tribal project but recently had been shifted to individual ownership, with eighty-eight Indians each owning about fifty head. The tribe held a $261,040 mortgage for the cattle that had to be repaid in eight years. Scott took this as a clear indication that Indians were moving in the direction of the self-sufficiency which Watkins, Berry, and others advocated. He believed Seminoles would eventually be capable of managing their own affairs; however, the tribal cattlemen, nearly all of whom were illiterate, still needed help from the agricultural agent and agency superintendent to run their business. If federal control of the reservations was withdrawn and the lands were taxed, the Indian cattlemen could lose everything. Scott also dismissed Watkins's suggestion that the State of Florida might serve as trustee for the tribe, citing massive Everglades drainage projects that threatened to inundate the reservations before the BIA and Seminole Indian Association intervened. Finally, he declared, "I really do not know why this bill was ever drawn concerning the Seminole Indians . . . but if there was ever a tribe that is not ready to go on its own, and will not be for some time, it is the Seminole Tribe of Florida."[28] To which Senator Watkins, in the first sign that he might concede the point, replied, "I will admit that it is not nearly as strong a case as the cases that have been made for other Indian tribes."[29]

An overwhelming majority of the statements submitted to the subcommittee by concerned citizens, civic groups, and experts on national Indian issues such as the Association on American Indian Affairs, emphasized the need for federal control and guidance to preserve the reservations. But in the hearings it became obvious that not all Florida Indians lived on federal lands, nor did they share common social and economic interests. About a third of them—the Miccosukee-speaking Trail Indians—lived in the Everglades and shunned the outside world. To complicate matters, the Trail Indians themselves were divided into several factions. These had been identified by a bureau official who traveled in Florida during February 1953 to investigate reports of Indian rights violations. He visited the camp of Mike Osceola and his father, William McKinley Osceola, the recognized leader of the Osceola band. Later he met with Jimmie Tiger who, with the medicine man Ingraham Billie, headed the other faction. These two groups followed diametrically opposite lifestyles. Mike Osceola owned a piece of land just west of Miami where he operated a store. He believed in educating Indian children and in complying with state and federal laws. The Tiger-Billie group believed Indian people were the rightful owners of any land they wanted to occupy in South Florida; it opposed education for Indian children and refused to recognize state hunting and fishing laws. So great were the differences between the two groups, the official noted, "that they now have two 'Green Corn Dances' or Councils."[30] Both Trail Indian groups had representation at the Washington hearings.

Larry Mike Osceola (generally called Mike), an articulate Indian entrepreneur claiming to represent seventy-seven Indians living on the east end of the Tamiami Trail, spoke forcefully for an immediate end to government control of Seminole affairs. He recounted his own experiences in public high school in Miami (where he had known Senator Smathers) and later training as an aircraft mechanic. In addition, he operated a business selling merchandise to tourists on the Tamiami Trail and owned cattle pastured at the Brighton Reservation. Osceola questioned the statement of Superintendent Marmon that over six hundred Indians spoke no English, claiming that he knew of only ten or so who could not converse with outsiders. He felt that Indians were capable of managing their own financial affairs without federal assistance, and therefore endorsed setting up a corporation to manage Indian lands. An attorney with close ties to the Osceola group, O. B. White, of Miami, submitted a statement recommending immediate termination of government supervision and establishment of an eleemosynary corporation to handle Indian property. He and Osceola also questioned the legitimacy of Miccosukee Seminoles in the "official" delegation who claimed to speak for off-reservation Indians.[31]

Rogers and Haley assailed the credibility of Mike Osceola, questioning whether he spent much time on the reservations or knew the people in the tribe well enough to state that most spoke English; furthermore, Smathers charged that Osceola might want termination because it would make him important to the tribe due to his connections in the white community. Osceola denied this accusation, claiming that he only wanted the best for his people. That was good enough for Senator Watkins, who told Osceola, "I think you are a splendid example of what can be accomplished when people are given their opportunity to do as you have done, to work, and particularly to stand on your own feet and develop. I congratulate you upon the success you have made. And I think instead of criticizing you for wanting to help your people, you ought to be complimented for that. The Seminoles would be much better off if they had a hundred just like you, who could lead the way out and help them with their problems."[32]

The Miccosukee General Council was represented by attorney Morton Silver and spokesman Buffalo Tiger. Silver had written to the secretary of the interior in October 1953 announcing that he represented the "General Council of the Seminole Indians of the State of Florida"—the name would evolve to become Miccosukee General Council—and it was the first time federal authorities realized such a group existed. The BIA initially suspected the "council" to be a numerically insignificant rump group of malcontents whose claims were spurious and possibly inflated by an unscrupulous attorney. Silver spoke first, claiming that the General Council represented a majority of Seminole adults in Florida. His clients had lived peacefully in

35

the Everglades, never recognizing federal authority over their land, and sent representatives to the hearings only to ensure that the government did nothing to affect their independence. But when Watkins noted, "I fail to see how much damage we are going to do them by withdrawing Federal supervision that they never had,"[33] the attorney then claimed that the council also represented many Indian people on the reservations and was protecting their interests as well; he also pointed out that the number of reservation Seminole delegates present was disproportionate to their true constituency. Silver's abrasive advocacy and evasive answers to questions about how long federal supervision should be retained obviously irritated some members of the subcommittee.

By contrast, when the low-key Buffalo Tiger testified, he was less confrontational. Although he lived in Hialeah, had a non-Indian wife, and sent his children to public school, Tiger claimed to speak for three hundred Miccosukee Indians who were opposed to any federal action that would impair their existing way of life. He estimated that six hundred Seminoles could not speak English. When asked if his people would consider sending their children to school, Tiger replied that Miccosukees were upset over the bill because they thought it would change their law and way of life: "It is a little too involved for Indians. I think they would be unhappy to do it right away."[34]

Senator Smathers sought to identify conditions under which the Indians might accept termination. He asked if they would object if the government assured them that their land could not be stolen, if their land was placed in an Indian corporation to be used for the general benefit of all their people. When Tiger still demurred, Smathers asked, "You say we should do nothing. Is that what you are saying, to leave everything as it is?" Tiger replied calmly, "It would be easier for you, I imagine."[35]

Smathers never convinced Buffalo Tiger that the bill could protect his people by vesting title to the land in the Indians themselves. Watkins, too, pursued the theme that the Indians would have ownership of the land, something that their children could inherit. He totally missed the point that the Indians believed they already had a right to the land through treaties and prior usage; they had no interest in the concept of property in severalty. "I will tell you now," Tiger replied, "I am pretty sure my people won't like that.... this bill you are speaking about now is just a bad thing for the Seminoles."[36]

The confusing and often contradictory testimony underscored both the political division existing between the on- and off-reservation Seminole factions and the fragmentation within the Trail Indian camps. Understandably Senator Smathers declared, "Mr. Chairman, I do not know where we are. I came up here to find out what was going on, and we succeeded in getting me even more confused about this bill than I was when we started."[37] By the time the hearings concluded the following day, a number of subcommittee members evidently shared Smather's confusion and were beginning to have doubts about including the Florida Seminoles on the termination list. No action was taken on a Seminole termination bill during the remainder of the session. Florida's senior senator, Spessard Holland, attended the second day of the Washington hearings and later wrote Mrs. Stranahan, "I feel that the Interior and Insular Affairs Committees of the House and Senate were wise in not reporting out the bill which would remove the Seminoles from the guardianship of the Federal Government, and I know careful consideration will be given to the desires of the Seminoles by these committees prior to any such action in the future."[38]

Following the congressional hearing that spring, Stranahan, Scott, and other Seminole partisans continued their lobbying against federal plans to withdraw services from the tribe. They emphasized that no matter what the outcome of the termination issue, additional lands should be secured for the Seminoles as provided for in the termination bill. As an inducement to gain Seminole acceptance of the bill, a provision had been inserted that transferred 27,086 acres of submarginal land at the Brighton Reservation to the tribe. Brighton encompassed 35,000 acres, 6,790 of which were secured with Indian Reorganization Act funds and 1,920 through exchange with the State of Florida, and the submarginal land was the carrot which assimilationists hoped would induce Seminoles to accept termination. The Resettlement Administration, a New Deal agency, originally purchased this tract in the 1930s for Seminole use. Title subsequently passed to the Department of Agriculture, with supervision transferred to the Department of the Interior by Executive Order 7868 on 15 April 1938. If the Seminole termination bill passed, the entire

35,000 acres at Brighton would be placed in an Indian corporation, or liquidated if the tribe chose to do so. But antitermination advocates warned that the tribe could lose its land to taxes unless federal trusteeship protection continued for at least another quarter century.

The hearings evidently persuaded Senator Smathers to clarify his position on termination. In April 1954 he engaged in a televised debate with Senator Watkins which aired on a Washington station; the topic was "Should the American Indian Be Given Full Citizenship Responsibility?" The debate climaxed when Watkins declared, "May I point out also that what the Indian really wants; he wants representation without taxation. He can tax all the rest of us and vote for people who do tax us; but he doesn't want to pay taxes himself even though he is able to do so." Smathers retorted, "Now I wouldn't go that far because every Indian that leaves the reservation and goes out and lives like the rest of us live, he is paying his fair share of taxes; he's in the service; he's doing everything everyone else is doing."[39] But this exchange masked a deeper philosophical cleavage. Smathers later confided that

> Watkins was a Mormon, and he took the position that they did not practice his religion. He was pretty tough about that stuff. . . . The best way to bring them into the twentieth century was to eliminate their subsidies (as he called them), which were government subsidized programs to keep them in villages and therefore they would be backward longer. The way to move them into the twentieth century and move them up was to cut off the funds and the help that we were giving Indians because they were Indians. . . . He was not a gradualist, he wanted to move them quickly, lock, stock and barrel, into the white-level community. He would say, "As of next year, all your kids are going to school, even though half of them cannot even speak English." He thought the way to do it was just to jerk them. He was going to make a big quick operation on them. Some of us said, "That is not right; it is unfair. Most people have an opportunity to have gradualism in to the movement." It was not right to take many of these people who had not had the education that some of us had.[40]

Smathers would be a powerful voice when deliberations on the Seminole bill resumed the following year.

Those who opposed termination were also concerned about the tactics of Morton Silver and the Trail Indians who claimed a historically separate existence from the main body of Seminoles. This position first surfaced during the Washington hearings; while the subcommittee was in session, a Miccosukee delegation made a dramatic presentation of their so-called Buckskin Declaration (the message was inscribed on a deerskin decorated with egret plumes) to a representative of President Eisenhower.[41] In this document the General Council set forth a brief history of relations between the Florida Indians and the United States since 1821, then turned to the land claim that had been filed with the Indian Claims Commission by a group of reservation Seminoles seeking monetary compensation for past injustices. The General Council disavowed any interest in financial compensation and held that the claim was adverse to their best interest. The document expressed their desire to continue a traditional lifestyle free of government interference. Finally, they declared they wished to deal directly with a representative of the president rather than the Bureau of Indian Affairs.

Following presentation of the Buckskin Declaration, Silver and Buffalo Tiger sent letters and telegrams to the White House, some of which were deemed disrespectful to the president and his office. President Eisenhower expressed sympathy for Indian concerns but rejected "independent action" and urged use of conventional channels. Silver then threatened that if no satisfaction could be obtained from the government, the General Council would submit their case to "the appropriate tribunals of national and international jurisdiction."[42] In August 1954 the president notified Silver that the commissioner would come to Florida for meetings with the General Council and the other Indians. Throughout the fall an exchange of querulous correspondence took place between Silver and the bureau, but eventually plans were solidified for the commissioner's visit.

In December 1954 Commissioner Emmons journeyed to Florida and met with all major Indian groups to hear their positions on a variety of issues. He was accompanied by Morrill Tozier, information officer for the bureau, who took notes during the consultations and compiled an official report. For five full days, 16–20 December, the commissioner held meetings at each of the three federal reservations, as well as with Mike Osceola, the faction led by his uncle Cory Osceola, and the General Council. The reservation Seminoles were generally in agreement on what they expected from the government. Specifically, they wanted prompt settlement of the $50 million land claim filed with the Indian Claims Commission; education for their children in public schools rather than in segregated BIA classrooms; improvement of their land resources to increase productivity; adult education to provide command of English; modern homes to replace thatched-roof chikees; a tribal organization based on majority rule; an additional twenty-five years of assistance and trust protection; and administrative transfer of the Dania Agency from the area office in Muskogee, Oklahoma, to direct supervision by the BIA central office in Washington DC.

Next, Emmons visited Mike Osceola's village on the Tamiami Trail. Mike lived there with a non-Indian wife and his elderly father, William McKinley Osceola, who had been a prominent figure in tribal politics during the 1930s. Although Osceola had advocated termination at the Washington hearings, during the meeting with Emmons his attitude toward termination was more subdued, and he conceded that some members of the tribe might be unprepared for release from federal supervision. From interviews the commissioner decided that Mike exerted little influence among the other Seminoles, particularly after his stand in favor of termination. The commissioner also visited the camp of Cory and John Osceola; although brothers of old William McKinley, they had little to do with Mike Osceola's village. This faction also was at odds with the General Council. Emmons learned that Cory Osceola operated within the same overall cultural framework as the General Council, and the cleavage originated in a personal dispute between Cory Osceola and the medicine man who headed the council, Ingraham Billie. The commissioner concluded that neither of these very small groups played a major role in the Florida Indian dispute. In the long run the acculturated Mike Osceola sided with the reservation Seminoles, while Cory Osceola's people were more attuned to the traditional constituency of the General Council.

Commissioner Emmons's primary purpose in coming to Florida was to meet with the Miccosukee General Council and to develop a clearer picture of its structure, which Indians it actually represented, and what it wanted. To this end two meetings were scheduled with the Trail Indians. On 19 December the initial session convened at Jimmie Tiger's camp on the Tamiami Trail some thirty-five miles west of Miami. At least a dozen newspaper and magazine reporters and photographers covered this public event. A private meeting was then held on 20 December at attorney Morton Silver's office in Miami. From these consultations Emmons and his staff gained a better grasp of the Indian situation in Florida. On the question of "legitimacy" they realized that the General Council was not an organization recently thrown together by a group of Indian extremists, or an ad hoc group fabricated by Morton Silver for his own ends. It evolved over many generations, having been formed by the medicine men as an outgrowth of the Green Corn Dance held each spring. Another issue involved the extent of the General Council's influence among the Seminole people. It was impossible to determine exact figures since no membership rolls existed, and federal officials discounted Morton Silver's claim that the General Council represented six hundred Seminoles; even so, they had a good turnout, estimated at seventy-five, for the meeting at Jimmie Tiger's camp, while none of the reservation meetings drew more than fifty Indians. Thus Emmons assumed that even though the General Council represented less than a majority of the Florida Indians, it spoke for a substantial minority and therefore should be included in policy deliberations. Indeed, officials concluded that "a large part of the current problem arises from the fact that it has been largely ignored or overlooked by the Government until very recent months."[43]

Another point arose from Silver's claim that there were two Indian nations in Florida—Miccosukees and Muskogees—and all Miccosukees followed the General Council's leadership. After exploring the situation, Emmons determined that although the Indians retained two languages, other cultural differences between Muskogees and Miccosukees appeared to be trivial. He found it noteworthy that one of the medicine men who played a key role in the General Council deliberations was a Muskogee, while many living on the federal reservations were Miccosukees. After examining the conflicting figures submitted by Silver and another attorney who represented the reservation Seminoles in their land claim case, Emmons concluded that the General Council spoke for about 375 Indians—at best a bare majority of the Miccosukee population. Therefore the most meaningful cleavage existing among the Florida Indians was not between Miccosukees and Muskogees, but between a mixed group of Miccosukees and Muskogees residing on the three federal reservations and a predominantly Miccosukee off-reservation population. The reservation Indians were generally perceived as accepting the framework of non-Indian society around them and wanting to improve their economic and social status within the broad pattern of that society. The Trail Indians, by contrast, deliberately rejected non-Indian society and preferred to continue living in a traditional subsistence-level hunting and fishing economy. Furthermore, the federal officials realized that these broad categories were not definitive; the lines were so fluid that there were probably families in each group which, if forced to choose, would join the other.

The most contentious issue to emerge in these meetings with the General Council was of federal recognition. It surfaced at Jimmie Tiger's camp when the Indians objected to BIA reports referring to them as "squatters" living along the Tamiami Trail. These Miccosukees were convinced that the land was theirs; they had occupied and used the Everglades for many generations. They were alarmed by recent development near their camps; livestock operators fenced large areas, there was dynamiting by oil explorers, and oil derricks had been erected within sight of the meeting location. Medicine man Sam Jones dramatically implored, "The land I stand on is my body. I want you to help me keep it."[44] Morton Silver stated that the Trail Indians were descendants of Seminoles who did not assent to an 1833 treaty mandating removal to the Indian Territory in present-day Oklahoma. Rather, they stayed and resisted American forces; he contended that the Miccosukees therefore owned a large part of south Florida under an executive order which confirmed the "Macomb Treaty" of 1839.[45] This was a dubious claim since the treaty had never been ratified in Washington. In summation, Silver repeated that Indians did not want usual legal title to the land, only a recognition of their rights to perpetual and exclusive use. They also demanded the prevention of further encroachment into their region, as well as federal recognition of the General Council. Silver's associate, Leo Alpert, emphasized that Indians held a sound claim to the land not only in terms of basic human rights and elementary justice, but also in specific legal terms that would stand up in court.[46]

During the Miami meeting Commissioner Emmons attempted to establish more precisely a common basis for understanding with the General Council. He emphasized the necessity and desirability of dividing Florida Indians into two broad groupings; there should be a referendum or plebiscite giving each adult Seminole an opportunity to chose which group to join. Furthermore, he hoped that membership would remain open so that when children reached age twenty-one they could make their own choice; this had already been broached with the reservation people and found to be acceptable. The commissioner sketched a plan for setting aside several thousand acres in the Everglades for the Trail Indians, but this might necessitate their giving up a share of any settlement from the Indian Claims Commission. Finally, Emmons expressed the hope that in the future Trail Indians would send their children to public schools. Buffalo Tiger had previously stated that once they settled the land problem and the Indians had tangible evidence of the government's good faith, they might change their minds about schooling. Tozier remained skeptical and recommended in his report that an Indian agreement regarding schooling be made part of any land settlement.

In response, Buffalo Tiger and Morton Silver indicated general agreement with Emmons. They then proceeded to mark on a map the exact area they claimed so Emmons could take the information back to Washington and develop a settlement plan. However, much of the area shown on the map included the State Indian Reservation that Florida's legislature had set aside for all Seminoles and that Big Cypress Reservation cattlemen already used. Toward the end of the consultation Tozier recapitulated the general understanding from his notes for everyone's agreement. Alpert repeated that the Miccosukees were a sovereign nation, and emphasized that recognition of the General Council was a vital issue in achieving a settlement. After Emmons returned to the capital he received a letter from Silver asking that the question of recognition receive top priority, and suggesting that the land problem be "deferred" for later consideration. Although Silver claimed to reflect the Indian position on the matter, neither Emmons nor Tozier could recall any Indians having raised the issue of their sovereignty, so they queried the attorney and received two justifications for his position. First, Indians were at a disadvantage in dealing with the local legal system and should be allowed to administer their own justice; this could best be achieved by recognizing their sovereignty. Second, if the government continued to deal with every "little chief," factionalism would increase and chaos would reign among the Florida Indians. While the second point was valid, this appeared to be yet another effort by Silver to secure some type of exclusive recognition for the General Council at the expense of other Seminole groups.

Commissioner Emmons realized it would not be a simple matter to resolve the Trail Indians' claims for land and recognition. When Silver deluged the White House and bureau with calls for immediate action on his demands, Emmons responded curtly,

> I am definitely of the opinion that the General Council should not be recognized at this time. . . . you have persisted in pressing this matter and have used a variety of tactical moves in an obvious effort to compel recognition before an understanding can be determined on other matters. As I have indicated to you before, I went down to Florida last December in good faith and with a sincere hope that we could confer with the Ingraham Billie group of Indians in an atmosphere of trust and mutual respect. I have not abandoned hope that this will be possible. However, I must say frankly that your continuing insistence on immediate recognition is having an adverse effect.[47]

Thereafter the bureau would focus its efforts on the economic and social development of the Seminole reservations with an eye to possible future termination.

When the Eighty-fourth Congress convened in January 1955, the sentiment for termination remained strong, and there was a possibility that the Seminole bill would be reintroduced. The House Subcommittee on Indian Affairs scheduled additional hearings to be held in Florida, and on 5 April 1955 Representative Haley, who had assumed the subcommittee chairmanship, presided at a day-long session in Clewiston, a town approximately equidistant from the Brighton and Big Cypress communities. Many who had testified at the Washington hearings in 1954 were again present. Haley opened the session by recalling that a year earlier he had brought members of the House subcommittee to Florida to investigate Seminole problems—although they held no public hearings—and there were still several matters that required study and clarification. "We hope to gather information," he noted, "which will help in preparing termination time schedules, if termination is desirable, information which will guide our thinking on the question of State trusteeship, and on the timing and basis for state assumption of welfare, law and order."[48] The latter issues were particularly important because Florida would become one of twelve states to claim civil and criminal jurisdiction over offenses committed by or against Indians under the provisions of Public Law 280 enacted by Congress during 1953.[49] Following Haley's statement, longtime subcommittee member A. L. Miller, of Nebraska, acknowledged the presence of Congressman Paul Rogers, who had been elected to replace his recently deceased father, Dwight Rogers.[50] The new congressman from the sixth district welcomed the subcommittee, saying, "I think we are very fortunate to have this committee take the time when the rest of the members of Congress are taking a vacation, to come down here because they are interested, deeply interested, in the conditions of our Indians."[51] At the subcommittee's invitation Rogers remained and participated in the proceedings.

Strong statements came from several local officials—a superintendent of schools, three county commissioners, and a county attorney—who agreed that taxpayers would expect the government to reimburse localities for the expenses of education and road maintenance, as well as medical and welfare services to the Indian population. When Haley asked an official whether the termination bill and attempts to interrupt government trusteeship over the Seminole Indians should be delayed until the present younger generation had reached adulthood and received a good education, the response was resoundingly affirmative.[52] Agnes Denver, a Seminole living with her family in

Utah, also made a statement. Denver, one of the first Seminoles to complete high school at the Cherokee Indian School in North Carolina, represented a progressive element within the tribe. She was living proof of an Indian's ability to function away from the reservations, yet she unequivocally declared, "The Seminole Indians are not ready to be terminated."[53]

Bill Osceola, acting as chairman of the board of directors for the three reservations, entered a statement reiterating the tribe's desire to extended federal protection for twenty-five more years. Even that sounded unacceptable to the Reverend Henry Cypress, a member of the delegation sent to Washington the previous spring; he expressed the sentiment of his small off-reservation group: "Some people said 25 more years extended, but I have said in Washington I want a lifetime."[54] Mike Osceola reiterated his position favoring termination. Initially he testified that the Seminoles should not be turned loose without a legally chartered organization to protect their interests. Questioning by Haley and Rogers disclosed that Mike Osceola had educational and economic advantages which other Indians did not enjoy, and he then became defensive. He declared that he did not believe in socialism, and if the federal trusteeship remained for twenty-five more years it would subconsciously indoctrinate the Indian people to socialism.

This struck a responsive chord with conservative Congressman Miller, who considered Mike Osceola to be a "fine example" of what Indians should achieve on their own. He, too, questioned the seemingly arbitrary request for extending federal supervision over the Seminoles: "This 25 years puzzled me. I think if we make them wards and give them something every day and feed, house and clothe them, and they make no efforts on their own, it will still be that way 25 years from now."[55] This, in turn, drew a strong rebuttal from Haley, who detailed federal neglect of the Florida Indians; he concluded by saying, "Of course, I take now the position that I have taken all along: I too want to see the Seminoles where they will fit in the economy and the social life of my State and their own community. I do not know whether 25 years is too much, but I do know, and I think it is plain to be seen, that 3 years is not the proper time, or 2 years. So I just hope that the gentlemen will assist me in maintaining a program that will bring the Seminole Indians of Florida some of the things that they should have been receiving many years ago."[56] This strong statement from the chairman—which provided the first public indication of his intent in the matter—drew applause from the largely antitermination audience.

The following day, subcommittee members reconvened at Jimmie Tiger's camp on the Tamiami Trail. The first person to testify was Buffalo Tiger, speaking for the Miccosukee General Council and its traditional leaders headed by the old medicine man Ingraham Billie. Tiger again made it clear that the Trail Indians were not a party to the Seminoles' $50 million claim pending before the Indian Claims Commission. "We don't want a claim for money," he stated, "we want a claim for land."[57] The next witness, attorney Morton Silver, clashed with the subcommittee members on a number of points. Some of the congressmen present still smarted from the Buckskin Declaration presented to President Eisenhower while the Washington hearings were in session, and they learned more about Silver's "grandstanding" tactics in behalf of his clients. In the course of occasionally hostile questioning, Silver revealed that he had attempted to quash the Seminole claim before the Indian Claims Commission, and continued to proclaim that his clients had a legal right to most of southern Florida. Moreover, in his opinion only the General Council legitimately represented all Florida Indians. In his zeal to validate this claim, Silver continued to advise the Miccosukees that they might be able to take their case before the United Nations.

Silver's was an extreme position, and even Buffalo Tiger took exception to his claim that the General Council should speak for other Seminoles throughout the state. Mrs. Stranahan admitted, "I am like the Indians, I don't know who owns this land out here."[58] She had never heard of Silver's claim that Indians owned most of Florida until it appeared in the newspapers the previous month. In his testimony, Bertram Scott, of the Seminole Indian Association, criticized the Miami attorney. He admonished the subcommittee: "The Silver business is a serious matter. . . . he has caused no end of trouble here."[59] Scott reminded the subcommittee members of Silver's positions on recognition for the Miccosukee General Council, his claim that the

Indians legally owned much of southern Florida, and the threats to take claims before the World Court and the United Nations.

The favorable tenor of these hearings convinced the antitermination forces that they had won the day. On 20 April, Bertram Scott informed Emmons that he had written to Haley requesting introduction of legislation to immediately transfer submarginal lands at Brighton Reservation to the Seminole Indians. He reminded the BIA official that "termination bills of the last session contained provisions for such transfer, but fortunately those bills never saw the light of day. There will be no such bills introduced into the present Congress, we presume, at least none affecting the Seminoles."[60] Haley responded, "I have not reintroduced the same bill that I introduced last year for the Seminoles because of a situation that has developed since I saw you last and which I will discuss with you next time I see you. I sincerely do not think that the passage of such a bill at the present time would be beneficial to the Seminole Tribe.[61] The situation alluded to was a report from Rep. Francis Walter, chairman of the House Committee on Un-American Activities, responding to Haley's request for information on Morton Silver, Leo Alpert, and others who had created a problem at the Tamiami Trail termination hearing. While committee records made no reference to Morton Silver, there was a file detailing Alpert's association with Communist front organizations in Maryland and his representation of members of the Communist Party.[62] This turn of events evidently reinforced Haley's support of the reservation Seminoles. Following Scott's suggestion he introduced a bill transferring approximately thirty thousand acres of land from the Department of Agriculture to the Bureau of Indian Affairs and officially creating the Brighton Reservation, which became law on 20 July 1956.[63]

In Fort Lauderdale, Ivy Stranahan also perceived a victory. The 1954 annual report of the Friends of the Seminoles contained a special report from its congressional lobbying committee which she headed. It highlighted the work of the members who attended the Washington hearings to support Seminole requests for additional time before termination. "So well did these delegates support requests and protests of the Seminoles," she wrote, "that the Interior and Insular Affairs Committee of the House and Senate did not even report-out committee bills No. s2747 and HR7321 terminating Federal Service to the Florida Seminoles. Your personal letters and telegrams to your Congressmen gave the much needed support. . . . This leaves the status of the Florida Seminoles the same as before the 83d Congress."[64] The committee report ended by lauding all groups that had worked for the Seminole cause, and extended special appreciation and thanks to the Florida congressional delegation.

Congress saw no Seminole termination bill introduced in the Eighty-fourth Congress or thereafter, thanks in great part to the determined opposition of Floridians, including Ivy Stranahan, Bertram Scott, and Dwight Rogers, as well as the Seminoles themselves. Discrepancies in information presented by witnesses during the congressional hearings—such as estimates of the number of Seminoles who spoke no English, which ranged from ten to over six hundred— must have convinced the solons that a great majority of Florida's Indians were unprepared to manage their own affairs and required federal trusteeship for the foreseeable future. Certainly the statements and subsequent actions of George Smathers and James Haley indicate that they had adopted a firm antitermination stance, at least where the Florida Seminoles were concerned, and moved to stifle such legislation. Nearly forty years later Senator Smathers was hazy on specific details of how he and other members of the Florida congressional delegation worked to thwart Seminole termination, but he firmly recalled, "We stopped the bill."[65]

Anthropologist Oliver La Farge, president of the Association on American Indian Affairs and a frequent critic of bureau policies, placed the Seminoles' experience in its proper perspective:

> Of the bills introduced under the Resolution, those to terminate the Flatheads, Turtle Mountain Chippewas, and Florida Seminoles were killed in committee. Opposition from the tribes concerned was strong and well presented, the states they lived in also opposed the bills; the legislation was obviously ill conceived. The Turtle Mountain Chippewas are strong contenders for the title of most destitute Indians in the United States; the Florida Indians have only recently had universal schooling and

retain a large group of members who speak no English. It is diffi-cult to conceive on what basis these two tribes were ever marked for termination.[66]

Once again Florida's Seminoles had thwarted an effort by the dom-inant society to destroy their tribal integrity, but they still faced an uncertain future. How could they survive economically in the face of severe funding cuts for employment and services on the reserva-tions? What would prevent federal or state authorities from revisiting termination in the future? Did the tribes retain any measure of le-gal and political sovereignty in the face of Public Law 280 and other congressional measures? There were no clear answers to these ques-tions in 1955, but the Seminole leaders moved to protect themselves as best they could, and that meant organizing some form of tribal government.

CHAPTER 3

Organizing a Tribal Government

Having avoided the likely disaster of termination, Florida's Seminoles began to resonate with early rumblings of the Indian self-determination movement. That they were able to do so was attributable in great part to those twenty-one anonymous Seminoles who voted in 1935 to accept Indian Reorganization Act provisions, and native people in Florida remained eligible to organize a government and business corporation under section 16 of the act.[1] This fundamental legislation of the Indian New Deal allowed tribes to organize a local government with limited powers vested in a constitution and bylaws. Upon receiving a petition from one-third of the reservation Indians, the secretary of the interior could issue a federal charter of incorporation empowering the tribe to conduct its business affairs. Both the constitution and the federal charter documents had to be submitted to ratification by a majority vote of all adult tribal members living on the reservations. Therefore the IRA initially served as a vehicle for the exclusive use of reservation Indians; those living off-reservation could participate in the planning and drafting of a constitution and corporate charter, but their reservation relatives retained control over adoption.

A loose coalition spearheaded the Seminole drive to gain tribal organization. It included both Miccosukee- and Muskogee-speaking leaders from the Dania, Brighton, and Big Cypress reservations such as Sam Tommie, Bill Osceola, Frank Billie, and Billy Osceola. All were Christians and some served their communities as lay ministers. As cattle owners they had an economic stake in the continued development of the reservation beef herd enterprise, which required technical assistance, supervision, and financial support from federal and state authorities. These men presented a combination of aggressive leadership and entrepreneurial skill that received strong support from the Seminole agency staff; their pursuit of a tribal government exacerbated the rift between reservation Seminoles and traditional Miccosukees.

Following his visit with the Seminole factions in late 1954, Commissioner Emmons remained convinced that no single organization represented all Indians in Florida since the reservation and non-reservation elements were separate and distinct. At first he hoped to organize both groups simultaneously, but the land and sovereignty issues raised by Trail Indians made this impossible. In addition, the reservation people had already taken a preliminary step toward self-government by setting up a tribal board of directors that could speak and act on their behalf; the Miccouskees were nowhere near that point of organization. In June 1955 Peru Farver, head of the tribal affairs branch at the bureau, visited Florida to discuss with the Seminoles a governmental organization as well as social and economic programs. He met with leaders on each reservation and discussed their needs for housing, education, credit, and a governing body to oversee all tribal business affairs—mainly the development of their pasture lands and cattle herds. Farver later recommended that the bureau provide support in each of these areas for at least five years. Initially he suggested organizing the reservation Indians under a Florida state charter, but the commissioner abandoned this in favor of developing a federal constitution and corporate charter, while leaving the Tamiami Trail group to live as they wished.[2]

There remained another aspect of the Seminole economy that the bureau's planners had to consider: the nascent tribal crafts industry. In August of the same year the general manager of the Indian Arts and Crafts Board, J. E. Davis, visited the Florida reservations, then reported to the commissioner that Seminole artisans were renowned for their fine patchwork sewing and there seemed to be a growing demand for colorful skirts, aprons, handbags, and dolls, as well as for baskets and wood carvings. Bureau teachers organized the Seminole Crafts Guild in 1940 without any operating capital, but received assistance in marketing their products nationally from the Indian Arts and Crafts Board. The business grew steadily and in 1954 sales reached $14,168 with more than $10,000 going to individual artisans. Davis recommended organizing the guild into a cooperative under the laws of Florida, with a permanent facility at the Dania Reservation, where year-round tourist traffic existed.[3] Even though arts and crafts had limited potential for generating high levels of income for the Seminole people, the bureau continued to promote this nonthreatening form of Indian economic enterprise.

Meanwhile, following the subcommittee session held at Jimmie Tiger's camp, the Miccosukee General Council continued to seek recognition from state and federal authorities. But growing opposition to the activities of Morton Silver surfaced. Two days after the hearing Robert Mitchell, president of the Seminole Indian Association, wrote to Buffalo Tiger denouncing the representations Silver made before the congressmen. Mitchell, a prominent nurseryman from Orlando and longtime friend of the Miccosukees, maintained his own camp in the Everglades and spoke their language fluently. He wrote bluntly, "I want to tell you now what the Bureau of Indian Affairs should have told you last December—that neither Mr. Silver nor anyone else can get for you all the land lying south of Lake Okeechobee; that talk of taking the matter to the United Nations is just a lot of bunk. . . . It is my honest opinion that he is doing you and your people a great deal of harm and that he knows that he cannot get for you, all of the things he has told you he could get."[4]

Morton Silver recognized that Mitchell and Bertram Scott were potentially his staunchest non-Indian opponents in Florida. Earlier he had written to Mitchell chastising him for derogatory statements reportedly made to Commissioner Emmons and the congressional subcommittee members, but suggested a conference to reconcile their differences. For his part, Mitchell would have nothing to do with Silver, while Scott constantly implored Emmons to move ahead with recognition for the reservation Seminoles. "Frankly," he wrote, "we cannot understand why you continue in your efforts to appease Mr. Silver. Those Indians, a clear majority, who are willing and anxious to adapt themselves to our way of life get a minimum of consideration from Washington."[5] Miami attorney O. B. White also advised Emmons that a dangerous situation had developed among the Trail Indians, charging that the faction counseled by Silver intimidated and threatened the others.[6] None of this deterred Buffalo Tiger and

Silver from continuing to push the General Council's agenda with federal and state officials.

Commissioner Emmons was in no position to take unilateral action against any group—or its attorney—while he attempted to resolve the Florida Indian situation. Increasingly, Silver muddied the waters by unrelenting letter writing to members of Congress, and by leaking information to the press; this left Emmons frequently responding to congressional inquiries concerning bureau policy. For instance, Emmons notified Ingraham Billie about Farver's impending visit to Florida to help the reservation Seminoles plan their own organization, but assured the old medicine man that the Trail Indians would remain wholly separate.[7] That letter immediately came to the attention of Representative Dante Fascell of Miami, who then queried Emmons on legal points pertaining to recognition of the reservation Seminoles' government; since these were issues which Silver had previously framed, it is reasonable to assume that he transmitted them to Fascell with the letter.[8] Emmons assured the congressman that Farver's trip was only exploratory, and he had no authorization to make any final decisions or to grant official recognition to any particular group at that time.[9] Disregarding the commissioner's assurances, Silver evidently feared that if the reservations were organized, federal authorities would lose interest in the Miccosukees.

More positively, Emmons informed Congressman Paul Rogers and Mrs. Stranahan that the bureau was initiating an adult education program on the reservations. Stranahan had contacted Rogers about delays in getting that program under way, and Emmons admitted it took a great deal longer than expected to get programs initiated for the benefit of the Seminoles. He recognized that many adult Seminoles had never attended school and could not speak or understand English, and he hoped to provide them with at least a working knowledge of the language; in that way they would be able to get better jobs and make adjustments to both the demands and opportunities of modern life. Emmons also recalled, "When the possibility of such a program was taken up at our three reservation meetings, I was amazed and deeply encouraged to find that practically all the adults in attendance raised their hands indicating a definite interest. So I have no doubt that our new adult education program will be well accepted at Seminole and that it will produce many far-reaching benefits."[10]

An amusing though apocryphal version of this event has made its way into the literature of the period. In 1955 Emmons initiated adult education programs on a number of Indian reservations to counteract national criticism of the federal withdrawal policy. According to Larry Burt,

> One BIA official in the education branch did not see the program as a wise use of tight dollars since it was not based on concrete information to determine the needs or projected benefits; he related an episode that allegedly was the impetus for starting the project, although he stressed that the story came to him indirectly, and he therefore could not verify it. While on a trip to Florida, Emmons supposedly asked a group of traditional Seminoles if they would like to learn to speak English, but the interpreter translated the question as "the Commissioner would like you to raise your hands." Naturally most of the Indians responded. Emmons was impressed and described the event on numerous occasions to show the enthusiasm toward his adult education program.[11]

If this did take place it serves as a reminder that federal officials, their interpreters, and Indian audiences were not always operating on the same wavelength.

Efforts to settle the Miccosukees' demands for land of their own remained stalled until Commissioner Emmons again visited Florida in the spring of 1956, and took an active role in moving the issue forward. Since his initial visit in 1954, Emmons had maintained that there could be no federal recognition for the Trail Indians until their land requests were settled. Even so, the Miccosukee General Council and its attorney continued to press their demands on both counts. Although the Miccosukees had backed away from the earlier claims to most of south Florida, at a Washington meeting in 1955 Buffalo Tiger, Morton Silver, and his new associate, George Miller, demanded exclusive and perpetual use of—but not necessarily legal title to—approximately 1,500,000 acres including all of state Conservation Area 3, as well as part of a 108,000-acre tract which Florida had set aside in 1935 as the State Indian Reservation, and other smaller parcels. By the next year this claim was reduced to exclusive hunting and fishing rights only in the western portion of the conservation area, and shared rights with non-Indians in the eastern part during the hunting and fishing seasons. The General Council also wanted the right to take frogs in Everglades National Park and for cypress logging near the Big Cypress Reservation. Since much of this area was not federally controlled, the bureau could do nothing and the issue remained deadlocked.

The Miccosukees' maneuvering to force federal recognition continued to undercut Emmons' efforts to organize the reservations. Their attorney frequently protested to state officials and the media that his clients were either being ignored or treated unfairly. Eventually the Miccosukees incurred the enmity of many individuals both in Washington and Florida by their involvement in the Seminole land claims case. As a result, Emmons took an increasingly hard line against the Miccosukee General Council and Silver. But there may also have been another reason for the commissioner's attitude. Larry Burt has placed the Emmons-Silver conflict in a different perspective, indicating a cold-war suspicion of infiltration by subversive elements: "By this time the general drive for quick termination and withdrawal from Indian affairs had faltered, and Emmons was willing to recognize another tribal organization. But rather than accept the Miccosukee leadership, he tried to isolate them and draw all Seminoles into a more controllable body. The commissioner checked into the background of the Miccosukee's lawyer, Morton Silver, and claimed he was an ex-Communist who was merely trying to use the Indian issues as a source of political agitation."[12] By later traveling to Communist Cuba and meeting with Castro, the Miccosukee leaders reinforced these suspicions.

Despite his distaste for a few individuals who represented the Miccosukees, Emmons continued to work for a settlement with the Florida Indian people. In March 1956 he went to Tallahassee to confer with Governor LeRoy Collins and the state cabinet on Indian matters. State officials agreed to consider setting aside a hunting and fishing refuge of 200,000 acres for the use of all Indians in Florida. The land issue was placed in the hands of the trustees of the Internal

Improvement Trust Fund (essentially comprised of the governor and cabinet), which had jurisdiction over Conservation Area 3. Collins and his colleagues wanted to establish clear direction for Indian policy, and an ad hoc committee of the cabinet recommended that a full-time head of state Indian affairs be appointed. The salary and office expenses for this position were to be paid from funds held in trust by the state government for all Florida Indians, derived primarily from payments for oil and gas leases on the State Indian Reservation. On 30 October 1956, Max Denton, a former air force colonel, was appointed commissioner of Indian affairs for Florida. His charge was to review state laws and requests by Indians and make recommendations to the governor and cabinet.[13]

Denton claimed no previous experience in negotiating with Indians, but throughout his tenure he worked closely with the Trail Indian elements attempting to resolve disputes and solve their problems. It was not an easy task as the factionalism among Miccosukee villages became more pronounced. In the fall of 1956 Ingraham Billie notified Governor Collins that his group had dismissed Morton Silver as its attorney and Buffalo Tiger as its spokesman.[14] This precipitated a major schism among the Trail Miccosukees. A number of younger Indians led by the brothers Buffalo and Jimmie Tiger supported Morton Silver, and most of the Trail Miccosukees followed their lead in seeking federal recognition. Also, there were still small factions headed by Mike Osceola and by his uncles Cory and John Osceola. Occasionally talk was heard of an attempt to reconcile the leaders of the Trail Indians with the reservation leaders, but this came to nothing. The 1956 political realignment among the Miccosukees marked the emergence of Buffalo Tiger as political leader of the Trail Indian faction that aggressively pursued federal recognition as an autonomous tribe.

While Emmons's visit to Florida ignited a movement in the capital which eventually led to state recognition for the Miccosukees in 1957, nothing short of federal organization would satisfy the reservation Seminoles' advocates. Shortly after his return to Washington, the commissioner received several letters from Mrs. Stranahan decrying white exploitation of the Trail Indians by various groups in the Miami area. She recalled that during the 1955 congressional termination hearing on the Tamiami Trail, a representative of the Hialeah-Miami

Springs Chamber of Commerce went on record in support of the Seminole claim to "all of Florida," while a previously unknown group called the United Seminole Affairs Association of Miami appeared to support Morton Silver and the Indians he represented.[15] Stranahan also encouraged the government to proceed with organization of the Seminole reservations as quickly as possible. In fact, the Friends of the Seminoles society in Fort Lauderdale engaged an attorney to prepare a tribal charter and submitted it to the BIA for approval. Emmons deftly sidestepped the state charter issue by referring it to the bureau's legal department for study, but reassured Mrs. Stranahan, "Like you, I believe that the early establishment of a tribal organization will be the key to additional progress along many lines."[16]

The Seminole Indian Association soon weighed in opposing a state charter for the Indians as its protections would be too limited. Bertram Scott cautioned that the reservation people were discouraged with the delays and urged the commissioner to assure them that a federal charter would soon be forthcoming.[17] Ethnologist Ethel Cutler Freeman also provided significant information on the Florida Indians during this period. She resided on the Big Cypress Reservation in 1939–40 and visited her friends there frequently; thus Emmons believed she could provide crucial insights into the relationships between various tribal factions. It was her opinion that with Silver out of the picture, most of the older Miccosukees could be reunited within a single organization.[18] As it turned out, however, Freeman had seriously underestimated the cleavages existing between the Tamiami Trail camps and their reservation kinfolk.

At last Commissioner Emmons became convinced that the time was right to move ahead with organization of the reservations, so early in 1957 he assigned Reginald Quinn to work with the Seminoles. Quinn was himself an Indian, a member of the Sisseton-Wahpeton Sioux tribe, and had broad experience as a BIA tribal government officer.[19] Between 27 February and 12 March he consulted with many white Floridians; then he and other government officials conferred with the Indian people in open meetings on the reservations to explain what was involved in organizing.[20] These gatherings were open to all Indians listed on the tribal roll at the Seminole agency, and that included everyone on the federal reservations plus the Tamiami

Trail camps. Some forty Indians attended the initial meeting held at the Dania Reservation. Among the non-Indians present were Max Denton, Ethel Cutler Freeman, and Ivy Stranahan, plus a number of reporters from local newspapers. Paul Fickinger, the BIA area administrator from Muskogee, Oklahoma, spoke about constitutions and charters authorized under the Indian Reorganization Act, as well as the right of Indian people to organize and select their own leaders. He also explained how the election would be conducted.[21]

The session was not without incident, however, as Buffalo Tiger came accompanied by Morton Silver. Prior to the meeting, Tiger sent telegrams to Florida's national political leaders protesting Quinn's assignment and claiming that Commissioner Emmons had broken his word by not coming himself. When Silver spoke he challenged the idea of forming a single organization. Quinn replied that there might be more than one organization in the future, so the attorney questioned why there could not be organizations on each reservation. The government officials explained that it was technically possible but too expensive, plus each member of the tribe had an undivided interest in lands on all the reservations. Then Silver raised the issue of whether the off-reservation Indians could vote on the constitution and charter, and officials informed him they could vote on the former but not on the latter. It became clear that the attorney meant to obstruct the process, and many of the Seminoles were incensed. They spoke heatedly in their own language objecting to his presence; then an Indian woman rose and in English made it clear that she thought the meeting was for the Seminoles only. At that point Silver and Buffalo Tiger left the meeting and never returned.

The afternoon session went very smoothly with Rex Quinn discussing the inherent rights of tribal self-government and the necessity for having spokesmen with authority to act. The government officials recommended that a committee be selected to work with Quinn, so the Indians elected a small panel to write a constitution and corporate charter. The committee of seven individuals, who served for ten dollars per diem and mileage, represented the various constituencies associated with the reservation Seminoles, plus a few who lived in independent camps. The committee members were: Larry Mike Osceola, from the Tamiami Trail camps; Billy Osceola and John

Henry Gopher, representing the Brighton Reservation; Bill Osceola and Jack Willie, from the Dania Reservation; and Jimmie O'Toole Osceola and Frank Billie, speaking for the Big Cypress Reservation.[22] Because of the role played by Quinn and Marmon in both the selection process and the actual writing of the documents, one critic has charged that the committee functioned as a "puppet" of the Bureau of Indian Affairs.[23] Also, the fact that fewer than fifty tribal members in attendance at the Dania session selected a committee that helped shape a government for over six hundred Seminoles raised concern about the lack of democratic process.

These shortcomings notwithstanding, all reservations were represented and most Seminoles viewed this election as a positive step in the direction of long-term economic and political stability. Earlier, even prior to the Washington termination hearings, there were several efforts to develop a Seminole constitution, but the Florida Indians and federal officials could never agree on a document. The Seminole trustees, desperately in need of funds to maintain and improve the reservations, came to realize that unless they organized a tribal government, the United States would not release Seminole funds held in trust. These funds had accumulated from the sale of rights of way and easements to the Florida Turnpike Authority and earnings of the tribal cattle program. The State of Florida also held substantial funds derived from oil leases on the State Indian Reservation in trust for the Seminoles.[24]

The constitutional deliberations had a profound impact on those Seminoles involved in the process. The committee members learned quickly from their government mentors and moved rapidly away from the old consensual form of governance. According to Bill Osceola, chairman of the original constitutional committee:

> One day this man came and said "My name is Rex Quinn, I come to help you write and set up the Constitution and By-Laws and Corporate Charter, I am an Indian." He was an Indian from far north. This was the opportunity we were waiting for, a teacher to help us with writing and setting up the Constitution and By-Laws and Corporate Charter. We met with Mr. Quinn and with our people and let them know who he was and why he was there.

He said he needed a committee to work with. The people selected a committee and I was one of the committee to work
with Mr. Quinn. He instruct[ed] us how to go about writing
and setting up a Constitution & By-Laws and Corporate Charter. He told us which the other Indian tribes uses and which is
good and which is not good. Some tribes have only the Tribal
Council. He recommended to us that it would be good to have
Corporate Charter, which meant we would have two governing
bodies. He kept teaching us until everyone understood the program and then to the people on the reservations and explained
to them what was happening. We went to the Tamiami Trail but
the people were not interested in organizing the tribe.[25]

Rex Quinn was also a Baptist and quickly developed a rapport with
the committee, guiding it in directions that were compatible with
long-term federal goals for tribal self-sufficiency. The documents
produced by the committee appear to be consistent with federal
guidelines for organizing tribal governments set forth in *Indian Affairs Manual 83-1, Tribal Government*, adopted in the fall of 1957.[26] In
any case, the bureau officials allowed the Seminoles wide latitude in
developing a plan which fit their needs; accordingly, they became the
only Indian tribe to organize with both a tribal council and a separate governing board of directors for its business corporation. There
remains a question as to whether the Seminoles originated this idea
or had it suggested to them as Bill Osceola indicated. Quinn later
claimed that the idea for a dual structure originated with the members of the constitutional committee, but he had been through this
process of constitution drafting with other tribes and knew how to
achieve a workable outcome. Moreover, he enjoyed the advantage of
being able to explain things convincingly from an Indian viewpoint
even while working through interpreters.

At the first committee meeting Quinn outlined the constitutional
powers on a blackboard and explained each of them carefully. On
another blackboard were listed all provisions of a charter. The Indians had many questions, and discussion of both documents took
all day. The committee talked of using state services in education,
health, and welfare. They discussed the issue of law and order on

the reservations at great length but did not address it in the constitution. The question of tribal membership also presented a potential problem. They agreed that no one should be forced to join and yet enrollment would remain open so those who changed their minds could join later. The idea of being able to tax and license businesses on the reservation had appeal, but everyone admitted Bureau help would be needed on this issue in the future. A heated debate ensued on whether a person could serve on the tribal council and board of directors simultaneously; they decided to allow it.

The committee discussed a corporate charter at length and agreement emerged that a board of directors should have very specific authority. Many of the questions centered on tribal lands and the proposal that all land not used for housing should be placed under a tribal management program. They proposed zoning for the Dania Reservation to prevent housing from being built in areas better suited for business development. Improvement of the cattle program emerged as a high priority, with housing and small business loans. There were business opportunities on the reservations that had to be planned in cooperation with the BIA. They discussed dividends from tribal businesses and agreed that only profits would be distributed. The committee spent four days of effort getting these two documents ready for presentation to the people. Meetings to explain the proposed constitution and by-laws and corporate charter to tribal members were scheduled at Dania, Big Cypress, Brighton, and in Everglades City for the Tamiami Trail group.

The most controversial member of the constitutional committee was Mike Osceola, primarily because he had testified at both the Washington and Florida congressional hearings as an outspoken proponent of termination. How he became a member of the committee is in dispute. The popular version holds that he was the political creation of Superintendent Marmon, who needed to show that the Trail Indians in his charge had a voice in the organizational process. Because Marmon had no entrée with the Trail Indians he reportedly promoted Mike as the spokesman for the off-reservation people. Admittedly Mike Osceola was too young for consideration as a traditional leader of the Trail Miccosukees; only the council of elders were considered true political leaders. When questioned some years later,

Rex Quinn recalled, "At that time he [Osceola] was having difficulty with the Trail people, so he affiliated himself with the Dania people, but continued to represent the off-reservation group.... I think he was actually a strong political figure" (as opposed to traditional leader).[27] As to his influence on the committee, Quinn remembered Mike as a persuasive personality who was respected among the Indians. They did not like him but they respected him: "He was pretty vocal compared to most of them. While they did not agree with him in many instances, they did not publicly disagree with him either. They just voted him down."[28]

It is also possible to question whether the other committee members would be considered Seminole leaders in the traditional sense. None could lay claim to any historic leadership role such as medicine man, and all were converts to Christianity who lived on the reservations. Quinn responded that he had never called them leaders.[29] The reservation Seminoles were asked to select a group of people to draw up the constitution and business charter; once they organized the new government, a separate process selected individuals to lead the tribe. Interviews with surviving members of the constitutional committee confirm that most believed they were selected to do a job with no implication of being "tribal leaders."[30] For many years Quinn served as head of tribal affairs for the BIA; as a result, he possessed insight into how Indians across the country selected their leaders as a result of changing realities in reservation life. The process had begun long before passage of the Indian Reorganization Act. The older chiefs, lacking a command of English and therefore unable to sit down and negotiate on complicated issues, selected younger, better educated "spokesmen" to deal with whites. At first they were simply interpreters who spoke English and conveyed specific positions to non-Indians. Soon they became more independent, often at the urging of government officials, and the tribal leaders had less influence on them. Eventually the interpreters began to be accepted as leaders in their own right, particularly by persons outside the tribe. These assertive, experienced Indians with particular talents such as the ability to read and write English, keep accounts, or manage a cattle program were soon elected to leadership positions in tribal government. As the tribes organized themselves with new constitutions and business charters, the traditional Indian political leadership roles passed out of existence or were greatly diminished. This became the paradigm for the Florida Seminoles when the reservation constituencies required, indeed demanded, a new style of leadership.

The makeup of the constitutional committee also confirmed the political influence which Seminole Baptists had achieved over a very short period of time. Billy Osceola, from the Brighton Reservation, personified this religious shift. He was one of the five Seminole men who attended the Florida Bible College in 1946 and returned home to become a lay minister. Still, during the early 1950s Christian Indians remained a minority at Brighton and were not allowed to hold church services or prayer meetings on the reservation. Most of the Muskogee-speaking families who lived there still attended the Green Corn Dance and adhered to the leadership of their medicine man and a council of elders. Therefore a Baptist church was built on donated land adjacent to the Brighton Reservation, with Billy Osceola serving as the minister. At the Big Cypress Reservation, Miccosukee-speaking Bill Osceola had ministered to the mission church's congregation since 1950. A small Baptist congregation continued to worship at the Dania Reservation, with pastoral duties shared by Billy and Bill Osceola, but the Southern Baptist Convention also assigned an ordained missionary there. Following an Indian church schism in the late 1940s, independent Baptist congregations were also formed on the reservations. So when time came to organize the Seminole Tribe of Florida, a significant Baptist element existed on all three reservations.

A recent study examined the ideological concerns which had to be reconciled in the process of conceptualizing Seminole tribal governance. The original 1957 constitution was designed to gain approval from Seminoles then living on the reservations. The document balanced various interests and prevented any one reservation from becoming politically dominant. This suggests that the constitutional committee was well aware that the three reservation populations had little in common with each other. Furthermore, there remained internal stresses on each reservation, such as Christians versus religious traditionalists, mixed-bloods versus full-bloods, and opposition to cattlemen by nonowners who were concerned that the cattle enterprise was being treated preferentially. Therefore the process of developing a viable constitution "was a throwback to the traditional practices of the Seminole leaders in [gaining] almost unanimous support in their aims and directions."[31]

An analysis of key features in the constitution tells us much about the Seminoles' attempt to achieve political balance on the eve of their new government. The article dealing with membership read, "Any person of Seminole Indian blood whose name appears on the census roll of the Seminole Agency of January 1, 1957, shall be eligible for enrollment, regardless of blood quality or place of residence, upon written application to the tribal council."[32] There are several possible explanations for this nonrestrictive stance. One is that the committee remained unsure just how many full-bloods would participate in the balloting, and wanted to open the way for generally progressive mixed-bloods to vote to accept the document. Nationally this had been the pattern among most Indian tribes since 1935, when mixed-bloods usually voted to accept or reject the Indian Reorganization Act while full-bloods predominantly boycotted the elections. However, the number of mixed-bloods among reservation Seminoles at that time was probably so negligible as to be insignificant. Another possibility is that the committee simply attempted to build consensus by encouraging the broadest participation possible. Such a provision would also be consistent with the bureau's emphasis on having tribes incorporate democratic procedures into their constitutions. Some Seminoles who welcomed the new tribal government did not want to live on the reservations; by eliminating a residence requirement the committee hoped to attract as many off-reservation members as possible. Also, although probably not clearly understood at that time, the size of the tribal roll would have significant implications in the future, when land claims funds were distributed among the Florida Indians.

The governing body known as the Tribal Council consisted of eight members, each of whom had to be a qualified voter of the tribe over twenty-one years of age. The chairman and vice chairman would be chosen from the council membership, but it could select "from within or without the membership of the tribe a Secretary and a Treasurer and such committees as may be deemed necessary."[33] This recognized that some qualified individuals might not choose to seek office and that the tribe would need technical assistance and guidance from outside the Indian community. The voting for council members took place within four discrete geographical and political subdivisions. Three of these were the federal reservations; the fourth included all nonreservation Seminoles, most of whom lived in the Tamiami Trail community. Residents registered at a particular reservation voted for their own representative, but not those from other reservations. They also cast ballots for five at-large positions. Nonresident electors could not cast ballots for reservation representatives; they voted only for the at-large candidates. This arrangement showed an awareness that each reservation had different needs and should be assured a voice in the government. The provision—"There shall be elected five at-large members of the tribal council, two of whom shall be nonresidents of the reservations"[34]—ensured that no single reservation could gain a majority, though technically it did not prevent one reservation from capturing four of the eight positions. The document thus attempted to create a balance of power enhancing tribal unity rather than pitting reservations against each other.

The Seminole government was never intended to be totally autonomous, and its constitution reaffirmed the limited nature of tribal sovereignty conferred by the Indian Reorganization Act of 1934. Historian Laurence Hauptman makes the intriguing argument that in implementing the IRA Commissioner John Collier "retarded the eventual self-rule of American Indians by increasing, not lessening, federal supervision over Indians. The act actually required approval by the secretary of the Interior and/or commissioner of Indian Affairs in eleven of eighteen sections, ranging from all aspects of land use, business incorporation, the writing of constitutions and by-laws, and drafting of new regulations in hiring Indians for government service."[35] Although Seminole tribal organization occurred almost two decades after the Indian New Deal ended, their constitution and charter suffered from similar restrictive provisions.

The secretary of the interior maintained review power over actions of the Tribal Council. Elections were to be held every two years, and if the council failed to call one within sixty days of a regular election date, the secretary could set a date. Interestingly, in the initial voting to approve the constitution and bylaws and to select a council, electors and officeholders had to be twenty-one years of age, but in subsequent balloting they were only required to have attained their eighteenth birthday.

The powers of the council were subject to limitations imposed by the U.S. Constitution and federal statutes as well as by the tribal constitution and bylaws. Although it had the right to negotiate with federal, state, and local governments and other entities on behalf of the tribe, the council possessed only limited power "to employ legal counsel for the protection of rights of the tribe and its members . . . subject to the approval of the Secretary of the Interior, or his authorized representative."[36] While the council prepared an annual budget request for funds deposited to its credit in the U.S. Treasury, this had to be approved by the secretary of the interior as well.

The constitution granted the Tribal Council power to "manage and lease or otherwise deal with tribal lands and communal resources in accordance with law."[37] This ostensibly allowed the tribe to administer policy within its own domain with guidance from the Department of the Interior. However, government "guidance" became more pronounced when it came to dealing with individuals outside tribal parameters. For instance, the council could only "levy taxes on persons doing business on the reservation subject to the review of the Secretary of the Interior."[38]

The full extent of the bureau's influence over council affairs is found in an article dealing with review procedures. Regarding those sections of the constitution which were subject to federal review, it held that "if the [local BIA] superintendent shall approve any ordinance or resolution it shall become effective, but the superintendent may within ninety days from the date of the enactment rescind the said ordinance or resolution for any cause, by notifying the tribal council of such decision."[39] The article also contained a provision for tribal appeals on such decisions to the secretary of the interior. It has been conjectured that this control was more benign than it appears. Given the fact that federal officials such as Quinn, Marmon, and Emmons all showed a genuine concern for Seminole welfare, the article appears to have been included to counter any nonproductive legislation passed by the council members through their ignorance of government operations—that is to say, the government did not want the Seminoles to "harm themselves."[40] But the essential point remains: federal authorities retained ultimate power to override all council decisions.

Finally, the article dealing with amendments revealed the Seminoles' ability to navigate the line between tradition and a more democratic system of government advocated by federal officials. It was imperative that members of the tribe be made comfortable with major decisions that a tribal government inevitably had to make. The traditional Seminole way of handling significant change rested on achieving unanimous consent; barring that, they avoided conflict by never confronting an issue directly. On the other hand, the tribal government would have to make decisions and act on them expeditiously. Therefore they arrived at a compromise, which stated, "Whenever the tribal council, by a unanimous vote of all members, or the tribal membership by a petition signed by twenty (20) percent of the eligible voters, calls for the submission of an amendment, the Secretary of the Interior shall call an election upon the proposed amendment to the Constitution and Bylaws."[41] Thus if the failure to achieve consensus functionally paralyzed the government, a fifth of the tribe could get the process moving again. At the same time, the opposition should be mollified knowing that they could still vote against an issue with which they disagreed.

Crafting the Seminoles' corporate charter involved a similar process of balancing interests. That article of the constitution and bylaws which delineated powers of the Tribal Council specifically authorized the existence of a tribal corporation with its own charter, a separate management, and independent sphere of action. Known as the Seminole Tribe of Florida, Inc., it became a federal corporation with rights of perpetual succession. The corporation's stated purpose is to "further the economic development of the Seminole Tribe of Florida by conferring upon said Tribe certain corporate rights, powers, privileges and immunities; to secure for the members of the tribe an assured economic independence; and to provide for the proper exercise by the tribe of various functions heretofore performed by the Department of the Interior."[42] The charter vested management in an eight-member Board of Directors—two elected from the Dania, Brighton, and Big Cypress reservations and two elected at-large with no restrictions as to place of residence. This structure meant to broaden the participation base beyond reservation Seminoles, who were the only ones allowed to vote on creating a corporation. Directors would serve four-year terms and select their own officers consisting of president, vice president, secretary, and treasurer. In contrast to the extremely involved procedure for recalling council members, any director could be removed at any time, without cause or charges, by a plurality of voting shareholders who had elected the individual—for example, only Brighton voters could recall a Brighton director. All enrolled members of the tribe were considered shareholding members of the corporation and shared equally in any per-capita distribution of profits. This constituted yet another attempt to bring the off- and on-reservation interests together by participating in the common effort. The charter mandated an annual meeting of shareholders and authorized the corporation to make per-capita distributions of its profits.

At first glance it appears that the Seminole people were allowed very wide latitude in conducting their affairs. But a closer scrutiny of the "corporate powers" article reveals just how tightly the Department of the Interior controlled Seminole business affairs. The corporation's powers were subject to any restrictions contained in the U.S. Constitution and laws, as well as by the constitution of the Seminole tribe. Moreover, a number of actions were expressly prohibited without permission of the secretary of the interior. The corporation could not sell or mortgage any land, or interest in any land, including water, oil, gas, and other mineral rights. Neither could it sell, mortgage, or lease any land within the reservations for a period exceeding ten years, nor execute any other leases, permits, or contracts relating to those lands. It could not borrow money in excess of $10,000 from the Indian Credit Fund or other resources unless authorized by the secretary. The charter also empowered the corporation to negotiate legal contracts of every description "provided that any contract involving payment of money or delivery of property by the corporation of a value in excess of $10,000.00 in any one fiscal year shall be subject to approval of the Secretary of the Interior or his authorized representative."[43] Even the distribution of per-capita dividends required the secretary's approval. In addition, no activities could be undertaken by the Board of Directors which might destroy or otherwise injure the tribal grazing lands, timber, or any of its other natural resources.

The Seminole's corporate charter could not be revoked or surrendered except by an act of Congress—which constituted a major protection against the ultimate exercise of bureaucratic interference. It should be noted that the Seminole constitution did not enjoy any such specific immunity. In addition, any amendment to the charter proposed by the directors or by twenty percent of the electorate had to be approved by the secretary of the interior before it could be submitted to the adult shareholders for ratification. With these governmental limitations on the board's freedom of action, the charter should be viewed as only a first step toward eventual exercise of the tribe's sovereignty.

While the constitutional committee moved forward in its deliberations, Morton Silver escalated his efforts. He also visited Quinn at his hotel and delivered a detailed critique of the entire process. The Miccosukees would, he claimed, oppose anything that the reservation residents adopted because they believed the government should have initiated organization with the Tamiami Trail people. He criticized the makeup of the committee, especially the presence of Mike Osceola as spokesman for the off-reservation Miccosukees. In fact, the attorney didn't like much of anything taking place beyond his control.

Then Silver abruptly attempted to reach an accommodation with the government official. As reported by Quinn, "he intimated that if we worked well together he could easily swing the important people in favor of organization, but that if he felt we were being unfair to the Trail people he would swing the influence the other way. He indicated he could not be seen consorting with BIA people, but that if we were really going to do a good job he would go along even if he couldn't do it openly. He said he wanted to see an organization, otherwise he couldn't hope to get paid. He indicated he thought he had some $1,900 coming to him for services rendered to date."[44] Quinn rejected all overtures from Silver and his law partner, George Miller, to meet privately and reported the incidents to his superiors in Washington. Bureau officials deliberated and decided to ignore statements in the press, most of which reiterated Silver's threat to take the Miccosukee case before the United Nations. Although certain regional newspapers such as the *Miami Daily News* and the *Fort Lauderdale Daily News* tended to sensationalize the story, especially the wild premise that Miccosukees could claim all Florida under an old Spanish treaty, the *Miami Herald* ran a balanced appraisal of the situation which explained Quinn's role in helping the Seminoles develop a new government.[45]

The community meetings scheduled with the reservation Seminoles went smoothly and followed a similar pattern. A member of the constitutional committee introduced Rex Quinn to the people, and through an interpreter he explained their right of self-government, the stability of organization, and the general powers of the Tribal Council and Board of Directors. The committee then threw the session open for discussion over the next hour or so, or until the people were satisfied that they had heard enough. Laura Mae Osceola, who served effectively at the Washington hearings on termination, played an equally important role at this juncture. She translated for Quinn on all three reservations, explaining issues and conducting the informal votes on adoption. The constitutional committee reported to Quinn that the people on each reservation had given virtually unanimous assent to the documents presented.

As expected, the gathering at Everglades City with the Trail Indians became quite heated when all factions put in an appearance. Ingraham Billie was not present when the meeting began, but his son Jimmie and fifteen supporters were in attendance. Their interpreter, a young man named Billie Doctor, tried to provoke Quinn with strong antigovernment language, but the experienced official remained unflappable during the verbal sparring. Cory Osceola, now reunited with his brother William McKinley Osceola, indicated that they were not associated with the Mike Osceola village and asked the sheriff of Collier County to speak for them at the meeting. Buffalo Tiger and Morton Silver formed still another contingent. When the session began, Quinn launched into a detailed explanation of the tribe's right to organize, the method of electing leaders, and the fact that any Seminole could join without having to move to a reservation. To allay fears of interference with the Everglades camps, he emphasized that a tribal government's jurisdiction would be limited to reservation lands. Quinn realized that most of his audience were traditional people with strong religious convictions, so he emphasized that hundreds of Indian tribes had already chosen to organize under the Indian Reorganization Act, citing the Hopi's retention of the Snake Dance to illustrate that forming a government and conducting tribal business did not necessarily interfere with traditional beliefs and rituals.

When Quinn began to explain the constitution, Silver interrupted the presentation and attempted to get the Indians present to take sides. He warned that only seventy-five people could determine the outcome of the vote and tribal government would then be imposed over all Seminoles, including Trail Indians. Again he called for a separate organization for the Tamiami Trail group. Quinn accused the attorney of trying to obstruct the proceedings and prevent the Indians from understanding what was taking place; he thought Silver's legalistic approach to problems only disturbed and confused the people. Buffalo Tiger also spoke out for a separate Trail Indian organization, then left the meeting. Morton Silver expressed anger over the whole affair, but lacking support also withdrew.

On balance, the Everglades City meeting must be considered inconclusive since those attending made no decision regarding tribal organization. Billie Doctor spoke for the Ingraham Billie faction, saying they had no interest in a constitution; they had their leaders and needed no new ones. He also reiterated that they were not interested in money, just their land. Cory and William McKinley Osceola, speaking through Sheriff Doug Hendry, indicated that they wanted nothing to do with any reservation government; however, their sons had cattle on Big Cypress Reservation and indicated they would join an organization, so Quinn thought the old men might eventually come around. As it turned out, the Trail people sent emissaries to the Big Cypress Reservation in an attempt to stall approval of the new tribal organization, but this effort failed. In Quinn's opinion, the Trail Indians finally realized that a majority wanted the organization, and if they fought it openly and failed, they would lose prestige. Thereafter they remained passive and did not openly campaign against the organization, so there could be little doubt that the reservation people would approve the new government.

A number of non-Indian observers also attended the Everglades

City meeting, and they were convinced that the lack of support among the Trail Indians would not set back the drive for organization. As usual, Robert Mitchell and Bertram Scott became incensed at Silver's tactics and thought Quinn should have run a tighter meeting; overall, though, they felt encouraged that the process was moving along. Deaconess Harriet Bedell, an Episcopal missionary who had worked with the Trail Indians for several decades, believed the meeting had gone about as well as possible and volunteered to continue explaining the matter to Ingraham Billie's group.

When analyzing the Florida situation for his superiors in Washington following the meetings to discuss a constitution and charter, Rex Quinn affirmed that this conflict should not be considered a split between Muskogees and Miccosukees as much as "a division between modern progressives and those who want to cling to tribal traditions. It was not uncommon to find brothers on opposing sides and fathers and sons in contention."[46] He thought the Trail people had been in the limelight so much that they believed they were the leadership element even though a majority of the tribe lived on the reservations. By contrast, the reservation leaders had stepped into new roles and were at a disadvantage contending with the seasoned medicine men of the Tamiami Trail group who commanded great personal loyalty. It would be difficult to coalesce all of these elements into a single organization, and Quinn suggested that the bureau move forward immediately with tribal government organization on the reservations. The natural resources of the reservations offered many economic opportunities to the Seminole people, but there were also problems that would have to be considered, especially "distance, internal conflicts, new and inexperienced leaders, problems of technical assistance in resource development and the whole spread of problems in human affairs with a tribe looking towards conformity with the American way of life in religion, domestic affairs, business, education, health, etc."[47]

Because the tribe had so many needs, and because the Indian people would expect them to be met quickly or risk discouragement, Quinn urged that comprehensive planning begin immediately. Also, liaison should be established with the State of Florida and its counties regarding education, health, welfare, law and order, and other services. This would be difficult because the reservations were located in three different civil jurisdictions. Tribal leaders and members were inexperienced with the problems, possible solutions, and ways and means of carrying out tribal programs. They would need consistent expert support and assistance, as well as guidance in developing social and economic activities for the people. Quinn concluded with the assessment that the Seminole agency staff needed a human relations specialist because administering human affairs among the Indians would be more difficult to handle than the technical ones of developing natural resources. The entire process should be under the overall supervision of a strong and experienced administrator who could carry the heavy load during the trying years ahead.[48] Unwittingly, Quinn had described the role that he fulfilled for the Florida Seminoles over the next decade. Superintendent Marmon retired the following year and the bureau often sent Quinn, who the Seminole leaders trusted, to help iron out problems encountered by the new tribal government. In 1965 he returned for a two-year stint as superintendent of the Seminole agency.

By July 1957 it had become obvious that the Trail Miccosukees would take no part in the new government planned for the reservation Seminoles. Governor Collins nevertheless attempted a last-minute effort to effect a reconciliation and bring the groups together in a united tribe. On 13 July the governor, accompanied by Max Denton and a member of the cabinet, met with the Seminoles on the Big Cypress Reservation and called for an end to factionalism. He even proposed the creation of a nonvoting Indian delegate to the state legislature to represent a unified tribe.[49] The following day Collins met with the Miccosukees at Jimmie Tiger's camp on the Tamiami Trail and reiterated his plea for unity. It might have become a contentious affair as Mike Osceola confronted the governor's party with charges that the state was creating a fake tribe of off-reservation Indians in an attempt to retain control of Indian funds and lands. Osceola had already sent a telegram to Senator Smathers stating these charges and asking him to intervene in the matter, but the senator declined.[50] Denton diplomatically turned this challenge aside and the meeting continued in peace.

The situation appeared hopeless; neither the reservation Seminoles nor the Miccosukees would budge from their positions. Buffalo

Tiger was quoted as saying, "Unification seems hopeless at this time. We're too far separated on basic issues to possibly get together."[51] Governor Collins could not have been pleased with the *Miami Daily News* article which headlined, "Seminole Elders Rebuff Governor."[52] Denton, too, became discouraged that the groups refused to cooperate, noting, "This is something that will probably take a long time. Maybe we can't work it out now, but perhaps the dream of a unified Seminole nation will become reality for your grandchildren to enjoy."[53] It is unlikely that anyone remained enamored of tribal unification other than officials in Tallahassee (they did not want to deal with two independent tribes). The BIA commissioner was reconciled to having two Indian groups in Florida. Inexorably the Miccosukees asserted their separate identity as a people and pursued recognition, while the reservation Seminoles were equally determined to have a government which they controlled.

During the next few months the bureau took no action on the Seminole constitution and corporate charter, which were being reviewed by its solicitor. Several changes had to be made in the documents, so Quinn shuttled back and forth between Washington and Florida securing the necessary approvals. This delay generated concern among individuals in Florida who strongly supported tribal government for the Seminoles. It may account in part for Mike Osceola's accusation that Emmons and Denton were conspiring to sabotage the Seminole constitution. When Mrs. Stranahan inquired about the matter in April, Commissioner Emmons assured her that "steps are now under way to give the people an opportunity of voting in the near future on a proposed constitution and charter under the provisions of the Indian Reorganization Act.... as for the Trail Indians, the position we have taken is that they are entirely free either to join the proposed organization or abstain, as they wish."[54] Another month passed without any action on the documents.

Meanwhile a minor crisis developed when the bureau's Muskogee area office established an office of land operations at the Seminole agency and proposed spending up to $250,000 of tribal trust funds held in the U.S. Treasury to begin improving reservation lands. There were also plans to impose higher grazing fees on Seminole cattlemen and to cut tribal timber to replenish the trust funds. Robert

Mitchell contacted Emmons complaining that the Seminole tribal trustees never approved these plans; they felt betrayed and did not want their funds expended before a tribal organization was in place. He warned that if the project was not squelched the Seminole's trust and confidence in the bureau would be seriously impaired. He concluded, "The tribal trustees also want to know what has become of the organization papers they signed. Mr. Quinn, when he was here urged immediate organization."[55]

Mitchell sent essentially the same letter to Representative Haley, as well as to Senator Smathers, who contacted Emmons's office expressing concerns regarding the land development issue. The Association on American Indian Affairs quickly took up the issue—Mitchell's Seminole Indian Association was their Florida affiliate—and raised questions with Secretary of the Interior Fred Seaton concerning the legality of the proposed expenditure of Seminole trust funds to improve lease lands on the reservations without approval of the Indians themselves. It also asked for a clarification of bureau policy since the Seminole constitution had been approved pending a ratification vote.[56] The associate commissioner, H. Rex Lee, quickly assured Haley and Smathers that any funds borrowed from the $250,000 held in trust for the Seminoles would easily be made up through an increase in grazing fees that had already been agreed to by the Indian cattlemen. Smathers communicated this to Mitchell and told him that the Seminole situation seemed to be well in hand.[57]

Emmons also wrote to Mitchell and apparently alleviated most of his concerns about the land development scheme. More important, though, he announced that the Assistant Secretary of the Interior Roger Ernst had approved the proposed constitution and charter for the Seminoles on 11 July and simultaneously authorized Superintendent Marmon to proceed with arrangements for a tribal referendum.[58] The superintendent of the Seminole agency could set the date twenty to sixty days following posting of a public notice.[59] Accordingly, Marmon scheduled the election for August.

The Seminole Tribe of Florida officially ratified its constitution and bylaws in balloting on 21 August 1957 "by a vote of 241 for, and five against, in an election in which at least 30 percent of those entitled to vote cast their ballots."[60] A tribal council thus became the

governing body of the tribe, replacing the traditional council of elders that had functioned within the busk groups. It also ended once
and for all any lingering confusion surrounding the multitiered tribal
trustees/directors structure imposed during the 1950s. At the same
balloting, a corporate charter issued to the Seminole Tribe of Florida,
Inc., was ratified "by a vote of 223 for, and 5 against."[61] The election
results were certified by Bill Osceola and Mike Osceola, chairman
and secretary of the constitutional committee, and by Superintendent
Marmon. Yet even as the Seminoles celebrated their new tribal government, forces were gathering to gain control of the apparatus. It
signaled the end of an era and the beginning of a modern, increasingly
complex, and occasionally divided Seminole polity. Bill Osceola, a
candidate for one of the new government's leadership positions, suc-
cinctly captured the spirit of the moment: "The tribal organization
was finish[ed] and the election of officers was on."[62]

CHAPTER 4

The Lean Years, 1957-1971

The Seminoles launched their new government at a time when the federal Indian policies of the Eisenhower administration were coming under fire from many quarters. In addition to national Indian organizations, the critics included leading intellectuals, media commentators, university scholars, and liberal politicians who opposed termination. To counter this criticism the commissioner of Indian affairs announced a broad campaign to meet tribal health, education, and economic development needs. However, congressional budgetary constraints and policy mandates, plus a lack of private sector investment on the reservations, limited the bureau's ability to act. As a consequence the Seminoles received limited support in setting up business enterprises and developing tribal lands. Lack of funds was complicated by the fact that very few Seminoles had a formal education or were experienced in business. Furthermore, many reservation groups remained distrustful of each other and religious factionalism persisted.

Following tribal ratification of the constitution and charter, the next step was setting a date for an election to select eight Tribal Council members and an equal number to sit on the Board of Directors. The constitutional committee supervised the election and, following consultation with Superintendent Marmon, appointed the poll workers who actually ran the process. Of the nine election officials, four were female—at least one served on each reservation—signaling the new, more active role women assumed in tribal political affairs.

On 19 September 1957 polling places on the three reservations remained open from eight in the morning to seven in the evening with an election judge, teller, and clerk assigned to each site. Color-coded ballots helped those Seminoles with limited English skills and minimal understanding of the process: ballots listing the names of candidates for the council were printed in red ink, while those for the board were produced in purple ink. In keeping with the constitution, residents of each reservation were eligible to vote for both a council and board member representing their particular venue, as well as for at-large members to each body. Nonresident voters were restricted to voting for the at-large candidates. Interestingly, an individual could simultaneously be a candidate for each of the respective branches, and several persons were elected to both bodies.

The selection of Charlotte Osceola to hold both the council and board seats from the Dania Reservation while her husband Bill Osceola gained an at-large board seat triggered the first Seminole election dispute. The challenge ostensibly involved a technical violation of the election laws, but the cause seems to have been a concern that one faction or family appeared to be acquiring too much power on the small Dania Reservation. Bill Osceola was born in the Everglades and grew up hunting, fishing, and trading with white men. In 1944 his family settled at Dania and became Christians; Bill later served as a Baptist lay minister but earned a living by operating heavy equipment and raising cattle. His wife, Charlotte, was also a respected member of the reservation community.

A losing candidate, Jackie Willie, who also served on the constitutional committee, charged that Bill Osceola engaged in illegal electioneering within two hundred feet of a polling place. Osceola responded that in his capacity as a member of the constitutional committee charged with election oversight responsibility he had to be present at the polls. A group of five persons—four members of the constitutional committee plus Superintendent Marmon—considered the charge and decided by a vote of three to two to deny Bill Osceola a seat on the Board of Directors.[1] As the deciding vote was cast by Jackie Willie, it created an uproar in the Indian community and the bureau sent Rex Quinn to negotiate a settlement.[2]

Quinn met with the Seminoles and explained that the election regulations under which they operated contained no penalty provisions, nor did he believe that their constitutional committee had any authority to prevent the seating of a candidate. He recommended that the tribe ask the bureau for a binding legal opinion, which was done. As Quinn suspected, the Department of the Interior's solicitor found the Seminole election regulations to be a statement of policy with no specific penalty provisions. Furthermore, the authority of the constitutional committee expired after the votes were counted and certified. A director could be removed from office only in a special meeting called for that purpose as provided in the charter. The committee dropped the matter, and Bill Osceola took his seat on the board.

As Quinn was already in Florida, he took the opportunity to work with the new council and board members for ten days. He cautioned them against hasty decisions and recommended that the first year be one of serious analysis and study of programs. Before they could administer effectively, the officers had to understand the tribe's problems. An industrial planning firm should be employed to find the most profitable use of the Dania Reservation's valuable commercial properties; the council also needed to cooperate with BIA specialists to determine the best use of natural resources at Brighton and Big Cypress. The council members elected Billy Osceola chairman and Betty Mae Jumper vice chairman, and appointed Laura Mae Osceola as secretary. The non-Indian wife of a Seminole agency employee served as the first treasurer. The council organized four standing committees reflecting its main emphases: enrollment, budget and finance, elections, and community planning and development. A budget of $12,000 was adopted for the ensuing year. The first resolution of the council delegated authority to the Board of Directors to conduct the tribe's business affairs.[3] The board members elected Frank Billie as their president and Bill Osceola as vice president, but shared the secretary and treasurer with the council. Within a year Frank Billie resigned the position after finding the distance and frequent travel from his home at Big Cypress to tribal headquarters in Dania too great a burden, so Bill Osceola became president. The standing committees for the board were budget and finance, land use and development, industrial development, and credit. To carry out its functions, the board developed an initial budget of approximately $12,000.

The success of this new government would depend on the quality of the individuals selected for leadership positions. In the early years the Seminoles were fortunate to choose individuals who worked effectively in a transitional era as the tribe moved from the old consensual form of governance to the new structure demanded by their constitution and charter. A study of Seminole leadership points out that "traditionally, the Seminoles are passive in their dealings with one another; they do not like being told what to do, and it is antipathetic to their cultural norm to presume to tell others what to do. Decisions affecting large groups of people have always been arrived at by consensus, with much discussion among spokesmen whose judgment was valued."[4] Both Bill and Billy Osceola were Baptist ministers who frequently won reelection to their posts during the first decade of Seminole tribal government, between 1957 and 1967, yet as Rex Quinn observed, "Bill and Billy were not spokesmen in the traditional sense. They knew what the tribe wanted and what was best for it. They were independent.... While these two may not have been the best leaders in the Seminole Tribe, they were the most willing ones."[5] The Seminoles' willingness to accept their leadership may also indicate that Christianity provided a vehicle for legitimizing a behavior pattern—telling others what to do—that was objectionable in traditional Seminole culture. The preacher could make recommendations without becoming known as a "Big Shot."[6] Both of the Osceolas were men of integrity and greatly respected by their peers, so it is likely that as time passed the authority of their governmental positions melded with their ministerial roles and personal popularity.

A second source of nascent leadership for the Seminole government came from the cattle program. The earliest efforts to develop a leadership cadre among the Seminoles began with the selection of cattle trustees on the Brighton Reservation in the 1930s. Initially the trustees were limited to approving decisions affecting the cattle program that was actually run by the state extension agent; but over time the BIA came to consider the trustees spokesmen for their reservations. Upon this base Superintendent Marmon had fabricated his quasi-official two-tiered structure (reservation trustees and tribal trustee/directors) for Seminole governance in the late 1940s. As a result, those trustees had a leg up on election for the council and board positions. Frank Billie, from Big Cypress, exemplified this access route. Not only was he a major cattle owner who served as both a reservation trustee and tribal trustee, but at the time of tribal elections he also held an office in the Big Cypress Cattlemen's Cooperative Association. The reservation elected Billie to both the Tribal Council and Board of Directors, and he remained on one or the other for over twenty years. Occasionally individuals demonstrated a combination of various claims to leadership. For example, although Bill Osceola resided at the Dania Reservation, he owned cattle on the Big Cypress and served as president of their cattlemen's cooperative, giving him yet more purchase on power. But leadership in the cattle program did not automatically translate into political power. At the Brighton Reservation the cattlemen's association president in 1957 was Frank Shore, a revered medicine man and traditional leader who never sought or held a position in tribal government.

While documenting the rise of this Christian, cattle-owning leadership element, one study of the emerging Seminole polity suggests that an atavistic relationship existed between clan membership and political leadership: "In the mid-twentieth century, the Seminoles were encouraged to adopt a system of government for which they were culturally unprepared. Yet it appears that the traditional way of doing things may not have been entirely legislated out of existence. The clan which is presently providing the major tribal officers is numerically the strongest of the moiety which had supplied leadership in earlier decades."[7] To emphasize this point a tabulation of officers chosen in seven elections held between 1957 and 1975 shows that the Bird clan, numerically the most important of the white moiety, held eighteen of the twenty-eight offices. Yet the Bird clan was the second largest clan among the reservation Seminoles, with a high likelihood that someone from that group would be selected. Large clans could provide the votes regardless of their historical role in providing leaders. As the Birds who held two principal offices, chairman and president, were continuously reelected to their posts during the first decade of tribal government, it was not a case of the Seminoles electing a succession of Bird clan members to high office but rather retaining a few of them. Clan membership appears to be coincidental rather than determinative in the selection of Bill and Billy Osceola (both Bird clan) who represented the growing strength of the Christian, cattle-owning element.

Seminole women were the most conspicuous new group to achieve institutionalized power as a result of tribal organization. Among the postremoval Florida Seminoles, women had played a crucial role as cultural conservators. The Seminoles followed a typically Southeastern Indian—most particularly Creek—pattern of clan and kinship.[8] They practiced matrilineal descent in which individuals inherited lineage through their mother. The mother and her lineal kin transmitted knowledge of clan origins, functions, and ritual roles to the children. This influence was reinforced by matrilocality, in which a married woman and her husband went to live in the camp of her mother, surrounded by the females of her clan and their families. Although the old Creek town system had disappeared in Florida by the midnineteenth century, these extended family camps, headed by a "grandmother," *posi*, provided a nexus of psychological support, social interaction, physical protection, and the context for child rearing. Large multiclan settlements prevailed in the period between 1850 and 1900; after that, small family camps dispersed across the south Florida landscape.

In the old Creek town organization the clans were separated into two political divisions known as moieties. The towns chose a political chief (*mico*) from clans of the white or peace moiety, while the war chief (*tastanagi*) was selected from clans of the red or war moiety. The Creeks were a patriarchy and only males served as town officials; women were excluded from the town square and played no formal political role.[9] As opposed to the Cherokee "war women" or the Iroquois "clan matrons" who wielded true political power within their tribes, the role of Creek "beloved women" is unclear. They seem to have been influential rather than powerful and to operate behind the scenes. This exclusionary pattern persisted among the Seminoles after they abandoned town life at the time of the Seminole Wars of the midnineteenth century and reconstituted as busk groups. Ceremonial busk groups consisted of camps that came together to celebrate the annual Green Corn Dance with its associated social and judicial functions headed by medicine men and a council of elders. Even in this attenuated form of political interaction among a greatly diminished population, Seminole women were allowed no formal input.

Early in the twentieth century the Seminoles' prosperous hunting and trapping economy disappeared with the growth of Florida's population, the ensuing drainage of the Everglades, and the outbreak of World War I, which removed European markets for their goods. There were several Indian responses to this radical change in their economic condition. Many landless and virtually destitute Seminole families became migrant laborers and lived on the land of white farmers. The traditional Seminoles maintained their camps in the Everglades south of the Tamiami Trail and survived by subsistence agriculture, hunting, and fishing. Many of these Indian families also spent part of each year in residence at commercial "tourist villages" in Miami and other coastal cities. There they engaged in alligator wrestling and other performances and sold handicrafts to tourists. Several Seminoles operated their own small commercial villages along the Tamiami Trail during the winter months. It was an extremely difficult time for Indians, especially with the onset of the Great Depression. In this economic crisis Seminole women frequently led the way in finding new sources of income. They were the first to engage extensively in agricultural wage labor and adapted their sewing skills to produce colorful patchwork dresses, jackets, and dolls that were prized by tourists.

In the 1930s many Seminole families took up residence on the three federal reservations, and for the first time Indian youngsters had an opportunity to attend government schools; most who did so on a continuous basis were females. But when the day school at the Dania Reservation closed in 1936 the children had no alternative but to drop out—they were generally excluded from Florida public schools by segregation laws—or attend the federal Indian school at Cherokee, North Carolina. Again, the girls as a group seemed to benefit most from this experience, and in 1945 Betty Mae Jumper and Agnes Parker became the first Seminoles to receive a high school diploma. Over a twenty-year period other Seminole youngsters would follow, attending Cherokee or federal boarding schools in Kansas and Oklahoma. In the late 1930s the bureau opened a day school on the Brighton Reservation at the request of Indian parents. By the time of tribal organization there existed a cadre of Christian, educated Seminole females ready to take leadership roles. At the first election three women were elected to the council and board in addition to the four female poll officials. These Indian women received support as well from the local white community; BIA officials lauded them as exemplars of positive acculturation. Superintendent Virgil Harrington found Betty Mae Jumper to be "a very pleasant and likable person who is interested in the welfare of her people," and Laura Mae Osceola to have "a remarkable memory and knowledge of the Seminole Constitution and Bylaws. A sincere and devoted tribal leader."[10]

The new council of 1957 got off to a shaky start. It soon became so distressed with attorney O. B. White, who handled everyday legal affairs, that his contract was rescinded. He was replaced with A. J. Ryan, who would represent the tribe for many years. White had made ill-considered statements regarding pending leases on the Dania Reservation which were published in the *Miami Daily News*. White and Mike Osceola tried to defuse the affair but the council, perhaps fearing that White had mishandled a lease which they desperately needed for income, would not be mollified.[11] This became the first of many personality clashes within the council in which Mike Osceola played a central role; in 1960 he charged Billy Osceola with gross neglect of duty and willful misconduct reflecting on the dignity and integrity of the council. The chairman's offense? He used a tribal car to take a petition to the reservations opposing the council's decision to open the Seminole tourist enterprises on Sundays.[12] Bill Osceola weathered this storm and remained as chairman, beating back Mike Osceola's attempt to assume that position.

The Seminole government began with virtually no operating funds. Although approximately $300,000 held in trust by the federal government became available, most was either earmarked for reservation land development or was not released immediately. Indian families needed cash but tribal government had only a limited amount of federal revolving credit funds to distribute. In 1958 the council requested release of some $75,000 held in trust by Florida's Internal Improvement Trust Fund; the monies were to be distributed on a per-capita basis to 1,025 Indians enrolled at the Seminole agency. The state released only $18,000 and in the fall of 1958 over 500 Seminoles collected $25 apiece. The Trail Indians refused to take part in the distribution for political reasons—they were negotiating a separate settlement with the federal government—so a surplus reverted to the tribal treasury. In 1959 the state transferred the remaining trust funds to the Seminole tribe, but this provided limited relief.

Throughout its early years the tribe operated with so little money that even the chairman of the Tribal Council was not considered a full-time employee. Billy Osceola remembered, "They don't pay me salary. Sometime they give me fifty dollars, hundred dollars, you know, that's it.... The fourth year that I was on the Tribal Council they started about seventy-five dollars a week, I think, and then a little bit increase each year."[13] It was not until the 1960 fiscal year that they budgeted the position at a salary of $5,200 per year; even so, there were no funds available to pay the incumbent.[14] The council's projected budget for 1961 was $48,250 but economic conditions continued to worsen; tribal expenses grew and there was no source of funds except continued borrowing from the federal government. By 1964 the budget had been reduced to $36,178 and the few tribal employees were given only a $125 raise. Although the Seminoles made a payment to attorneys pursuing the land claims case in 1962, the attorneys were notified that it would be impossible to pay future expenses.[15] Attorneys Roy Struble and Effie Knowles agreed to stay on the case despite the tribe's economic difficulties.

By the early 1960s political relationships among the Florida Indians had changed dramatically. First, the tenacious Trail Indians had received federal recognition as the Miccosukee Tribe of Indians in 1962 and were no longer considered members of the Seminole tribe. Now only a few enrolled Seminoles still lived at a distance from the reservations. Second, after several years of operating under their constitution and charter the reservation Seminoles had time to consider the strengths and weaknesses of the organization and to recommend needed changes. This also presented an opportunity for the Christian cattle owners to consolidate their power.

In 1959 a petition signed by 135 Seminoles brought an election to amend the constitution and five changes were eventually approved.[16] However, that was just the beginning of a protracted amendatory process. Because the tribe's economic woes continued in 1961, the council discussed revising its organization to have just one governing body, creating savings of over $12,000 in salaries and expenses. They also considered cost-cutting alternatives while retaining the existing dual structure. Meanwhile, stirrings at the grass-roots level evinced dissatisfaction with the government. Over the council's objection a petition circulated on the reservations calling for revisions in the constitution and charter, especially for direct election of major tribal officers. The bureau accepted the petition in 1962 and Rex Quinn returned to Florida to guide the Seminoles in revising their fundamental documents. At that point tribal leaders had assumed the lead in pushing for far-reaching revisions. Quinn spoke to a joint meeting of the board and council warning them,

> the Bureau has taken much pride in the way this tribe is set up and the Commissioner feels this is the way they should be set up to handle all the problems which you have to face. If you reorganize you will not lose any of the problems, they will just have to be handled in a different manner. You must still carry out all the duties and functions which are now being carried out. It is very important that the tribe be represented the way it should be. The Federal Law is directed at the Tribal Council much more than at the Board of Directors.[17]

The Seminoles heeded Quinn's advice to move carefully before making any radical revision in their structure and scrapped the idea of a unified governing body. Nevertheless, the sixteen amendments adopted prior to 1970, when considered as a whole, reflect significant changes within the Seminole polity during the decade following organization. One of the trends which emerged in this period was the Seminoles' creation of a new synthesis of American democratic governance with traditional cultural values.[18]

The first amendment proposed reflected a growing Baptist influence within the tribe. It changed the constitution's preamble to read, "We, the members of the Seminole Tribe of Florida, seeking divine guidance under God, in order to promote...."[19] Evidently Christians were no longer concerned that non-Christians might be offended by the mention of God since the latter were free to join the Miccosukee tribe, which still observed the traditional religious rituals.

The electorate amended the article on membership to state that "any person of one-fourth or more degree of Seminole Indian blood born after the adoption of this amendment both of whose parents are members of the tribe shall be enrolled as a tribal member"[20] Previously no blood-quantum requirement existed and only one parent had to be listed on the tribal roll. Also, any person whose name appeared on the census roll at the Seminole agency as of 1 January 1957 would be eligible for membership if approved by a majority vote of the Tribal Council; before that date membership was automatic upon application. This represented an attempt to tighten the eligibility requirement for membership to prevent individuals of limited Indian ancestry from applying in hopes of financial benefit. Additionally, this meant to keep political control in the hands of those of Indian blood, as it required that no person admitted to tribal membership by adoption would be eligible to hold an elected office in the Seminole Tribe of Florida.

The article detailing organization of the governing body was revised in its entirety to restructure the Tribal Council. This represented a move away from the traditional Indian search for consensus to a more streamlined decision-making process. It reduced the council's size from eight to five members, each with full voting rights. The council's chairman would be elected at-large, giving all Seminoles a role in selecting their chief executive officer and preventing a cabal within the council from controlling that increasingly important office. With the movement to a directly elected tribal chairman the bylaws were amended to give that official full voting powers in the council (formerly the chairman voted only in case of a tie).

The elected at-large president of the Board of Directors filled the position of council vice chairman. The president of the board also became more powerful; the original charter allowed board members to select the president from outside the tribe due to the need for technical management decisions, although the board never took that action. Similar amendments to the charter reduced the board to five members and authorized the tribal chairman to sit ex officio as vice president of the board.[21] This provided greater interface between the legislative and business arms of tribal government. However, if the chairman or president could not finish their term, a new at-large election filled the vacant office; in that way there could never be a situation in which one person functioned as both chairman and president by virtue of the ex officio crossover. The other three council and board members were elected from and exclusively by residents of the Dania, Brighton, and Big Cypress reservations; nonresidents lost their previously guaranteed representation on the council.

A section of the constitution redefining eligibility to run for office stated, "Any member of the tribe having reached the age of 21, and who has been in residence on Dania, Brighton or Big Cypress reservation for a continuous period of four years immediately prior to an election, shall be qualified to be a candidate for election to the council."[22] The revised charter contained a similar restriction on candidates for the Board of Directors. This residency rule effectively restricted the right to hold tribal office to the reservation Seminoles; it also left most council members accountable to single constituencies and fostered parochialism in the decision-making process. This was somewhat offset by another provision which created a more or less permanent tribal bureaucracy by stating that all officers and employees "are appointed or employed in permanent positions and shall serve unless removed or their services terminated" for cause.[23] The charter revision included a similar statement.

These amendments restructuring the governing bodies were strongly opposed by Mike Osceola, who perceived a plot to remove him from the council by preventing nonresidents from seeking office. He increasingly became a voice of dissent within the government and frequently clashed with Billy and Bill Osceola. His argument that the best and brightest of the Seminoles who moved away and became educated were being disenfranchised and could never hold tribal office fell on deaf ears. Prevailing sentiment within the tribe held that anyone who really wanted to become politically involved would return and live on a Seminole reservation. Mike Osceola could not relocate because his home and business were on the Tamiami Trail, so his political career came to an end.

The amended article on nominations and elections made twenty-one the age for voting and holding office. It also introduced a structure to prevent a monopoly on power by any individual or group within the council. The chairman's term remained at four years while the term of a council member was reduced to two years. This allowed the chairman to exert strong leadership in developing policies, planning, and implementation of programs, but with the possibility of facing new council members halfway through the term. Extreme or unpopular policies could be checked in council after two years by the simple expedient of electing new representatives.

Standards for performance and attendance were also raised, again with greater accountability to the reservations. A member of the council who failed or refused to attend two meetings in succession without a valid excuse forfeited the office and a special election would be called to fill the vacancy. In extreme circumstances the council could remove a member or the chairman by a four-fifths affirmative vote where before a simple majority was required. This was a protection for the incumbents and a recognition of factional squabbles within the tribe. However, each reservation could initiate recall of its representative with a petition signed by twenty percent of the eligible voters. On the other hand, a recall of the chairman demanded a petition signed by twenty percent of all tribal voters who participated in the election.

The revised article on amendments revealed another effort to move the tribal government away from the consensual model toward more speed and efficiency. It allowed the submission of an amendment to be triggered by a majority vote of the Tribal Council or a petition signed by twenty percent of the eligible voters; then the secretary of the interior would call an election. Prior to this change it took a unanimous vote of the council or a petition from twenty percent of the eligible voters to initiate an amendment. A new article allowing referendums, added to the constitution in 1963, introduced Seminoles to the use of that parliamentary device. A referendum on any enacted or proposed ordinance or resolution of the Tribal Council could be initiated by either a petition signed by twenty percent of the eligible voters or an affirmative vote by a majority of the members. The council had to take action on a referendum vote within thirty days. These two articles moved the tribe toward speed of decision making over unanimity.[24]

A bill of rights, also new in 1963, represented a melding of democratic process with recognition of traditional Indian social and religious values. It guaranteed tribal members "equal political rights and equal opportunities to participate in the economic resources and activities of the tribe, and no person shall be denied freedom of conscience, speech, association or assembly, or due process of law, or the right to petition for the redress of grievances."[25] This assured all Seminoles the basic rights of citizenship regardless of their clan affiliations. A second aspect of the bill of rights guaranteed that "the members of the tribe shall continue undisturbed in their religious beliefs and nothing in this Constitution and Bylaws will authorize the tribal Council to interfere with those traditional religious practices according to their custom."[26] This recognized that a significant number of Seminoles still held traditional religious beliefs and followed the medicine men; it also indicated a fear of the possibility of religious persecution from the growth of Christian influence on the reservations. Baptist congregations had already forced the traditionalists to conduct the Green Corn Dance on private land outside the reservations, and that seemed only a step away from imposing a religious test for participation in tribal government. By guaranteeing religious freedom as a constitutional right, the leaders averted a potentially acrimonious struggle within the communities.

Other amendments to the bylaws provided more democratic procedures in the way the tribe conducted business. The council moved from monthly to bimonthly meetings to accommodate the increased volume of business. With the council reduced in size, three members constituted a quorum and could call a special meeting; previously only the chairman had this power. Moreover, meetings could now be called for any purpose; before they were called only for matters of serious concern. All committees served at the pleasure of the council rather than for fixed terms. This allowed greater flexibility in appointing or removing individual committee members. An important change to the charter expanded corporate powers allowing the Board of Directors to borrow funds, make and perform contracts, and pledge or assign future corporate income in amounts up to $100,000 (previously the limit had been $10,000).[27] This acknowledged the expansion of Seminole corporate enterprises and their growing sophistication in fiscal matters.

These amendments to the constitution and charter reveal that the Bureau of Indian Affairs had relaxed many of the controls imposed on Seminole government at the outset. Experienced bureau officials understood that for the tribe to develop socially and economically, it had to exercise expanding degrees of autonomy in making decisions.

Even with this new freedom the board had its hands full trying to generate income. As longtime member Willie Frank recalled, "We did not know [how] to go about in starting business or operation of business. Whenever we ran into something that we needed answers, we would [have] BIA staff help us with problem. We had no funds to get the operation going so BIA informed us that we need to set up Credit Office and use loans for the people to start their businesses. . . . Tribal members make loans to build their homes and to purchase cattle to start their own business."[28] Although the board occasionally authorized a small dividend to tribal members—usually at Christmastime—this was taken from Seminole trust funds held by the federal and state governments; otherwise, the board operated with money borrowed from the bureau's revolving credit account. The 1959 tribal budget amounted to $90,643—$14,000 for the council and $75,000 for the board—virtually all from a federal loan. The Seminoles desperately needed to increase cash flow from the rental of their commercial properties, oil and gas leases, and other revenue sources. Limited leasing for oil and gas exploration in the Big Cypress had been in effect since the late 1940s, but the agricultural leases at Brighton and Big Cypress produced little revenue; the latter were valuable primarily for land development rather than income. For example, S. and M. Farms, of Fort Pierce, leased 870 acres of land for five years at $2,500 per year; the land would be returned as improved pasturage for the cattle program.[29] This left the tribe dependent upon the commercial properties at the Hollywood Reservation as its primary source of lease income.

An impediment to leasing was a federal law restricting reservation land leases to twenty-five years with an option for an equal additional period. The council passed a resolution urging Congress to amend the existing law to allow leases up to ninety-nine years. Representative Haley visited the Seminole agency and offered his assistance in having the law changed, as well as in increasing the BIA's revolving credit fund available to tribes. The council welcomed his support because it had committed an enormous amount of money to the cattle program, "expending all Tribal funds available plus loan advancements that have been made available to the Land Development Enterprise from the Bureau of Indian Affairs Revolving Credit Fund."[30] The Seminole government also asked Congressman Paul Rogers to introduce a bill granting the tribe $150,000 per year for five years to develop and maintain their pasture lands.

The Seminoles never received a large special appropriation for their cattle program, but Congress eventually authorized the tribes to engage in long-term leasing of reservation properties—although Haley's committee refused to grant blanket permission for ninety-nine year leases. One observer believes this policy was a real service to the tribes: "The House Subcommittee on Indian Affairs, led by Congressman James Haley of Florida, refused to authorize a blanket lease and insisted on hearing each tribe present its reasons why it should be allowed to lease its lands for the longer term. On the other hand the Senate Indian subcommittee generally favored long-term leasing, and Secretary Udall encouraged this manner of using Indian lands. . . . Had Haley not stood firm against the policies of the Democratic administrations, there might be few Indian reservations today in the hands of Indians."[31]

A review of the Seminole revolving credit program for the years 1961 through 1971 shows just how acute the tribe's financial situation had become. In 1961 the amount committed to the loan contract between the United States and the Seminole Tribe of Florida, Inc., was $950,000, of which $455,000 had already been advanced. Of that amount $100,000 was in loans to individuals (at 2 percent interest) for the purchase of homes, cattle, and so on, and $355,000 was lent (at 4 percent interest) to tribal enterprises. Included in this was $210,000 for the arts and crafts center and Indian village, $40,000 to build a tribal office building, and $105,000 for land development (pastures) on the reservations. The principal on these loans was not due until 1969, but the tribe was to pay the annual interest payments. By fiscal year 1963 the amount of government loan funds committed to the Seminoles had risen to $1,750,000, with $1,027,000 already advanced. There was over $450,000 in outstanding individual loans and $557,000 advanced to tribal enterprises. Already the Seminole arts and crafts center and Indian village could make only partial interest payments.

In 1967, board president Bill Osceola informed the commissioner of Indian affairs that the interest payment of $43,983, due since 30 June 1966, would have to be carried as delinquent. Why? The tribe had to invest $50,000 in a water and sewage system on the Hollywood Reservation before a major electronics manufacturing firm would agree to locate a plant there; also, another $50,000 was needed to furnish housing for Indians from other reservations who came to work at the plant. These improvements could not have been accomplished if they made the interest payment on time.

Earlier, the council created a Tribal Housing Authority to improve living conditions on the reservations. In addition to the workers' housing at Hollywood, an additional twenty units were scheduled for Brighton and Big Cypress. The funding for this home building program came from the Seminole Interim Financing Enterprise, which ran up a debt of over $114,000 by 1970.

The Seminole agency staff reported in 1967 that "during the past year Tribal enterprises have shown little improvement, if any. We believe this is a result of all enterprises being under financed with three very important ones having to be subsidized to keep them in operation."[32] And things continued to get worse. The revolving credit program balance sheet for 30 June 1968 revealed almost $1,600,000 of individual or enterprise loans and interest outstanding. Some relief came when the cattle program was shifted to the separately funded Cattle Improvement Enterprise in 1968. The Seminole debt structure seems to have reached a nadir in 1969 when they owed $1,772,133 to the federal government. The tribe wrote off over $109,000 in principal and interest due from the arts and crafts center and Indian village and asked the bureau to reduce its indebtedness by that amount. By 1970 things had begun to stabilize a bit for tribal enterprises, although individual debts remained high. That year the Seminole Tribe of Florida, Inc., was delinquent by $15,000 in principal and $197,228 in accumulated interest payments, so it requested a modification of the loan agreement whereby the tribe could keep current on its note and still have sufficient funds to operate. The bureau renegotiated the loan agreement on 20 August 1970 and the tribe's total debt was set at $1,317,000. The tribal board expected to meet the payments with income of $300,000 annually from real estate and oil exploration leases.

At last the tribe began to generate a positive cash flow from its property leases by 1970. Local businessman Joseph Antonucci leased several hundred acres of the Hollywood Reservation for a mobile home park as well as a manufacturing and sales facility. Thanks to the revised federal law allowing long-term leasing of Indian lands, the lease was for fifty-five years at a minimum lease base of $225,000 per annum; ten years earlier a similar lease on property at Hollywood brought the tribe about $10,000. There were several other small leases totaling about $50,000 for properties with commercial frontage on U.S. Highway 441. These long-term leases were well below the going market rate for commercial properties in the rapidly growing west Broward County area where Hollywood Reservation is located. Nevertheless, they represented a princely sum for the cash-starved Seminole tribal government. That same year the tribe received a onetime payment of $223,000 from Mobil Oil for oil and gas exploration rights on the Big Cypress Reservation, and Mobil would also pay $37,000 a year for five years to keep the lease in force.

Undoubtedly the most questionable industrial development project undertaken by the tribe was its contract with the Amphenol Corporation, which planned to locate a plant in the Seminoles' seventy-seven acre industrial park. The sixty-five year lease had never been projected to produce more than $4,000 in annual rents on ten acres of land, but the trade-off was to be below-market rents in return for Indian jobs. This became a recurrent theme in federal industrial development policy for Indian reservations throughout the United States during the Kennedy and Johnson administrations. Light industries were encouraged to locate on reservations for which they received low rental rates, tax benefits, and federal subsidies for training Indians; but when the benefits expired, companies generally abandoned the reservations, leaving behind empty buildings and disrupted communities. It was precisely such a state of affairs that so concerned Congressman Haley and his committee; Indians committed their land and funds but realized little in return. In announcing the Amphenol contract with the Seminole tribe a government official said, "We have great hopes for industrial development of Indian areas. There are now nearly 100 American companies operating plants of various sizes on Indian reservations or in nearby communities and providing employment for 7,000 Indians in their home areas."[33]

The Amphenol Corporation, headquartered in Chicago, is a manufacturer of electronic components for aerospace and telecommunications industries. It committed to build and equip a modern plant at an estimated cost of $500,000. The company also promised to hire and train Indians (with a BIA manpower training grant), promising that about one-half of the initial work force of two hundred would be Seminoles. The Seminole tribe invested over $125,000 in preparing the site and providing additional housing for workers. Associate Commissioner Theodore Taylor commented, "The Bureau of Indian Affairs is grateful for the confidence Amphenol has shown in the Indian people by deciding to establish this plant on the Hollywood Reservation. I believe the Seminoles have shown extremely good judgment in choosing to do business with this sound and far-sighted company."[34] Unfortunately, the results were not as planned. By December of 1967, a year and a half after the plant was established, only twenty-two of the 209 employees were Seminole; of $397,480 in annual payroll only $80,800 went to Indian employees. Moreover, the $8,400 BIA on-the-job training grant which called for training some seventy-five Indians had been scaled back to $5,568.[35] Shortly before the plant closed in the late 1970s there were fewer than twenty Seminoles among its 300 employees.[36] The Amphenol affair typified bad deals and cruel delusions which the government fostered during the 1960s—initially it looked promising but in retrospect neither jobs nor income were produced for the tribe.

Lack of education presented a major barrier to employment in the 1960s; few Seminoles possessed the education and social skills to compete successfully. Although the bureau operated a day school at Big Cypress, most Seminole children attended public schools; yet fewer than 150 members of the tribe had completed high school and only one was a college graduate. In a report to the Senate Subcommittee on Indian Education, the superintendent of the Seminole agency noted that sixty-seven percent of Seminole youths who entered the first grade in 1956 failed to graduate in 1968.[37] Many of the Indians who completed high school still exhibited English-language deficiencies and most were marginal students. Although a number received vocational training at BIA expense, they found it easier to work on the reservation than to compete in the alien world outside. Upgrading the quality of Seminole education and job training programs, while providing better employment opportunities on the reservations and in nearby communities, remained a challenge for Seminole administrations.

The Seminoles' tourist enterprise turned into another ill-fated venture. In 1959 the council eagerly endorsed the board's plan to construct the arts and crafts center and Indian village, as well as a tribal office building on the Dania Reservation. The board voted to name the new tourist attraction the Okalee Indian Village and authorized its construction on a site fronting state road 7 (U.S. 441), a major tourist artery before the opening of Florida's turnpike. The board also bought the inventory and supplies of the Seminole Crafts Guild at the Brighton Reservation. Although the tourism and crafts business never achieved financial success for the tribe—in fact, it created a major economic drain—it served an important social function. Rex Quinn believed that

> the purpose of the economic development program was to provide the financial means for them to develop socially.... We had a little [factory] they used to call it Quinn's Folly or Quinn's Hatchet Factory. I had a little plant going out at Big Cypress. We hired fifteen or twenty people, see. We never made any money, but we broke even ... sometimes we lost a little money. One year we lost ten thousand dollars, and everybody was pointing a finger at me. And I told the tribe, "Would you rather lose $10,000 in this thing, or would you rather put $50,000 into a welfare program and give it to them? Now what do you want to do?" I didn't think it was bad.[38]

The factory at Big Cypress produced small drums and hatchets as well as figurines carved from cypress knees. At Brighton the women brought their sewing machines to the recreation hall and turned out intricate Seminole patchwork by the yard. The patchwork was then affixed to shirts that had been bought by the gross from a commercial manufacturer. These items were brought to Dania for sale in the arts and crafts center. According to Quinn, "We were buying it by the yard—two or three dollars a yard. We had $3,000 worth of that kind of inventory on hand all of the time. We had boxes of that stuff."[39] He felt it was a worthwhile endeavor that gave the people some income and self-respect, as there could be no social progress where there was complete poverty. "We had women there who were making more money doing what they could do best than they could working in the fields, and they wouldn't get sunburned quite so bad."[40]

Both the council and board found it imperative to establish control over the Seminole cattle enterprise which, along with the Okalee Indian Village and Crafts Shop, accounted for most of a nearly $2,000,000 debt owed to the federal government. Since its inception in the 1930s the cattle program had never been financially sound. Nationally, Indian cattle enterprises repaid the government for starter herds with a portion of their annual calf crop, and the original Seminole agreement required that form of compensation. Unfortunately, the poor quality of the Florida range cattle kept other Indians from taking them, so the bureau pressed the tribe to pay in cash. Over the years better cattle management practices were employed, such as the use of better bulls to improve the herd quality. The tribe also greatly expanded improved pasturage by renting lands to commercial farmers, who turned it back to the tribe planted in good grasses and properly ditched and drained. In 1954 the tribal herd was dispersed to individual owners who assumed loans repayable to the tribe; also, two livestock cooperative associations were formed at Brighton and Big Cypress.

Cattle owners, used to having their own way, presented stiff resistance to centralized tribal authority. An overview of the Seminole cattle program in the late 1960s revealed that cattle owners formed an economic special interest group within the tribe even though they were not uniformly successful.[41] For years government officials had told the Seminoles that raising cattle would open the way to wealth and prosperity, and many families borrowed money to purchase a few cows. Also, a number of people inherited cattle, but many of them were women or infirm or elderly individuals unable to care for their stock; some absentee owners even employed other Seminoles to work their herd. In addition, many family herds were too small to be profitable. Government stockmen considered fewer than fifty cows inadequate to support a family because owners could not increase their herd unless they were allowed to keep the calves, yet they had to sell the calf crop to repay loans and have any operating income left over. Further, their presence on the limited improved range land hindered more aggressive Indian owners who wanted to increase their herd size.

Between 1959 and 1966 the Seminole tribe tried to develop a better cattle program through persuasion and example. It formed a cattlemen's association and required all cattle owners to become members for a fee of five dollars but no annual dues. The association elected its board of directors to work with the state extension agent and the Seminole agency staff. The extension agent managed the cattle program in the field while the board and superintendent supervised financial affairs. Although great effort went into explaining and illustrating good management practices such as rotation of fields, fence maintenance, and bull service, the owners paid little attention. Perhaps due to imperfect translation or lack of technical understanding, the board had no power to enforce compliance.

In 1963 the cattlemen's association established standardized cattle and pasturage regulations. Most of the available government loan funds were exhausted, so the cattle owners had to pay more to keep up the improved pastures or they would be unable to raise the more profitable Angus cattle. Pasture maintenance cost $218,000 per year. The bureau contributed about $100,000 annually, but that would not continue indefinitely. Thus the superintendent and agency staff pushed to have the board make the necessary decisions to keep the cattle program viable. The tribe guaranteed $50,000 per year leaving $68,000 to be raised. Faced with this the board, following meetings in the communities and with the cattle association members, authorized a complete revision of the rules for ownership and management of cattle on the reservations. Among other things it raised the grazing and labor fees of the owners significantly. Although the tribal leaders delayed taking action in hopes of achieving consensus—still important in the early years—this became one of the most controversial decisions of the new Seminole government and took years to implement.

The most immediate impact was a reduction in the number of cattle owners as those with small unprofitable herds sold out. Others objected to raising the fees, particularly when they learned that the regulations exempted tribal leaders from paying labor charges when they were away on tribal business and could not manage their own herd. This limited exemption violated the Seminoles' belief in equal treatment for all members. Seminole cattlemen failed to see that payments for better pastures and bulls really constituted an investment in their long-term prosperity; they only saw that larger monthly charges reduced their cash in hand. This put the Seminole leaders "in a position between two groups, white society and reservation society. They cannot make decisions in the face of intense opposition on the part of their own people even though they know that the decisions must be made in order to implement the cattle program."[42]

When Rex Quinn arrived to become superintendent in 1965, the cattle program still languished; there remained too many small owners, poor calf crops, and insufficient funds to continue developing improved pasture. While the government still maintained most of the pastures and fences and provided technical assistance, the Indians paid only $5 per head in grazing fees — about one-seventh of the actual cost. After a thorough examination of the situation Quinn and his staff developed a plan, which the bureau approved, to put the program on a paying basis. It established a schedule of graduated grazing fees and defined the rights and responsibilities of both tribal government and the cattle owners. Quinn presented his plan to the tribe at an all day meeting held in the United States Sugar Corporation's auditorium in Clewiston and it received general acceptance. Still, it would take the support of all of the reservations to make the plan work. As Quinn recalls, "We had our problems along this line, and some of our leaders got their nose bloody, politically speaking, trying to carry out these things. You're going to have some casualties — political casualties — in tribal affairs, I don't care who you are or what kind of program you have. But in the final analysis, the program worked excellently."[43]

On 1 January 1966 the Seminole tribe took over the direction of the cattle program for a four-year period. The board and Superintendent Quinn became the decision makers, and their directives were implemented by the state extension agent who acted as cattle manager. The cattlemen's association became merely an advisory, educational, and marketing organization. Under the new cattle regulations adopted by the board, every owner had to sign an agreement that clearly delineated rights, privileges, and responsibilities; penalties could be imposed on owners who did not adhere to the regulations. "The expectation was that a written agreement would stop the dissension and controversy arising from misunderstanding of the role of cattle raiser."[44] By the end of the year Quinn reported that the number of individually owned herds had been reduced to approximately sixty-seven and each was profitable. Yet after paying loans and fees, income was low: the twenty-six cattle owners at Brighton had an average income of $2,092 during the 1966–69 planning period; twenty-two cattlemen at Big Cypress averaged a slightly higher $2,290.[45] Beginning with fiscal year 1968 the financial burden of the cattle program was transferred from the Seminole land development account to the newly formed Seminole Indian Cattle Improvement Enterprise. At that time the loan due to the federal government for land development exceeded $411,000; within two years it would add another $250,000 to the tribal debt. The Cattle Improvement Enterprise consolidated the operations of six separate bull-improvement and cattle programs on the reservations. The comprehensive plan devised by Superintendent Quinn remained in effect for many years, while the cattle owners continued to be a contentious group within the Seminole tribe.

Not all of the tribal government's actions were political or economic in nature. It also came to grips with a broad spectrum of social issues within the Indian community, particularly those resulting from increasing interaction with the world outside the reservation. For example, council members realized that in the past most Seminoles had married following Indian traditions. Yet many younger people no longer married under tribal law or custom, but rather formed common-law unions. The council believed they needed church or civil marriages to have legal protection, and passed a resolution urging the community to "encourage all of the younger generation as they get ready to marry, to obtain a marriage license and have a ceremony through the civil and religious ceremony in order that these marriages may be recorded in a lawful manner for the future benefit of the children and all parents concerned."[46] The council also received and allocated funds donated by groups such as the Friends of the Seminoles, in Fort Lauderdale, or S. and M. Farms, of Fort Pierce, for community development and recreation facilities on the reservations. At the same time it went on record admonishing S. and M. Farms, the largest renter of Indian lands, that the village area of the Big Cypress Reservation was off-limits to its Mexican workers because of clashes with Indian residents. The council occasionally assigned funds to Baptist churches on the reservations, primarily for parties at Christmastime.

Mindful of the need for good public relations, the council frequently bestowed Seminole patchwork skirts and jackets on national, state, and local dignitaries. A gift of Seminole dolls was sent to the children of Vice President Richard Nixon, for which the tribe received a note of thanks. Nor was the council opposed to solidifying the tribe's relationship with neighboring communities. On 2 May 1966 a council resolution changing the name of the Dania Reservation to the Hollywood Reservation in honor of the surrounding municipality received approval from Secretary of the Interior Stewart Udall.[47] Among the most important matters to come before the council were applications for tribal membership. Individuals who qualified for membership under the admissions article of the constitution filed applications with the membership committee headed by Laura Mae Osceola, and these were acted upon by the council. Most often the council considered requests from dependent children of tribal members, but the most significant application accepted in the summer of 1962 came from Ingraham Billie and his family.[48] It signaled the old medicine man's total political alienation from those Trail Indians who had formed the new Miccosukee tribe.

The prevention of unauthorized hunting, domestic violence, "moonshining," and other illegal activities on the reservations had long been a problem, but the tribe's economic straits prevented it from implementing a law and order program. The employment and training of officers, provision of a jail and jailers, patrol vehicles, and the like would have exhausted their resources, so the council asked for assistance from local law enforcement agencies. Rex Quinn recalled, "When I was superintendent, we never had any problem with that. In two instances, the counties had non-Indians as deputies coming on the reservation. We arranged for police, the state patrol and the sheriff's department to circulate through the reservations regularly, and particularly on Saturday night."[49] Such arrangements were stopgap at best and had to be renegotiated every time a new sheriff was elected. In 1968 the Indian Civil Rights Act amended Public Law 280 and allowed states and counties to exercise both criminal and civil jurisdiction on Indian reservations with the consent of tribal governments.[50] This issue would be satisfactorily addressed only when the Seminoles could provide their own police force. That became possible in 1974, when the Florida legislature made statutory provision for the tribes to handle law enforcement on their reservations.[51]

The 1967 elections saw a major change in the leadership of the Tribal Council and Board of Directors. After a decade of routinely returning incumbents to office the Seminoles selected somewhat younger, better-educated people to head their government. Moreover, they chose a woman to fill a major tribal office: Betty Mae Jumper was elected chairman of the Tribal Council. Joe Dan Osceola, the first Seminole to graduate from a Florida public high school, was elected president of the Board of Directors. Jumper and Osceola represented transitional leadership as the Seminoles were moving from total dependence on the bureau to a state of quasi independence through federal War on Poverty programs. Even so, federally authorized Indian self-determination would not arrive until the next decade.

Joe Dan Osceola entered tribal politics at age thirty when he ran for president of the board. By his own account, "I won it by a landslide. I got more votes than all the other four guys put together, so the people had enough confidence in me through the election. There were several people, of course, who weren't going to be satisfied.... So, I did have political enemies—the people who used to be in it and also a lot of people who are not Indians and Indians from the other tribe as well. They tried to get me out of office. The first six months in the office, so we finally had to take it to the people, and have a vote on it again. I won the election again by 3-1."[52] The 1967 election reportedly became an acrimonious affair. There were accusations that BIA staff members had interfered in the election process by campaigning for a few candidates. A rumor also circulated that if his candidate won, Superintendent Quinn would resign from the BIA and become the business manager of the tribe. In the aftermath of the election, partisanship was rampant. Joe Dan Osceola recalled, "I was accused

of selling the tribal government properties and many other accusations that I was investigated on by the FBI three times and also the
Secretary of the Interior office. Of course, they found it negative."[53]
In retrospect, Osceola believed that being cleared by the investigation enabled him to secure a better job; he resigned before his term as
president ended to accept a position with the Indian Health Service.

Betty Mae Jumper and her younger brother, Howard Tiger,
provide an interesting study of education, upward mobility, and leadership within one Seminole family. She was born at Indiantown, near
Lake Okeechobee, on 27 April 1922, the daughter of Ada Tiger,
a full-blood Seminole, and a white father. Howard was three years
her junior. Their mother moved the family to the Dania Reservation in 1928 and both children attended the federal day school. They
were also among the first Seminole youngsters sent to the Cherokee
Indian School in North Carolina. After graduating in 1945, Betty
Mae attended public health training in Oklahoma before returning
to Florida, where she married Moses Jumper and started a family.
In 1943, a few days before his eighteenth birthday, Howard Tiger
left school to join the Marine Corps; he served with distinction in
the Pacific, seeing action at Guam and Iwo Jima. Following the war
he returned to Cherokee and married a former classmate, Winifred
Sneed, a member of the Cherokee tribe. After working in North
Carolina for several years, Tiger brought his family back to Florida
and became involved in tribal government. He served on the Tribal
Council from 1958 to 1963 and as president of the Board of Directors, 1961–63. During Tiger's term as president, he supported leasing
reservation lands to oil companies and other commercial interests, as
well as expanding tribal enterprises such as the Indian village and craft
shop and the cattle program. Shortly after leaving office he died in an
accident operating heavy equipment on the reservation. Betty Mae
Jumper served as vice chairman of the council from 1957 to 1959,
then was elected to the board for 1959–63; thus she had experience
on both governing bodies. After a period away from office, she ran
for chairman in 1967, promising to improve health, education, employment, welfare, law and order, and housing conditions within the
tribe. During Jumper's administration the Seminoles also took a leading role in organizing the first intertribal political organization within

the region. In 1968 the chairman met with the leaders of three other tribes at Cherokee, North Carolina, and signed an "Oath of Unity" preliminary to the formation of United Southeastern Tribes (USET).

As the tribe remained chronically short of funds, the chairman made numerous trips to Washington to meet with members of Congress and federal agencies to secure appropriations for Seminole programs. Thanks to the Kennedy and Johnson administrations' War on Poverty, a variety of federal programs became available to the reservations. The Office of Economic Opportunity featured a special Indian Desk, which channeled federal poverty funds directly to the tribes and reservations.[54] Like some sixty other tribes, the Seminoles saw a proliferation of programs based on the concept that the poor and minorities should design and manage the programs designed to lift them out of depressed economic conditions.

Seminoles were suddenly confronted with an array of agencies which became conduits for federal funds to the reservations. The Comprehensive Education and Training Act (CETA), Neighborhood Youth Corps (NYC), and Community Action Program (CAP), as well as Head Start, provided better employment opportunities for reservation Indians than most could find in the outside world. These programs also created a new venue for political activism and leadership training. In fact, many future tribal leaders got their introduction to federal bureaucracy by administering poverty programs. Grants from Housing and Urban Development (HUD) and the Economic Development Administration (EDA) also contributed to the rehabilitation of physical facilities on reservations. As a result, "tribal governments became surrogates for the federal government during the sixties, and this trend extended into the seventies, clothed ironically not as termination but in the new language of self-determination. Federal bureaucrats began to speak in hushed tones about the 'government-to-government' relationship they enjoyed with the tribes. In reality, the tribes were almost totally dependent upon the federal agencies for their funds and program ideas."[55]

These Great Society programs brought new energy and badly needed funds to American Indian reservations at a time when they had reached the point of economic exhaustion. They were no substitute for the tribes controlling their own social and political destiny, but that could only be achieved by developing additional revenue sources and fully regulating them through the exercise of sovereignty. Federal efforts to stimulate private-sector investment and job creation on the reservations had not succeeded, while tribal enterprises were spiraling ever deeper into debt. Virtually every aspect of tribal political and economic life was still tightly controlled by myriad federal regulations enforced by the Bureau of Indian Affairs. Many aggressive Indian spokesmen—from both the mainstream reservation constituencies represented by the National Congress of American Indians (NCAI) and National Tribal Chairmen's Association (NTCA), as well as more radical groups like the American Indian Movement (AIM) and National Indian Youth Council (NIYC)—articulated the position that meaningful progress would never come until tribal peoples were liberated from these restrictions and granted true social, political, and economic self-determination. Reluctantly the president, Congress, and the federal courts responded to this strident advocacy, and the Seminole Tribe of Florida found itself in the forefront of an Indian self-determination movement which matured during the 1970s.

CHAPTER 5

Howard Tommie's Legacy: Smoke Shops and Bingo

Annie Tommie was perhaps the best-known Seminole matriarch on the east coast of Florida early in this century. She had been the wife of Doctor Tommie, a famous Miccosukee medicine man who died in 1904, and became a highly regarded herbal healer in her own right. Her family made its camp on the North Fork of New River near Fort Lauderdale, and they were well respected by white residents of that region.[1] However, when a burgeoning population encroached on Indian lands during Florida's land-boom years, it was Annie who helped convince her people to seek refuge at the new federal reservation that opened a few miles west of Dania in 1926. She also cooperated with Mrs. Stranahan in encouraging Indian children to attend the public school.

Annie Tommie was the mother of six sons.[2] They were imposing men—over six feet tall and broad shouldered—who easily commanded public attention. Although Annie was a Muskogee, her children learned to speak both Indian languages as well as English, and non-Indians generally considered them to be leaders among their people. The most publicized of her boys, Tony, became the first Seminole youngster to enroll in the Fort Lauderdale primary school; he then attended the famous Carlisle Indian School, in Pennsylvania.[3] The flamboyant Tony later gained notoriety as headman at the Musa Isle Indian Village in Miami, and the local press often referred to him as a chief of the Seminoles—that would lead to conflict with traditional tribal leaders. In a 1927 newspaper account, a white spokesman for the Big Cypress medicine men and council denounced Tony Tommie as a "fakir and liar" who pretended to be chief of all the Seminoles.[4] Nevertheless, the Tommie family remained influential in the east coast Indian community.

Another of Annie's sons, Sam Tommie, converted to Christianity and attended Florida Bible Institute in 1946 to become a Baptist lay minister. Although not widely accepted as a tribal political leader, he worked closely with federal authorities to establish a Seminole cattle herd; Sam also helped convince his Indian kin to move to the Brighton Reservation during the 1930s. Only later did he receive recognition for these efforts. It was Sam's son, Howard Tommie, who emerged as an aggressive and dynamic Indian leader during the 1970s.

Howard Ernest Tommie was born on 28 May 1938 at the Brighton Reservation, the third of the Rev. Sam and Mildred Bowers Tommie's nine children.[5] As a child he learned to speak Muskogee from his mother, as well as the Miccosukee used by his paternal grandparents. He is a member of the Bird clan—one of the two largest Seminole clans and arguably one of the most powerful politically, since it produced so many officeholders during the early years of tribal government. When his family moved to the Dania Reservation the children attended public schools in Broward County, but Howard graduated from Chilocco Indian High School, in Oklahoma, where he lettered in football and basketball. He then served six months of active duty in the U.S. Army and eight years in the inactive reserve. Although Howard took some college courses, he worked in Miami as a truck driver and welder during the 1960s, when the Seminole tribe became a recipient of government-funded community development projects. This provided an opportunity for educated Seminoles to advance economically while assisting their people, so Howard returned to head the Neighborhood Youth Corps (NYC) program and learn the ins and outs of the grant-writing process. During this time he gained the reputation as an outspoken advocate of Indian self-determination, a concept which had recently captured national attention.

President Richard Nixon's congressional message on Indians of July 1970 was a defining moment in establishing the principle of Indian self-determination. Yet it could also be argued that the philosophical antecedents of self-determination are in the Meriam Report of 1928 and the Indian Reorganization Act, passed in 1934. Nixon's message outlined specific proposals for self-determination, and even though never fully implemented, Philip Deloria believes "it stands as the strongest official policy statement for Indian self-determination."[6]

Throughout the Great Society era a gradual momentum developed toward Indian control over tribal economic, social, and political affairs. The virtual monopoly of the Bureau of Indian Affairs and Indian Health Service in providing for tribal needs would be broken. Tribes adopted a strategy of establishing eligibility for the programs that were available to state and local governments, and to make tribal governments the primary delivery vehicle for these programs. While termination was no longer the official policy of the federal government, many tribal leaders believed that assimilationist sentiment lurked just below the surface; therefore, another part of their strategy was an attempt to lock in the role of the tribes in these delivery systems so that any attempt to resurrect termination would be difficult. Furthermore, with funds coming from an array of other federal agencies, it would be possible to target limited BIA monies on well-defined problems such as education and health. The vehicle for implementing this strategy was the War on Poverty, which channeled funds directly to tribes and bypassed BIA bureaucrats. Funds for CETA, CAP, NYC, and the like were the first discretionary funds that had ever been made available to many tribes.[7]

This financial windfall of federal dollars can be viewed as a mixed blessing. Federal funds generally had restrictions on their use, and many Indian leaders were unprepared for such limitations; they often had to restructure tribal governments to use the funds effectively. In addition, tribal priorities were often determined by the availability of funds for particular programs rather than by the needs of the people. While many Indians developed leadership and managerial skills running these programs, there was concern over how they would apply them once the Great Society faded into history. The logical development would be for tribes to assume responsibility for programs that had traditionally been conducted by the BIA, but that would call for a radical reassessment of the guardianship relationship between the federal government and Indians.

Congressional acceptance of Indian self-determination came with passage of the Indian Self-Determination and Educational Assistance

Act in 1975.[8] Ironically, it was shepherded through Congress by Senator Henry "Scoop" Jackson, of Washington, who in the 1950s had been an ardent advocate of Indian termination; two decades later Jackson's presidential aspirations tempered his approach to Indian policy. The 1975 act had two basic components: title 2, the Educational Assistance Act, authorized significant amendments to the Johnson-O'Malley Act that had guided Indian education since the 1930s. In particular, it required local committees of Indian parents whose children attended schools served by a federal contract; there were also provisions for expanded funding for Indian children in public schools.

Title 1, the Indian Self-Determination Act, held far-reaching implications for tribal life. It provided for direct subcontracting of federal services to tribal organizations, authorized discretionary grant and contract authority, permitted federal employees to work for tribal organizations without losing their benefits, and allowed the secretary of the interior to waive federal contracting laws if deemed inappropriate for specific tribal situations. This paved the way for aggressive Indian governments to assume many functions formerly performed by the BIA or IHS alone. Tribes like the Miccosukees opted to dispense with a BIA presence altogether. As Vine Deloria has summarized the situation, "Congress was thus taking the lock off the barn door and inviting Indians in to seize whatever they could pry away from suspicious bureaucrats."[9] Seminole and Miccosukee politics of the 1970s must be assessed within the context of these rapidly evolving changes in federal-tribal relations. Unexpectedly, two small Florida tribes would find themselves on the cutting edge of a national movement.

Howard Tommie won election as chairman of the Tribal Council in 1971, handily defeating incumbent Betty Mae Jumper. He represented himself as a new tribal leader and appealed to younger members of the tribe with the promise of Indian self-determination, especially direct contracting with the federal government as the Miccosukees had done. Jumper, an experienced tribal leader, had served the Seminoles for many years. Her Christianity also appealed to many of the older voters. Howard, though, bridged the generation gap and sold himself as a young rebel. He promised more aggressive policies than the older generation who had been bound by BIA policies which dictated the old style of limited Indian self-government and a high degree of dependency. Tommie recalled, "It was quite an upset when I came in with my idea of self-help. I said that we have to move forward by use of our own resources, and I captured the votes of the young."[10] On the other hand, the new chairman recognized that he had the support of the large Bird clan while Betty Mae Jumper belonged to the very small Snake clan. With a smile he confided to a reporter, "I do belong to a large clan and that was very helpful."[11]

Delivering on his promise to shake things up, the new chairman hit the ground running. He pressed forward on all fronts to assure that the tribe took maximum advantage of federal funding sources. The administration embarked on a furious cycle of grant writing, and money began to pour in. To coordinate the separately funded programs, Tommie created an umbrella Human Resources Division (HRD) with its own director and accounting department. For many years this division was run by Michael Tiger, a young, well-educated Indian who later became a regional Indian Health Service administrator. Included under HRD were reservation programs, social services, manpower planning, employment assistance, CETA programs, education departments, community health coordination, the Indian Action Team, food stamps, community health representatives, emergency medical assistance, mental health and alcoholism programs, and drug abuse counseling. The chairman also energized established tribal programs such as Head Start and the Native American Program. Meanwhile he encouraged the council to reorganize the Seminole Housing Authority and Tribal Utility Commission. He also promoted the construction of new health clinics on all reservations, as well as community centers and ball fields.

Chairman Tommie constantly sought funding for special education programs at the Ahfachkee Day School and for adult education. When parents were negligent in getting children to school, the Tribal Council passed a resolution reaffirming that all Seminoles must attend school until eighteen unless graduated from high school or married. "Education," the council stated, "is set as highest priority of the Tribe and children must be motivated to seek high school education."[12]

Improving law enforcement on the reservations remained a major goal for Tommie, and after the state legislature enacted a law in 1974 allowing the Florida tribes to police themselves, he secured Law Enforcement Assistance Administration funds to establish a tribal law enforcement program.[13] Next the chairman initiated a tribal legal assistance program to defend the tribe and its members, and the tribal attorney aggressively pursued Seminole land rights and sovereignty in the state and federal courts.

Howard Tommie gained national recognition as an articulate spokesmen for Indian causes. He represented the Seminoles in the National Tribal Chairman's Association and served as chairman of its culture and tradition committee. The committee was instrumental in negotiating a compromise with federal authorities over the Migratory Fowl Act, permitting Indians to legally possess eagle feathers for religious or cultural ceremonies. Tommie also served on the litigation committee of the National Congress of American Indians and testified in support of the 1975 Indian Self-Determination Act at the congressional hearings. Reflecting his interest in healthcare issues, Tommie received an appointment to the National Indian Health Board, which met quarterly in Denver to advise the government on policy issues; eventually he became its chairman. Throughout his administration Howard represented the Seminoles on the board of United Southeastern Tribes, serving one term as its president; in addition, he and Miccosukee leader Buffalo Tiger chaired the Florida Governor's Council on Indian Affairs. All in all, the energetic chairman brought a new dimension to Seminole leadership in an era of increasing tribal activism.

The 1971 election also brought change to the tribe's Board of Directors. The new president, Fred Smith, was born at the Brighton Reservation in 1939 and was therefore of the same generation as Howard Tommie. He graduated from Okeechobee High School and attended Indian River Junior College until 1963, and briefly held a seat on the Board of Directors before entering military service. After two years with the army in Europe, Smith returned to the reservation and managed a two-hundred-head beef cattle herd while taking extension courses in agricultural and business management. From 1968 to 1971 Smith was secretary-treasurer of the Seminole tribe. His family maintained residences at both the Hollywood and Brighton

Reservations, providing Smith with a broad base of support. When Joe Dan Osceola resigned as president of the board early in 1971, Smith determined to file for that post at the spring election.

Fred Smith's agenda for the Board of Directors generally complemented Howard Tommie's goals for tribal social and economic development; the council and board frequently held joint meetings and were generally in accord on most issues. The president was aware of the implications of Indian self-determination; as secretary-treasurer in November 1970, Smith had read a letter from the commissioner of Indian affairs to a joint meeting of the council and board advising tribes of Nixon's policy statement. As a result the council passed a resolution asking the government to turn over control of land operations, the cattle program, education, and employment assistance.[14] Smith planned to follow this lead and "traveled extensively throughout the United States, meeting with other tribal leaders and business consultants, touring their reservations, studying their enterprises and programs to enhance his home operations."[15] Under Smith's direction the board moved to upgrade and expand tribal business enterprises. They set regulations and restrictions for the tribe's commercial frontage along U.S. Highway 441 and made leases available to Indian businessmen. The tribe started a catfish farm on the Brighton Reservation and built a camp ground and marina tourist complex there with EDA funding. The board's EDA office also secured funds for community development programs including swimming pools and gymnasiums. As a cattleman Smith had definite ideas about that enterprise. He convinced the board to assume the cattle and range management program from the BIA and increase improved pasture acreage; the cattlemen's fees were then raised so the program would be self-sustaining. In addition, the board set up a retirement pension program for tribal employees. Only the Indian village and craft shop, despite numerous infusions of cash, continued to suffer significant losses.

The installation of new officers signaled a new parity between the council chairman and president of the board. The fiscal year 1972 budgets for the council and board listed salaries for both top officials at $10,660. This ended a long period in which the tribal chairmanship was treated as an unsalaried position. At the installation ceremony outgoing chairman Betty Mae Jumper remarked somewhat sardonically, "Four years ago we didn't have any money to work with and had to cash a bond in order to go on. I had to work elsewhere to get money on which to live, and still work as Chairman of the Council without pay."[16] Jumper received only a few dollars attendance money for council meetings and was employed by the public health office. Moreover, even the budgeted (but unfunded) salary for the chairman was only $3,600, less that the secretary-treasurer or clerk, and substantially below the $10,660 approved for the board president.[17] This disparity offers a glimpse into the sometimes byzantine nature of tribal politics. Evidently Jumper inherited the low or nonexistent salary that had been imposed on her predecessor, Billy Osceola. An undocumented but widely circulated story on the reservation is that Superintendent Quinn and Bill Osceola planned to transfer most of the tribe's economic assets, and thus its political power, to the Board of Directors at the expense of the council and its chairman. In the 1960s most of the money being spent on the Seminole reservations flowed into the land development and cattle enterprises which fell under the board, as did the commercial property leases. A lack of funds to pay the chairman's salary forced Billy Osceola to resign the chairmanship in November 1966 to head the Community Action Program. A few Seminoles still contend that Quinn planned to retire from the BIA and accept a position as tribal business administrator, but the upset election victories of Betty Mae Jumper and Joe Dan Osceola squelched that plan. In some circles it is still believed that the old guard on the council and board resisted Jumper and limited her effectiveness, and it could not have been lost on the first female chairman that the council approved a decent salary for her male successor.

In an interview Howard Tommie noted that to be effective, an Indian leader must command support from the people, and he believed he was the first Seminole chairman who fully gauged tribal sentiment. Admitting that he had no experience in tribal government other than directing NYC, he recounted:

> A lot of things made me feel like something needed to be done.
> I wanted to see things improve. I did not have much of an idea
> whether I could correct these things being chairman. We had two

forms of government, the board and the council. I went ahead and ran for the council, and, luckily, because of the fairly decent job I did with the Neighborhood Youth Corps, I won a lot of people on my side. Luckily they believed me. I was born and raised here, and everybody within the reservation knows me and that recognition had a lot to do with it. That is how I got into tribal government. I am not downgrading the people who were in there, but I just felt like they did not want to progress. But, in a way, I felt it could be done and still be able to keep harmony within the tribe.[18]

The new administration undertook a policy of contracting with the federal government for services, and tribal members replaced bureau functionaries wherever possible. "Of course, we had a Bureau of Indian Affairs. I do not want to say anything bad about them, but it is a bureaucracy. For some reason or another, they seem to do whatever their guidelines are, which are very minimal. They have never lived here, like I do."[19] He believed that the Tribal Council could make better use of the money allocated to the tribe. "For a guy sitting over there with a GS 15, 20, 30, whatever it is, I could hire two people and a secretary with that money."[20] Initially the chairman's plans encountered strong opposition from the federal Indian agent and his staff. Tommie believed that many of the government employees "did not really care whether an Indian kid got an education, or that an Indian kid got a job, or that the mother and father had a steady job. These were eight-to-five people. So we hired people that would stay on the reservation or that were qualified to go out and talk to people about what they would like to do."[21]

The chairman was convinced that during the early years of tribal government, local agency officials had directed revolving credit funds to a select group of Seminoles, namely, cattlemen or owners of heavy construction equipment. When asked if federal employees tried to influence the selection of tribal officers, he responded,

I felt the biggest influence that they had was on the federal purse strings. They would satisfy a certain part of the tribal government. I do not know whether there was any particular attempt to select these individuals, but they found that most aggressive

Indians would see the opportunities there, so they catered to them, I am sure. They made a substantial number of loans for the purpose of assisting the tribe. But a lot of times it would benefit the present administration's personal pocketbook.... I am pretty sure that goes on in most places.[22]

In an attempt to correct these abuses by government personnel, the chairman voided many contracts and adhered to a "buy Indian" policy wherever possible.

In 1975 Howard Tommie sought reelection. His opposition came from Betty Mae Jumper and Fred Osceola, the son of former tribal chairman Billy Osceola. Since Osceola belonged to the Panther clan and Tommie was a Bird, the election pitted candidates from the two largest lineages against each other. More important was which candidate could capture the vote of younger tribal members. It again became a campaign in which a youthful candidate (Fred Osceola was in his early thirties) sought to turn out a sitting chairman. Osceola adopted the slogan "motivate, rejuvenate, and educate" and was given a good chance of winning.

The older members of the electorate were left with a dilemma. "The Seminoles used to be ruled by the elders," explained tribal member Billy Cypress, a college graduate and army veteran employed as the bureau's community services officer in the 1970s. "You didn't have wisdom until you were 50 or 60. But today most of the elders don't speak English, so the question is if they can carry on the business of the tribe. Many of the old question the young, because the young have capability, but not the wisdom, to make decisions. What you need is a young man with wisdom."[23]

The Seminole tribe allowed only a month for campaigning between the close of nominations and election day. Most eligible Seminole voters were unlikely to be swayed by campaign literature or a media blitz. That placed a premium on intense face-to-face campaigning on all three reservations. Both Howard Tommie and Betty Mae Jumper were fluent in the Muskogee and Miccosukee languages; the latter was spoken by most tribal members and by virtually everyone at the Big Cypress Reservation. Fred Osceola, from the Brighton

Reservation, spoke only the Muskogee language of that community, leaving him at a disadvantage. All three candidates spoke English fluently, but it was important to articulate their positions in the native tongues of the old people. Seminole politicians must reconcile the conflicts that separate reservation constituencies, and this requires an ability to employ the nuances of native languages.

Seminole politicking is low key. "It's a guerrilla style of campaigning they use," observed Billy Cypress. "It's done more by backyard talk than big campaigning. There are subtle innuendoes by candidates attacking the other candidate's efficiency or integrity. When a candidate is talking to the Christian faction, he might say that he doesn't smoke or drink and tries to say that the others do all sorts of things."[24] The favorite campaign gathering is a cookout with an entire reservation eating together, hosted by a candidate. In his campaign, Osceola butchered and cooked two cows, one at Brighton and another at Big Cypress. Howard Tommie and Betty Mae Jumper held cookouts at the Hollywood Reservation, which they felt was crucial to their campaigns. The more-educated Indians lived there and worked for the Seminole tribe or the BIA; they were likely to cast ballots for the candidate who could most effectively address program and government issues. The rural Brighton and Big Cypress constituencies would probably vote on more local concerns.

Fred Osceola campaigned against what he called the downhill slide of the tribe since his father—who had passed away the previous summer—left office in 1966. He promised to return the tribe to the position of prestige he claimed it had enjoyed when his father and Bill Osceola dominated tribal government. Thus he became informally linked with the candidacy of Bill Osceola, who was running for president of the Board of Directors. Betty Mae Jumper made her appeal to the religious older voters by stating, "I believe if you don't put God before you, you're nothing."[25] She also understood the necessity of making specific campaign promises and pledged to build gymnasiums on the two outlying reservations so they would have facilities equal to those at Hollywood. Howard Tommie stressed his record, pointing to new facilities for adult education and remedial education, increased social welfare assistance, jobs, nutritional programs, and social activities for the elderly, and the placing of part-time doctors on the reservations, all obtained through federal funding. He admitted that more needed to be done and promised to work for additional funding for employment and cooperative food centers on the reservations.

With one of the largest turnouts in Seminole political history, Howard Tommie was elected to a second term as chairman of the Tribal Council. One south Florida newspaper credited the genial chairman with being the first Seminole leader to challenge the authority of the Bureau of Indian Affairs, noting that he had replaced government bureaucrats in health, education, and welfare programs with tribal members. The victorious Tommie was quoted as saying that "Using our own people, we're getting into a system where our interests are protected."[26]

The second term of Tommie's administration included the beginning of the most far-reaching social, economic, and political changes in modern Seminole history. Tommie was instrumental in initiating or vigorously pursuing four issues which became crucial in defining the extent of tribal sovereignty. First, he brought closure to the Seminole land claims case by urging tribal acceptance of the Indian Claims Commission's award in 1976, and then led a struggle with Oklahoma Seminoles over equitable distribution of the funds. Congress resolved the issue in 1990, and in the process implicitly recognized Seminole tribal sovereignty. A second legal action of Tommie's administration, known as the East Big Cypress case, set a major precedent in eastern Indian water rights. In 1987 Congress affirmed a settlement between Florida and the Seminole tribe, including a water compact regulating tribal water rights and usage; it also assured tribal sovereignty in its own lands. A third and controversial assertion of sovereignty came in connection with "smoke shops" selling cigarettes free of Florida sales taxes on the reservations. Most audacious was the introduction of high-stakes, unregulated bingo. The last two ventures were undertaken at some cost in adverse publicity for the tribe and were opposed by Indians opposed to smoking and gambling; they also generated legal challenges to the expansion of Seminole sovereignty.

In April 1979 a perceptive and somewhat critical article appeared in the *Miami Herald* highlighting many ambiguities of contemporary Seminole life.[27] The *Herald* noted that the tribal government no longer depended on ventures such as the arts and craft center (closed after five consecutive years of losing money) or the unfavorable land leases with mobile home park operators that netted less than five percent of the current fair rental value. Instead the Seminoles had developed a dynamic economy. At that time the greatest money maker for the tribe were the smoke shops that opened in 1976. Taking advantage of a federal court decision exempting the Colville tribe of Washington from paying state sales taxes, the Seminoles sold their cigarettes for $4.75 per carton, or $2.15 less than local merchants charged. In addition to tax-free cigarette sales, the tribe had become proficient in securing federal grants, and there were nearly eighty-eight contracts bringing money to the reservations. As a result, from 1968 to 1977 the tribal income soared from $600,000 to $4.5 million per year, enabling many social and economic ventures. The tribe's first full-time attorney, Stephen Whilden, was also busily involved in filing lawsuits challenging state and local governments that were arbitrarily using Seminole lands. Almost immediately the Seminoles were confronted with an assault on their smoke shop operations.

In July 1977 Broward County Sheriff Edward Stack, acting as a private citizen and taxpayer and supported by a local cigarette vendor, filed suit to require imposition of state taxes on the sale of cigarettes on the Hollywood Reservation. Stack claimed that the tribe cost Florida $275,000 per month by not paying taxes on its cigarette operations. Florida's Division of Alcoholic Beverages and Tobacco had not attempted to collect the state taxes because of ambiguities in the law. Untaxed cigarettes had long been available on military installations and in veterans hospitals, and Florida citizens could order them by mail from North Carolina. *Vending Unlimited v State of Florida* was transferred from Broward County, home of the Hollywood Reservation, to the state capital, Tallahassee, in Leon County. In March 1978 the Circuit Court of Leon County ruled that sales on Indian reservations were not taxable by the state, and the plaintiff appealed. The First District Court of Appeals of Florida affirmed this ruling on 22 November 1978.[28] The appellate court cited *Confederated Tribes of Colville v State of Washington* in its decision.[29] Nevertheless, contradictory rulings by federal courts in similar cases involving Indian cigarette sales cast some doubt on the continuation of tax-free sales to non-Indians; therefore the tribe's attorney adroitly negotiated with state officials and the Seminoles became directly involved in supporting political candidates. In 1979, following a lobbying effort by the Seminoles and their backers, the Florida legislature passed a bill authorizing the tribe to continue its sale of tax-free cigarettes on the reservations.[30] This act was challenged in subsequent legislative sessions, but it has been successfully defended on the grounds that smoke shops operated by the Seminole tribe assure continuing economic independence for the Indian people of the state.

Still, many within the Indian community complained that money was not a cure-all for tribal problems, and that all Seminoles were not benefiting equally from the wealth. Critics argued that federal grants only created a new form of dependency and that whites and blacks received the best jobs on the reservation while many Seminoles remained unemployed; one 1970s estimate had unemployment at Hollywood hovering around 35 percent with even higher rates on the rural reservations. More than half of the residents at Hollywood received some kind of government aid, while 75 percent of the employed Indians worked either for the tribe or the Bureau of Indian Affairs. Moreover, many newly affluent tribal members often lived side by side with those on welfare, thereby exacerbating the growing economic disparities.

Discontent became more pronounced as the tribe prepared for an election in May 1979, and Tommie found himself at the center of controversy when it was learned that he drew a large salary. During his eight years in office the chairman's salary had grown from less than $10,000 to $35,000, all paid from federal funds on the premise that Tommie functioned as primary administrator of the various government contracts. The Tribal Council had encouraged this course of action due to a reversal of financial fortune. In 1973 the Seminoles' income was projected to exceed $500,000, with over four-fifths of that sum derived from commercial property leases at Hollywood. Consequently the council approved $13,000 salaries for the chairman and president, while tribal employees received 11 percent raises the following year. But funds became tight in 1975 as a result of three lease cancellations which forced the council to suspend its annual cash dividends.[31] The chairman suggested that until matters improved, his salary could be taken from various programs under the Human Resources Division. A council resolution not only endorsed this approach but encouraged the chairman to increase his salary to $20,000 from such sources.[32] Rather than being defensive, Tommie expressed pride in having been able to secure so much of the federal largess. "You can't knock it," he said. "It was there: hot meals for the elderly, an ambulance for the Big Cypress Reservation, two pairs of shoes for a kid -- that's shoes the Indian would have never had otherwise."[33]

Despite these improvements in welfare, Tommie's detractors pointed out that non-Indians held many of the jobs in the smoke shops and even in the chairman's office at tribal headquarters. Tommie defended his white secretary on the grounds that he had tried Seminole secretaries, but they did not have the requisite skills for the position; he also complained that many Seminoles believed they were entitled to a job regardless of whether they were competent or not. On the other hand, one of his opponents conjectured that the chairman did not want an Indian secretary because in such a tight-knit community there would be no confidentiality. The CETA programs he supervised were particularly criticized as not preparing Indians for advancement in the job market, especially away from the reservation. James Billie, a young Vietnam veteran who sat on the Tribal Council and was a candidate for the chairmanship in the coming election, was quoted as saying that government training programs "sure don't help any. They seem designed to keep you on the reservation, and that's all."[34] Some Indians were also concerned that the chairman had become too autocratic, pointing to a council resolution that granted him final authority to fire tribal employees.[35]

The *Miami Herald* singled out Howard Tommie, Bill Osceola (who had replaced Fred Smith as president of the Board of Directors in the most recent election), and entrepreneur Marcellus Osceola for their large new automobiles, airboats, swamp buggies, and other signs of affluence that set them apart from the rank and file; they were the most obvious beneficiaries of the new smoke shop prosperity. Again, Tommie would not apologize. He admitted that the sale of cigarettes on the reservation was his idea and that he had brought Marcellus

Osceola together with financial backers. The partners were to pay 4 percent of income to the tribe as sales tax and 15 percent as rent. The tribe agreed that Osceola and his backers would have an exclusive smoke shop franchise for five years; in return they assumed all costs of litigation connected with the enterprise. Tommie later informed the council that the agreement with Marcellus Osceola was not intended to be an exclusive franchise. Osceola was supposed to wholesale cigarettes to other tribal members; however, when the Tribal Council granted franchises to other Seminoles, Osceola unsuccessfully challenged the decision in court. The new smoke shops on the reservations, owned 51 percent by Seminoles and 49 percent by white partners, paid approximately $1.6 million to the Seminole tribe's budget by 1980.

Buoyed by judicial and legislative victories vindicating the smoke shops, Seminoles now entered an even more lucrative and controversial venture: unregulated, high-stakes bingo games. In the fall of 1978 the Tribal Council received an economic development proposal from a group known as the Seminole Management Association in which Howard Tommie held majority ownership with over 51 percent of the stock. It encumbered nineteen acres fronting along U.S. 441, the most valuable vacant land remaining on the Hollywood Reservation. The investors planned to spend $2.5 million developing the Seminole Indian Plaza, including a smoke shop, a strip shopping center, and a bingo hall to seat over 1,500 patrons. The tribe was to receive its usual percentage from the smoke shop, all the rent from the shopping center, plus 20 percent of the profits from the bingo. Tommie promised to present a complete financial proposal showing how the non-Indian investors who put up the capital would be repaid. The Tribal Council reportedly discussed this proposal with chairman Tommie absent from the room, then voted 4-0 for acceptance. Thus the tribe's elected leader could become its leading entrepreneur.

The ease with which the proposal passed led many tribal members to accuse the council of favoritism. Some grumbling ensued that members of the council had been bought off with offers of jobs or even a piece of the action. Joe Dan Osceola, the former board president who had announced his candidacy to become chairman, conjectured, "It could have been everyone scratching everyone else's back."[36] Furthermore, he questioned whether Tommie was really the majority owner or just a front man for non-Indians who put up the money.

These accusations infuriated Tommie, who countered, "I really don't think I've taken the tribe for anything. Why should I be treated differently than anyone else who wants to go into business? It doesn't seem fair that I should be excluded just because I'm chairman."[37] He explained how he arranged for the $2.5 million from two backers, Eugene Weisman and George Simon. However, some tribal members and public officials questioned whether the chairman's associates represented organized crime. Simon had an office at the Flagler Dog Track in Miami and identified himself as a "financial consultant" to the track, but not a full-time officer. According to the *Herald* his name had surfaced in the media several times in the past: in one deal, Morris Lansburgh (the hotelman convicted of a Las Vegas skimming operation), Jack Cooper (a longtime Simon acquaintance and a partner in the dog track), and Simon were mentioned as being involved in negotiations to buy World Jai-Alai, Inc. Another time, Simon was questioned about his financial interests by a U.S. Senate committee looking into influence-peddling activities. In 1964 Simon testified at a trial about a $3 million loan from a Teamsters pension fund.[38] Weisman was a Pittsburgh investor whose family had been involved with other bingo operations. Weisman and Simon each produced about half of a "long list" of investors whose stake totaled $2.5 million. Yet by the summer of 1979 no contracts had been signed.

More fuel was added to the fire that year when Marcellus Osceola sold his smoke shop interests to Howard Tommie for a rumored $400,000 plus another $100,000 for inventory. The council obligingly canceled Marcellus Osceola's lease on a three-acre site and transferred it to Howard Tommie.[39] At the same time the council passed a resolution declaring a five-year moratorium on establishing new smoke shops at Hollywood, citing the danger of saturating the market and thereby reducing tribal income from sales.[40] Still another resolution made price wars illegal and set a minimum sale price of $4.75 per carton.[41] Although Tommie was nominal majority owner, critics again claimed that outside money really controlled the business. Some suggested that the plan all along had been for Osceola to sell his holdings to Tommie, but the chairman vigorously denied any collusion. "I honestly could say that people could understand it that way," he admitted, but "we didn't want to move in that particular way. . . . Never had an agreement per se between me and Marcellus, and there were differences of opinion" which led to lawsuits. "In a humorous way, we asked him to sell out. Because we didn't want any competition. In a joking way. But he changed his mind and arrived at a figure."[42] As part of the deal Osceola reportedly retained a share of the profits from the first shop and subsequently leased another smoke shop, although at a less accessible location. It was a joke on the reservation that Howard Tommie, like Marlon Brando's movie character in *The Godfather*, had made Marcellus "an offer that he couldn't refuse."

A proposal by the chairman for tax-free liquor sales on the reservations became another volatile issue. A joint meeting of the council and board decided that the issue should be brought before the people at community meetings.[43] Predictably it drew a storm of protests from religious conservatives in the Seminole community, especially Southern Baptists. Following a raucous meeting held in the Hollywood Reservation gymnasium, the Tribal Council voted 5-0 against the proposal. Even Howard Tommie could not win a confrontation with the antiliquor sentiment prevailing among older Seminoles. When asked about this issue, he explained, "It came about during my administration many, many times. The people, of course, were highly Baptist. They told me that they did not want it. I really got into hot water with them one time, because I did authorize the sale of beer at one of our tribal fairs one time. They worked me over pretty well in tribal council. . . . So after they shot it down in the community meeting, I just said 'Okay. Now I know that you really do not want it.' It was not a cop-out or anything, I just wanted to find out what they wanted."[44] Some tribal members supported liquor sales to provide emergency services—primarily ambulances—for the rural reservations, so the chairman gave it a try. But he expected the old-timers to say they did not want the services, that they could take care of themselves. Also, he understood the Baptists were set against liquor because they had seen what problems it could engender on the reservations.

Even though he backed away from liquor sales, Tommie remained convinced that his vision of the tribe's future had as much validity

1. Billy Osceola greets Commissioner of Indian Affairs Glenn Emmons on his visit to Florida in 1954. Courtesy the Seminole/Miccosukee Photographic Archive.

2. Top left: Meeting to discuss Seminole constitution and charter, Dania Reservation, March 1957. Left to right: BIA official, Rex Quinn, Josie Billie, Joe Bowers (in background), Kenneth A. Marmon, Billy Osceola, Jackie Willie. Courtesy the Seminole/Miccosukee Photographic Archive.

3. Bottom left: Seminole tribe constitutional committee, March 1957. Left to right: Rex Quinn, Mike Osceola, Frank Billie, Jackie Willie, Bill Osceola, John Henry Gopher, Billy Osceola, Jimmy O'Toole Osceola. Courtesy National Anthropological Archives, Smithsonian Institution.

4. Above: Meeting to discuss Seminole constitution and charter, Brighton Reservation, March 1957. Seated at table, left to right: Rex Quinn, Billy Osceola. Courtesy the Seminole/Miccosukee Photographic Archive.

5. Top left: Seminole constitution and charter committee meeting, March 1957. Tribal constitution outlined on blackboard. Left to right: Jimmy O'Toole Osceola, John Henry Gopher, Rex Quinn, Bill Osceola, Frank Billie, Billy Osceola, Jackie Willie, Mike Osceola, Kenneth A. Marmon. Courtesy the Seminole/Miccosukee Photographic Archive.

6. Bottom left: John Henry Gopher casting his ballot for tribal government, August 1957. Courtesy the Seminole/Miccosukee Photographic Archive.

7. Above: Meeting of Seminole Tribal Council, May 1959. Left to right: Frank Billie, Mike Osceola, John Cypress, John Josh, Billy Osceola (chairman), Laura Mae Osceola (secretary), Betty Mae Jumper, Charlotte Tommie Osceola, Howard Tiger. Courtesy the Seminole/Miccosukee Photographic Archive.

8. Left: Tribal Council member Betty Mae Jumper, 1959. She would later become the first woman elected chairman of the Seminole tribe. Courtesy the Seminole/Miccosukee Photographic Archive.

9. Above: Laura Mae Osceola, secretary and treasurer of the Seminole tribe, 1959. Courtesy the Seminole/Miccosukee Photographic Archive.

10. Top left: Miccosukee delegation arriving in Havana, Cuba, July 1959. Courtesy Historical Association of Southern Florida.

11. Bottom left: Miccosukee delegation meeting with representatives of Castro government, July 1959. Far left: Morton Silver; fifth from left, Buffalo Tiger. Courtesy Historical Association of Southern Florida.

12. Above: Billy Osceola, chairman of the Tribal Council, and Commissioner Glenn Emmons, 11 November 1959. Courtesy the Seminole/Miccosukee Photographic Archive.

13. Howard E. Tommie, chairman of the Seminole tribe, 1971–79. Courtesy Howard E. Tommie.

as that of religious conservatives who thought things were changing too fast. He told them,

> The thing that you have to understand—I cannot impress this upon you too much—is that I am an Indian, too. I live here. I have just as much right to say something, whether I am a tribal chairman or not a tribal chairman. I see things that are happening. There is only one way that something is going to get done, and that is if we do it.... if another Indian steps up to me and asks me why are you doing this, I am going to tell him. I am just as much an Indian as he is. Just because you go to church and you have your values does not mean that I would not like to have these benefits at my disposal.[45]

The national debate over appropriate forms of Indian enterprise ratcheted up sharply during the late 1970s, as more tribes sought additional sources of revenue such as tax-free cigarettes and gambling. State and local governments became equally opposed to what they perceived as unwarranted and illegal activities on Indian reservations. As a result, the 1980s witnessed numerous legislative and legal challenges to Indian economic sovereignty. Howard Tommie, having introduced tax-free cigarette sales and bingo to the Seminoles, decided to become a full-time businessman and did not seek a third term as chairman. He withdrew as head of the bingo consortium and devoted his time to Howard E. Tommie Enterprises, which included a substantial smoke shop in a prime location on the Hollywood Reservation. It fell to the administration of his successor, James Billie, to deal with the legal assault on Seminole bingo.

In the summer of 1979 the Seminole tribe contracted with Seminole Management Association to run the bingo emporium for 45 percent of the profits.[46] By operating their games daily, offering large jackpots, and bussing in players from long distances on bingo excursions, the tribe expected to realize about $1.5 million from bingo the first year, or approximately what the smoke shops generated.[47] However, a new Broward County Sheriff, Robert Butterworth, threatened to intervene and close down the bingo hall before it opened. According to Butterworth the tribe violated the Florida statute which regulated bingo operations. The statute restricted the operation of bingo games to qualified (that is, charitable or nonprofit) organizations. Operators could hold games only two days per week, with jackpots limited to one per session with a top value of $250. As the Seminoles ignored all three of these sections, the sheriff intended to enforce the law and make arrests. Operators of qualified games formed a strong anti-Seminole bingo lobby, claiming that the tribe operated illegally and would cut into their business; law enforcement officials were also concerned about possible underworld involvement in Indian bingo.

In *Seminole Tribe of Florida v Butterworth* the tribe's attorneys asked the federal district court to permanently enjoin Sheriff Butterworth from enforcing Florida's bingo statute on the reservation. The court issued a preliminary injunction in December 1979 that permitted the bingo hall to open. Florida assumed criminal and civil jurisdiction over Indian tribes in 1961 under the provisions of Public Law 280; however, the Supreme Court had held that it did not confer general state civil regulatory control over Indian reservations. For the state to have enforcement power over bingo on the reservations it must rely on the grant of criminal jurisdiction contained in Public Law 280. The case then turned on whether the state's bingo statute was civil/regulatory or criminal/prohibitory in nature.[48] On 6 May 1980 the U.S. District Court for the Southern District of Florida held the statute to be civil/regulatory; but Congress had never authorized Florida to impose its civil regulatory power on Indian lands. The court granted injunctive relief, finding that "in view of the Congressional policy enunciated in Public Law 280, the court must resolve a close question in favor of Indian Sovereignty."[49] On 5 October 1981 the U.S. Fifth District Court of Appeals affirmed the lower court decision, thus paving the way for expansion of Seminole bingo.[50] The Seminoles experimented with bingo at both Brighton and Big Cypress with mixed results, then opened a major bingo hall on its small reservation in Tampa. By 1985 tribal income from all sources would exceed $10 million per year, the bulk of it coming from bingo and cigarette sales.[51]

By the end of Howard Tommie's administration the Seminoles were able to deal with a major economic problem that had plagued them since the tribe's organization. The federal loan used to create a revolving credit fund was initiated in 1958, and it increased over the years. The BIA became concerned when the delinquency on the loan continued to grow each year. Although a portion of the original loan had already been forgiven by Washington authorities, on 30 June 1979 the Seminole revolving credit fund owed the federal government over $1.5 million, including almost $330,000 of interest. Accordingly, that year the BIA required the tribe to develop a plan for retiring this debt.[52] Tribal enterprises owed the revolving credit fund over $1.4 million in principal and interest. The loans ranged from $18,000 due on the tribe's office complex to $334,617 for the Land Development Enterprise, plus $293,999 on the Indian village and arts and crafts center. Various cattle programs accounted for another $330,000. The Tribal Council and Board of Directors also allocated an additional $145,000 to social programs.

Federal authorities saw that this debt had been built up over decades and would take years to eliminate, but claimed repayment had to begin somewhere. The plan proposed by the BIA called for the tribe to make substantial payments between 1980 and 1985 and to be current on principal and interest payments by 1982. A systematic repayment schedule was drawn up requiring each tribal enterprise to make specified annual payments to the tribal government, then the Seminole tribe could repay its debt to the federal government. It called for an initial payment of $195,000, with most of that coming from a $160,000 cash balance remaining in the revolving credit fund. This ambitious scheme depended upon the tribe sustaining a high level of income from its business endeavors. Because the Seminole enterprises have prospered, by 1993 the remaining Seminole debt reportedly amounted to less than $50,000.

In reviewing his administration almost a decade after leaving office, Howard Tommie spoke of the difficulty in developing progressive policies and programs to benefit the tribe, while preserving and honoring the traditional conservative values of his people. Conservative and progressive may just be convenient labels used by outsiders to describe what were essentially more complex social and political relationships within Indian communities. Certainly Seminoles on the three reservations did not display a uniform degree of conservatism and resistance to change despite their religious orientation; they exhibited a wide range of acculturation, and there were multiple factors at play which led to political factionalism. Even so, the tribal government encountered a resistance to many of its programs. When asked how he responded to this conservative opposition, the former chairman replied, "I am in the age group that I am the progressive. So you have to walk a fine line for political reasons. In other words, elections are going to come, and you do not want to offend too many people. You had to walk a fine line."[53]

Another impediment to Seminole progress stemmed from the fact that many Indian people retained primary loyalty to their reservation community; they did not consider themselves members of the political entity known as the Seminole Tribe of Florida, and that perception colored the actions of their representatives on the Tribal Council and Board of Directors. Such parochialism was never fully overcome during Tommie's administration despite his efforts at unification. "I think we recognized that there were some benefits by working together. But I think that you also have to understand that there were two different cultures, even languages. I would not say that I was successful in it."[54] The Tribal Council had some success in bringing children from the reservations together for workshops and summer programs, and intertribal athletic competitions were popular, but basically the groups remained divided. Reflecting on this division, Howard conceded, "I do not think that they want [anyone] to bring them together. The main reason is that we were told so often that we are our own people and cannot be told [what to do], not by the tribe, but by the Bureau."[55]

The failure to resolve these differences also accounted for what Tommie considered one of his greatest defeats as a tribal leader. He strongly favored having the tribe contract to operate the Ahfachkee Day School at the Big Cypress Reservation which the BIA had run since the 1940s. The school had a record of poor attendance, marginal teachers, and below-standard academic performance; moreover, most Indian parents on the reservation were apathetic toward education. A few adults who were interested in their children's schooling agreed with the chairman that the Tribal Council should take charge of the facility—certainly it could do no worse. However, the Tribal Council expressed great reluctance to assume responsibility. Representatives from the other reservations argued that should the BIA contract fail to cover all expenses, then tribal funds would be siphoned away from other projects to meet costs. There were also questions concerning who would direct the school, hire teachers, set curriculum, as well as an unwillingness to leave affairs in the hands of the Big Cypress community. BIA education officials in Washington had also raised questions about the tribe's ability to run a school. In the face of such resistance even the chairman, who had a reputation for getting his way, could not push the council to agree on contracting:

> As strong as I was, that is one of the things that I felt I could have done to help that school a whole lot. We had three meetings; we held public meetings to contract it. We talked about a lot of things, and everything was positive. I guess if I had tried it the second time maybe I would have been successful. It really boiled down to the people trying to save their jobs out there. The government employees trying to keep their jobs. They muddied up the whole water, and I just walked away from it. If I was going to accomplish a whole lot, I think it is one of the things I should have done, contract that out, because I think we could have done it.[56]

His critics concur that Tommie was remiss in not aggressively pushing for contracting as his successor did, and point to the achievement of Seminole children since the tribe began running the school in 1982.

The most sensitive issue during Howard Tommie's administration concerned the profits that he and his associates apparently reaped from the smoke shops and bingo. Tommie earlier alluded to the BIA rewarding a few aggressive Seminole leaders prior to his tenure. Now media reports—some might call them exposés—such as the *Miami Herald* piece had essentially accused Tommie of similar actions, noting that he was one of a small group within the tribe profiting from the business ventures. I asked him directly: How much did the entire tribe benefit economically under your administration from these new ventures? The response evolved into a lengthy justification of the benefits which his administration had produced for the tribe, and if in the process a few individuals had become wealthy, well, that was a natural outcome of the entrepreneurial, capitalist system. On the whole, he believed that while a few individuals were enriched the entire tribe had gained more:

> That is a very broad question because anytime that you have to do something it involves economics. In other words, the whole budget would have been $150,000 or $200,000 when we first started. That kind of puts you in a dilemma. As far as monetary value, I would like to think that what I did benefited everybody. Every member of the tribe gets $300 every six months. That is money that they could stick in their pockets. We were used to having volunteer lawyers come out and take care of some of the little business that we had, like land leases or maybe a chikee that needed to be built on the area. During that time we did not have a legal department. Now the Indians can come over here, because we have a full legal department. . . . I would say maybe there are a few of them that are in the cigarette business, but the tribe taxes, and they use that money. From what I understand, Disney World does not pay any taxes. . . . but the taxes they collect benefits everybody. What I am saying to you right now is that there are people going around saying it benefits only a certain amount of people. Sure, it is like that all over the world. You can say that. It does not offend me. The paper can say that. As far as aggressiveness is concerned, we introduced something that the whole tribe can benefit from. There were some aggressive people in the tribe, and aggressive people were only looking after themselves. I can sit here and say this because I can defend myself. When money came to the tribal council [in the past], somehow it would benefit the cattle people; it benefited only the cattle people and their families. Here we are benefiting the whole tribe.[57]

Howard Tommie's candid account of his administration provides insight into the motivations, conflicts, and concerns driving many American Indian tribal leaders during the self-determination era. From it comes a greater appreciation for the broad range of social, political, and technical issues that tribal leaders are required to deal with in the modern context. Yet there exists a cultural continuity which links modern tribal leaders to their progenitors: respect and support for both rested on the exercise of wisdom coupled with cultural empathy. The memoir also illustrates how easily leaders—Indian or non-Indian—can blur the line which divides personal and public interests. Ironically, the very enterprises which generated great wealth for the Seminole tribe also encouraged entrepreneurial skills that produced private gain. While such activities were not illegal, in the early stages they benefited relatively few Seminoles directly and created social and political cleavages within the Indian community. As an exercise in leadership, Howard Tommie's chairmanship was a great success. He exploited every facet of the Indian self-determination movement and delivered the Seminoles to the brink of economic and political independence while guaranteeing their sovereignty—yet, perhaps undeservedly, at a cost to his personal reputation. That may be the price that dynamic Indian political figures must ultimately pay to serve their people.

CHAPTER 6

The Seminole Land Claims Case

L ong before the Florida Seminoles moved to seek federal recognition under the Indian Reorganization Act, they had engaged in a vigorous defense of their tribal rights. Two major legal cases—one involving compensation for Seminole lands taken prior to the Second Seminole War,[1] and the other aimed at securing Seminole water rights on the Florida reservations—had their origins in the 1950s before tribal government was established and functioning.[2] In both instances it took congressional action to finally resolve the issues in favor of the Seminole tribe. The much-heralded land claims case deserves attention because it had a profound impact on the long range well-being of the Florida Indians, not only in the sense of bringing a monetary award, which had been expected for nearly four decades, but also through its broader affirmation of Seminole tribal sovereignty.

The Indian Claims Commission Act became law on 13 August 1946.[3] It was part of that controversial legislative package passed by a conservative Congress to end once and for all federal obligations to the tribes.[4] Under its provisions any tribe, band, or other identifiable group of American Indians could file a petition with the commission setting forth any claim—of a nature delineated in the act—against the United States which had occurred before that date. The act provided a five-year window within which the tribes had to file; any claim that had not been filed by 13 August 1951, could not thereafter be presented to any administrative agency or court, nor would Congress entertain any such claim. Those tribal governments that the secretary of the interior recognized had the exclusive right to represent their tribes in any claims proceedings. If no such organization existed, or failed to act on behalf of its constituents, claims could be presented by any member of the tribe as the representative of all members of that tribe. Each tribe could select its own attorney, subject to approval of the secretary, to present its claims. Regulations required the commission to send a written explanation of the act to each identifiable group of American Indians and to the superintendents of the Indian agencies who were directed to assist the tribes in pursuing their claims. Regardless of whether the Indian Claims Commission Act grew from the urge to promote the ultimate assimilation of the tribes, clearly the government intended that all Indians have ample time and opportunity to file their claims.

By 1949 almost half of the five-year period for filing claims had passed, yet the Seminoles of Florida still had taken no action, due primarily to a lack of organization. Given the absence of a recognized Seminole tribal government, the three Seminole reservations operated with their own governing bodies, each tacitly approved by the Bureau of Indian Affairs. Brighton and Big Cypress each elected three persons as trustees, an outgrowth of their cattle programs begun in the Depression years. At the small Dania Reservation three individuals acted as a business committee. In addition, the federal government authorized three tribal trustees to give overall direction to tribal affairs; Brighton and Big Cypress selected two members, while the agency superintendent appointed a third, at-large member. At the urging of Superintendent Marmon this entire group of twelve Indians, elected by residents of the federal reservations, contacted Jacksonville attorney Roger Waybright to explore a claim.

Initially Waybright was reluctant to take the Seminole case. He had no background in Indian law, but knew that it would require a great deal of work and money over a period of many years to achieve success. The Seminoles had no tribal funds available for legal expenses, and attorneys would receive no compensation unless they were successful. The amount of legal compensation would be fixed by the Indian Claims Commission and could not exceed 10 percent of the amount recovered. Thus it was not financially attractive to a competent attorney to handle such a case. Nevertheless, after an initial investigation Waybright "became convinced that the claims of the Seminoles of Florida were of considerable merit, and that they had been oppressed and defrauded by the United States to an extent unusual even in the sordid annals of the treatment of American Indians generally."[5] Since the tribe had no regular attorney to pursue the work and time was running out, Waybright agreed to undertake the claims presentation on behalf of the tribe. His two associates in the case were attorneys John Jackson, of Jacksonville, and Guy Martin, in Washington DC.[6]

The parties executed a contract on 15 October 1949, and the commissioner of Indian affairs approved it in January of the following year. Earlier, Superintendent Marmon wrote to the commissioner of Indian affairs urging approval of the contract and identified the Seminoles who signed it: "Brighton reservation is represented by Frank Shore, Jack Smith and John Henry Gopher, present Trustees. Big Cypress reservation is represented by Morgan Smith, Junior Cypress and Jimmy Cypress, present trustees. Dania reservation is represented by Sam Tommie, Ben Tommie and Bill Osceola who act as a Business Committee. Seminole Tribe Trustees who signed their names are Josie Billie, John Cypress and Little Charlie Micco."[7]

The Indians who negotiated the contract were, according to Waybright, "duly elected Trustees of the tribe, authorized to execute the contract. . . . it is interesting to note that the 12 Trustees came from each of the three reservations where the bulk of the tribe is concentrated, and were divided about equally between those of Miccosukai [sic] and those of Cow Creek descent."[8] Apparently a reorganization took place on the reservations shortly thereafter, for Waybright reported that Bill Osceola represented himself as the head of a new "Board of Directors for all three reservations."[9] His understanding was that an overwhelming majority of the Seminoles were in favor of pursuing the claim. It now appears that Waybright may have been either misinformed or misled concerning the number of Trail Indians and the extent of their opposition to any claim that might threaten their own demands for land and autonomy.

After seven months of investigation and research to locate evidence necessary to support the claim, the Seminoles filed their petition before the Indian Claims Commission on 14 August 1950. Assigned docket number 73, the petition set forth four causes for action: a claim for $37,500,000 plus interest—the value of 30,000,000 acres of land taken under the Treaty of Camp Moultrie in 1823; a claim for $5,040,975 plus interest for 4,032,940 acres of land taken under the

Treaty of Payne's Landing in 1832; a claim for $6,250,000 plus interest for the value of 5,000,000 acres of land taken under the Macomb Treaty of 1839; and a claim for $992,000 plus interest for 99,200 acres of land taken for the Everglades National Park in 1944. The claims on all four causes of action totaled $47,782,975 plus interest. After delays and legal maneuvering by government attorneys to have the Seminole claims dismissed through summary judgment, on 22 January 1953 the Indian Claims Commission entered an order denying the government's motion and ordered it to answer the Seminole petition.

Earlier, another complication had developed which the commission was forced to resolve before the case could go forward. In July 1951, about a year after the filing of the Florida Seminole petition and only a short time before the filing period expired, the Seminole Indians of Oklahoma—calling themselves the Seminole Nation and the Seminole Nation of Indians, of the State of Oklahoma—entered their own petition, which became docket number 151 before the Indian Claims Commission. The Oklahoma group advanced substantially the same claims found in the first two causes of action set forth by the Florida Seminoles; they also made additional claims based upon their experiences after removal to Oklahoma. The Oklahoma Indians also filed a motion to dismiss the Florida Seminole petition, asserting they were the only group entitled to sue for the true value of Florida lands. Waybright challenged this Oklahoma motion, and it was dismissed by the commission on 22 January 1953.

At the same time the commission also split the Florida Seminole claim into two cases. The first three causes of action for the value of lands taken in the treaties of 1823, 1832, and 1839 were left in docket number 73. These were consolidated for the purpose of trial with the causes of action set forth by the Oklahoma Seminoles in their petition, docket number 151. The Seminoles' fourth cause of action dealing with the value of land taken for Everglades National Park constituted a separate case under docket number 73-A. The attorneys for the Florida Seminoles considered this relatively small claim to be the weaker of the two cases.

Over the objection of Waybright, government attorneys secured from the commission a number of extensions for replying to the petition in docket number 73. Even the intervention of the two Florida senators failed to hasten matters. The government did not file its answer to the Florida and Oklahoma petitions until 17 December 1954, some four and a half years after the Florida Seminoles had originally filed for a trial date. Attorneys for the Florida and Oklahoma Seminoles agreed that they would be ready for trial by June 1955, but the government held out for January 1956.

While the government was delaying the case, Waybright faced opposition from attorneys purporting to represent substantial numbers of Seminoles who disavowed the claim. One of these lawyers, O. B. White of Miami, who had long been associated with the Mike Osceola group, supposedly represented Indians from five south Florida counties who had never been informed about or consented to the claim. When a meeting was held with the Trail Indians so that attorneys could explain the claim, White attended and advised tribal elders to disassociate themselves from the action. Waybright believed that White wanted to be associated as an attorney in the case, and when he was rebuffed he fomented discord.

More serious was the intervention of attorney Morton Silver, who represented the Miccosukee General Council and its spokesman, Buffalo Tiger. At that time the council spoke for forty or fifty traditional families living along the Tamiami Trail but did not include two factions headed by William McKinley Osceola and Cory Osceola. In 1953 Silver initiated an exchange of correspondence with the Indian Claims Commission, the Bureau of Indian Affairs, and the Seminole attorneys denouncing the petitions before the commission. He announced that his clients would never accept money from the United States of America—fearing it might jeopardize their future rights to Florida lands—and demanded that they be specifically excluded from the claim. The Seminole attorneys refused. Failing to attain the desired response, Silver attempted to enter the litigation. In September 1954 he filed a document for "Special Appearance and Motion to Quash" on behalf of Ingraham Billie, Jimmie Billie, and thirteen other individuals acting as the "General Council of the Miccosukee Seminole Nation."[10]

The Seminole attorneys opposed this, and in April 1955 the Indian Claims Commission denied the General Council a hearing, finding that those who filed the claim represented virtually all Indians living in Florida. The U.S. Court of Claims dismissed Silver's appeal of this decision on 5 December 1956.[11] Despite a letter from the American Civil Liberties Union, which raised the issue of whether the constitutional rights of the Miccosukees had been fully protected, the motion for rehearing also failed. The Indian Claims Commission and the courts had thwarted all attempts by the Trail Indians to intervene in the claims process, asserting that their interests were adequately protected.

The year 1957 was a turning point in the history of the Florida land claims case because Roger Waybright resigned as lead attorney. Two political actions apparently triggered this move. First, the federal government granted official recognition to the Seminole Tribe of Florida by approving a constitution and corporate charter which the people adopted. The fact that about one-third of the 448 adult Indians who were eligible to vote for a Seminole government had boycotted the balloting evidently came as a shock to Waybright. He had assumed that the twelve Seminoles with whom he contracted in 1949 spoke for the tribe and that there was virtual unanimity for pursuing the land claim. Second, the State of Florida extended recognition to the "Everglades Miccosukee General Council" in July 1957.[12] Up to that point Waybright had remained convinced that Silver and Buffalo Tiger were speaking for only a small dissident minority of the tribe.

In an interview granted twenty years after his resignation Waybright noted, "I regarded that election result as a rather queer demonstration that about one-third of the adult Seminoles in Florida were opposed to presenting the claims of the tribe to the Indian Claims Commission.... I did not care to continue as an attorney attempting to present the claim of a group of people, one-third of whom did not want me to do it. That, in essence, is the reason I stated for wanting to withdraw."[13] In this and other interviews Waybright has intimated that his distaste for the infighting with the Trail Indians and their attorney also prompted his resignation. He also calculated that he had already put in $50,000–100,000 in legal work plus unreimbursed expenses on the case which still faced long, uncertain litigation; therefore he resigned on 11 October 1957. Roger Waybright, who went on to a long and distinguished judicial career, never received a cent of compensation for eight years' work on the Seminole claim.[14]

The case continued under attorneys John Jackson and Effie Knowles—the latter had been retained primarily as a legal researcher—but the matter remained stalled. At various times other individuals including Morton Silver and the firm of Millard Caldwell (a former governor) negotiated with Jackson to have themselves joined as attorneys in the claims case, but nothing came of these efforts. In 1959 at the urging of Effie Knowles, who knew the Seminoles would be happier with a male lawyer, the Seminole Tribal Council hired Roy Struble, of Miami, as attorney for the case, with Charles Bragman, of Washington, as his associate.[15] Jackson died in 1963, and rifts between the remaining attorneys initiated a long and confusing struggle over allocation of fees that would eventuate in several suits long after the Seminole claim was settled.

In 1962 the Miccosukee Tribe of Indians of Florida received federal recognition and six years later made its final attempt to intervene in the claims case. By this time Silver had split with Buffalo Tiger and no longer represented the General Council. A Washington attorney, Arthur Lazarus, was given the bureau's permission to file a motion to intervene in dockets 73 and 73-A. For the first time the Miccosukees appeared to be making a request for monetary compensation; yet this was never clarified because their motion failed. The commission once again held that the Miccosukee interests were adequately represented in the proceedings. This removed the last legal roadblock to resolving the claims case.

On 13 May 1970, the Indian Claims Commission delivered its opinion. Of the four original claims in the suits, only the first—for additional compensation for most of Florida excepting three enclaves and one reservation held in 1823—and the second, for additional compensation for the reservation taken in 1832, were considered in dockets 73 and 151 consolidated. The third claim, concerning the Macomb Reservation, and the fourth claim, based on transactions creating the Everglades National Park, were consolidated in docket 73-A. The commission found that in 1823 the Seminoles held aboriginal title to 23,892,626 acres with a fair market value of $12,500,000, which were ceded by the Camp Moultrie treaty. At that time the

Seminoles had received consideration in the amount of $152,500 for the ceded land. In 1832 the Seminole reservation in peninsular Florida north of Lake Okeechobee comprised 5,865,600 acres having a value of $2,050,000.00. By provisions of the Treaty of Payne's Landing the Seminoles had been compensated in the amount of $2,094,809.39. Therefore the commission found: "The payment of $152,500.00 for land having a fair market value in excess of $12 million was clearly unconscionable and on this count the plaintiffs will recover the difference, $12,347,500.00. Equally clearly, the payment of $2,094,809.39 for lands having a fair market value of $2,050,000.00 was not unconscionable, and on this count the plaintiffs will recover nothing."[16] The commission entered an awarded of $12,347,500 to the plaintiffs. The government was allowed certain offsets which it claimed for funds already expended on the tribe; therefore the commission made a revised award of $12,262,780 to the Seminoles on 22 October 1970.[17]

Both the Florida and Oklahoma tribes appealed, and the Court of Claims remanded the case for more specific findings as to the value of the land.[18] But in 1975, to avoid prolonging an appeal process with no assurance of realizing a substantially larger award, both the Oklahoma and Florida tribes agreed to seek a compromise settlement for $16,000,000. The Seminole Tribal Council approved the settlement by resolution, but to meet the commission's requirements for full discussion of the issue, a general meeting of the tribal membership and other interested Indians was held in January 1976. Chairman Tommie presided and Roy Struble gave a lengthy presentation on the proposed settlement, which was translated into both the Muskogee and Miccosukee languages. Of the 376 Seminoles present only 7 opposed the resolution accepting the compromise settlement. On 27 April 1976 the commission entered its final judgment and award "in full settlement of all claims in these consolidated documents" for the amount of $16,000,000.[19] In its findings on docket 73-A, which involved the Florida Seminoles alone, the commission disallowed any claim for the so-called Macomb Treaty reservation but upheld the claim for additional compensation in the Everglades National Park acquisition. An award of $50,000 was made on 20 April 1977.[20]

The Macomb claim was based on a treaty supposedly sanctioned during the Second Seminole War. The United States charged its commander in Florida, Gen. Alexander Macomb, with bringing the hostilities to a conclusion. In 1839 Macomb made contact with a number of Seminole chiefs and offered them a substantial portion of southern Florida as a reservation to conclude the war. Apparently they accepted and officials in Washington approved the arrangement. President Martin Van Buren issued an executive order setting aside the land, but a treaty was never signed or ratified. For that reason the Indian Claims Commission found that the Seminoles had no legitimate claim. Nevertheless, attorneys representing the Florida Indians periodically revisited the issue to gain leverage in negotiations with the state and federal governments.

Not all Indian families living in the vicinity of the Tamiami Trail had become members of the Miccosukee Tribe, and a small group calling itself the Traditional Seminoles remained adamantly opposed to any settlement. In March 1976, just as the commission was about to enter its final award and judgment, a class action suit was filed in the Federal District Court of Washington DC by Guy Osceola, son of Cory Osceola, a leader of the traditional Indians opposed to the claim. The suit sought to enjoin the commission from entering a judgment and sought a declaration that the Indian Claims Commission Act was unconstitutional on its face and as applied to plaintiff because, among other reasons, it deprived the Traditional Seminoles of their rights and property without due process. The three-judge court denied a temporary restraining order on the grounds that the commission's judgment would not affect Seminole rights. As the case progressed other traditional Seminoles joined the suit, contending that the treaty guaranteed the right to live on their lands. The Department of Justice argued that the United States had the right to take Seminole land without due process or compensation. In short, Seminole property was not protected by the Constitution or any other law, and therefore the commission's actions could not be challenged. In its final decision on 11 March 1977 the district court adopted completely the Justice Department's argument that the United States was free to take Traditional Seminole property without due process and dismissed the complaint. The U.S. Supreme Court declined to hear the case on appeal on the grounds that the lower court decision was not based on the constitutional merits of the case.

On 19 November 1976 the Indian Claims Commission entered an order allowing attorneys fees based on the award of $16,000,000 to the Oklahoma and Florida Seminoles in docket 73 and 151 consolidated. The commission recognized that Paul Niebell and the estate of Roy St. Louis, Charles Bragman, Effie Knowles, and Roy Struble were entitled to fees as contract attorneys in the amount of $1,600,000, which represented 10 percent of the final award. The attorneys were to divide that sum according to their contractual arrangements.[21]

The Indian Claims Commission's 1976 award ushered in a political struggle over distribution of the funds that continued for another fourteen years. The central problem was that the commission, following its usual practice, gave no direction for the distribution of the monies among the Seminole Nation of Oklahoma, the Seminole Tribe of Florida, the Miccosukee Tribe of Florida, and the independent or traditional Seminole Indians of Florida. The Bureau of Indian Affairs set out to devise a formula for a division of funds between Florida and Oklahoma and to address a plan for allocating funds among the Florida groups. It was recognized that an equitable distribution could not be based on 1976 enrollment figures in Oklahoma and Florida. The Seminole Nation of Oklahoma had no blood-quantum restrictions for membership and thus had enrolled thousands of members with little Indian ancestry. By comparison the federal tribes in Florida had one-half and one-quarter blood-quantum restrictions for membership, while the traditional Seminoles were virtually all full-blood. The bureau plan accepted the Oklahoma Seminole census figure of 2,146 from the 1906–14 period when all persons on the tribal roll had blood-quantum designations. In Florida the first reliable census was that of 1914, but it had to be reconstructed to include a number of persons omitted from the official roll. The final reconstructed roll for Florida contained 700 names. Thus the BIA recommended that approximately 75 percent of the funds go to Oklahoma and 25 percent to Florida, to be divided among the Seminoles, Miccosukees, and Traditionals.

When Florida Seminole leaders refused to accept the BIA plan, a legislative division became necessary. Both the Oklahoma and Florida tribes had legislation introduced in Congress to alter the distribution in their favor. These bills represented fundamentally different philosophies and approaches to the distribution process. Senators Dewey Bartlett and Henry Bellmon of Oklahoma authored bill s2000, which proposed a division based on the number of Oklahoma Seminoles by blood in 1914 as reflected in the Seminole roll of 1906 and 1914, and the number of Seminoles in Florida as they appeared on the Florida census of 1914. In short, it accepted the BIA proposal as the basis for a settlement.

Senators Lawton Chiles and Richard Stone of Florida introduced bill S. 2188, which directed the chief commissioner of the U.S. Court of Claims to determine a fair and equitable division based on all relevant factors, including any difference in the past benefits received by the Oklahoma and Florida Seminoles. This position rejected per-capita distribution and postulated that Oklahoma's Seminoles had already received economic and other benefits from the government over the years, while the Florida people were ignored, and that therefore they were entitled to a differential settlement to rectify past neglect. Moreover, they demanded a disinterested third party to arbitrate the dispute.

On 2 March 1978, the Senate Select Committee on Indian Affairs held a hearing on both bills. Senator Bartlett chaired the session, at which a number of interested parties appeared as witnesses or submitted statements.[22] These included the sponsoring senators, officials from the Bureau of Indian Affairs, and attorneys and leaders from the Indian tribes. The Seminole Tribe of Florida was represented by its chairman, Howard Tommie, and Washington special counsel Marvin Sonosky. They emphatically stated that the Florida Seminoles believed a reconstructed 1914 census—even one that increased their head count from 526 to 700—was still seriously flawed because the Indian people then had little to do with the government. Furthermore, they charged that the BIA official who recommended a division based on comparative census rolls from 1906 to 1914, Stephen Feraca, was biased against the Florida Indians. He had alienated many of the tribe while serving on the Seminole agency staff during the 1960s, and once received an injury in a scuffle with an Indian youth.

Interestingly, Feraca had recommended against a division of funds based on contemporary tribal rolls in Oklahoma and Florida; he also supported the bureau's $9,000 grant for the Florida Seminoles to produce a reconstructed 1914 tribal census. In addition to their allegations of bureau personnel bias, the Florida tribe contended that the Oklahoma Seminoles had already received vast sums from the federal government for housing, health, and education services following their removal to the Indian Territory in the 1830s. By contrast, the remnant Seminole group remaining in Florida had received virtually nothing from Washington until relatively recently.

The Oklahoma Seminole delegation was headed by Principal Chief Richmond Tiger, who testified that his council had attempted to negotiate with the Florida tribe on two separate occasions, at meetings in Nashville and Oklahoma City, but with no results; therefore they had turned to the BIA to draft a plan. They believed that a just and equitable division of the award could only be made on a per-capita basis. Guy Osceola and attorney Robert Coulter, of the Institute for the Development of Indian Law, in Washington, spoke for the Traditional Seminoles.[23] Coulter reiterated his clients' position that they had not been a party to the claims, and he sought to halt any action on the bills authorizing distribution of funds. Failing that, the attorneys requested that any legislation enacted include a proposed amendment which would not jeopardize or extinguish their rights to the Florida lands where they currently resided. But an associate solicitor representing the BIA observed that the Traditional Seminoles could not have it both ways. Since they were specifically designated as recipients of an Indian Claims Commission award that extinguished all future claims against the lands in question, they could not also expect to retain aboriginal title.

On 4 April 1978 the Department of the Interior submitted a distribution plan to Congress as required by the Indian Judgment Funds Act of 1973. If either house did not veto it within sixty working days, it automatically became law. The Florida Seminoles urged Congress to defeat the plan and return to the regular legislative process, but the bills introduced by the Oklahoma and Florida delegations were never acted upon. In the interim the Florida Seminoles challenged the BIA plan in the U.S. District Court in Washington, which ruled that the secretary of the interior had not submitted the plan within the time limits prescribed by law, and it was therefore void.[24] Unexpectedly, however, the court left the way open for the secretary to make an arbitrary division of the funds. The Seminoles appealed, and, with agreement of the Justice Department, the U.S. Court of Appeals entered a judgment that the secretary had no authority— absent legislation—to divide the Seminole funds.[25]

Throughout the early 1980s there were various initiatives to bring the Oklahoma and Florida tribes to a settlement. The new Seminole tribal chairman, James Billie, instituted a tribal legal office with an in-house attorney, Stephen Whilden, whose efforts were coordinated with the firm of Sonosky, Chambers, and Sachse, in Washington. Senators Lawton Chiles and Paula Hawkins, supported by members of the House, also stood behind the tribe's position and introduced a new settlement bill calling for a fifty-fifty division between the Florida and Oklahoma groups. In addition, the Department of the Interior actively promoted its own package. Meanwhile, the monies held in escrow multiplied at a rapid rate. In 1980 Chairman Billie wrote to his Oklahoma counterpart recommending that they divide the amount— which had grown to $20 million—$8 million for the Florida people and the remainder to Oklahoma. This overture was met with indecision. The BIA would not advise the Oklahoma group to accept or reject the Florida tribe's proposal. Furthermore, the Seminole Nation of Oklahoma was under pressure from two bands of Seminole Freedmen which sought a share of the settlement. These were descendants of black slaves who had come west with the Seminoles during removal and became citizens of the Seminole Nation in 1866. Excluded from the Indian Claims Commission award, they filed suit to be included as Oklahoma Seminoles. Eventually their claim was disallowed by the federal courts, but at that time the outcome was still unclear.

In 1981 James Billie approached the new chief of the Oklahoma group, this time offering a take the lesser part of a sixty-forty split (although the legislative claim for a fifty-fifty division was not abandoned) of the ever growing funds, then estimated at about $22 million. It looked for a time as though the impasse would be resolved only to be short-circuited by a schism among the Oklahoma

Indians. For some months two separate governmental groups claimed to represent the Oklahoma Seminoles.

By 1987, because of the accrual of interest, the judgment fund for docket numbers 73 and 151 held in escrow had reached the sum of $40 million, and the stage was set for a final effort to settle. The popular James Billie had been reelected to his third term as tribal chairman. He moved aggressively on a number of economic fronts and wanted to bring closure to an issue that had been pending for almost four decades. Also, the Seminole Tribe of Florida now had as general counsel one of its own members, Jim Shore—the first Seminole to receive a law degree. Unlike his predecessor, Shore was inclined to negotiation rather than confrontation. In addition, the Washington firm of Hobbs, Straus, Dean, and Wilder, which was already involved in the Florida Seminoles' water rights case, also began to advise them on the claims dispute.

The negotiating strategy they developed to achieve a settlement was based on a number of points. First, the Florida Seminoles continued to object to a split of the judgment based on population figures arbitrarily developed by the Bureau of Indian Affairs and that ignored the different history of the Oklahoma and Florida groups and the history of the claims litigation. Second, because of the benefits received by the Oklahoma Seminoles—which were not shared by the Florida Seminoles—the Florida group argued that the award to the Oklahoma tribe should be significantly reduced. The Florida Seminoles demonstrated that the Oklahoma Seminoles had received over $7 million in treaty payments and 265,000 acres of land as well as substantial appropriations for health, education, social services, and the like. The land was allotted to individual Indians and subsequently sold, thereby providing significant additional compensation to the Oklahoma people. By contrast, the Seminoles who remained in Florida shared none of the benefits but suffered all of the detriments from events which occurred in the previous century. Due to the intensity of feeling in this matter it sometimes appeared that the Florida Seminoles would rather accept a settlement mandated by Congress than negotiate an agreement giving the Oklahoma tribe a greater portion of the funds.

This reasoning would soon be tested. On 4 March 1988 Senator

Don Nickles of Oklahoma introduced bill s2150, which called for a distribution of 75.404 percent of the funds to the Seminole Nation of Oklahoma and 24.596 percent to the Seminole Tribe of Florida, Miccosukee Tribe of Indians of Florida, and the unaffiliated Seminoles of Florida. It also mandated distribution of the funds awarded under docket 73-A (then about $110,000) among the Florida Indians. In his strong floor statement Nickles noted that all attempts at settling the dispute had failed, so the BIA had prepared the bill being introduced. He also tried to drum up sympathy for his constituents, stating, "While I have been reluctant to introduce legislation to settle this problem without an agreement between the two tribes, it is apparent to me that Congress is going to have to step in and dictate an appropriate division. The 75/25 percent division is very reasonable and is rather generous to the Florida Seminoles. I might add that while the Florida Seminoles have been doing rather well economically, the Oklahoma Seminoles have not been so fortunate."[26]

In an astute political move the Nickles bill and a companion measure introduced in the House by Rep. Wes Watkins specifically provided that funds awarded to Oklahoma would be held in trust for the present-day Seminole Nation of Oklahoma to be invested or used for the "common needs, educational requirements, and other long-term economic and social interests of the Tribe," without regard to Indian blood quantum.[27] This meant that the Oklahoma Seminole Freedmen who could demonstrate no Indian blood quantum and who had earlier been excluded from the award by the Indian Claims Commission and federal courts would now become eligible to share in the funds. Previous bills had called for a "by blood" distribution to the Oklahoma Seminoles, and now that wording had been eliminated. This became a powerful argument for congressional civil rights advocates in favor of passing the Oklahoma measure.

Florida Seminoles moved to protect their interests in the Washington proceedings. The first defensive move was to put forward a Florida Seminole position on the Nickles bill through a letter from Chairman Billie to Senator Daniel Inouye, chairman of the Senate Select Committee on Indian Affairs.[28] It set forth the Seminole rationale for demanding a more equitable distribution, and also opposed the bill's broad definition of independent Seminoles—essentially anyone of Indian descent not affiliated with a recognized Florida tribe—which might lead to thousands of persons in Florida who claimed Indian ancestry applying for part of the funds. Another objectionable provision of the bill precluded distribution of anything but interest to the tribal governments, while secretarial approval was required before this money could be invested in any manner. The Florida Seminoles perceived this as a radical departure from the treatment afforded other tribes when distributing judgment funds.

The second step was to have the Florida congressional delegation introduce its own bills offering the Florida Seminoles' plan for distribution. For over a decade Sen. Lawton Chiles, a powerful committee chairman and seasoned legislator, had lent strong backing to the Seminole cause, and his retirement in 1988 was a crucial loss. Some Capitol Hill observers believe that the Nickles bill would never have passed the Senate as written if Chiles had been present. Nevertheless, the Florida delegation remained supportive of the Seminoles. Sen. Bob Graham authored the requested bill as s1336; a bipartisan companion measure, HR2838 was introduced by Reps. Larry Smith, of Broward County, and Tom Lewis, of Palm Beach County. In the first session of the 101st Congress Senator Nickles reintroduced his bill as s1096 and Representative Watkins submitted HR2650. The stage was set for a confrontation. The House Committee on Interior and Insular Affairs held a hearing on the opposing measures, HR2838 and HR2650, on 14 September 1989.[29]

This was a final opportunity for the Florida Seminoles to make their case for a favorable division of the funds. In a last-ditch effort to forestall what appeared to be a rush to pass the Oklahoma version and be done with the whole affair, Chairman Billie requested additional time to negotiate with the Oklahoma Seminoles. If at the end of thirty days negotiations had failed, he agreed "the time has come for Congress to act."[30] The Traditional Seminoles still maintained that they wanted no part of the money under any conditions and continued to oppose any plan for distribution that did not contain an amendment to protect their claims to lands in Florida.

Principal Chief Jerry Haney of the Seminole Nation of Oklahoma and their attorney, Paul Niebell, presented persuasive arguments for immediate congressional action on the bill favored by the Oklahoma delegation and the BIA. The thrust of their presentation was to show that the Florida Seminoles had not suffered from neglect; rather, they had secured a large amount of federal trust lands and this was the basis of their current prosperity. Ross Swimmer, a former assistant secretary of the interior—who vowed that he had not been directly involved in the case during his tenure in Washington—appeared as co-counsel for the Oklahoma Seminoles. Swimmer's assertion was bizarre in that he had reportedly presided over an earlier meeting in which attorneys for the Florida and Oklahoma groups attempted to reach an agreement. Also, his appearance had the potential of lending quasi-official support for the Oklahoma position. Representative Wes Watkins delivered a strong statement claiming that nearly thirteen years of negotiations had brought no progress. Appealing to the politics of racial inclusion, he emphasized that all Oklahoma Seminoles— including the Seminole Freedmen—would share in the distribution.

The Senate passed Senator Nickles's bill on 21 November without debate.[31] The House approved the measure on 6 February 1990, but amended it to give the Florida Seminoles 27 percent and Oklahoma 73 percent of the funds.[32] Although a conference committee restored the original 75-25 division, the final language of the legislation was a bit more palatable to Florida interests.[33]

First, it included a specific definition of who could be accepted as an independent Seminole. These individuals had to be listed on or be lineal descendants of persons included in the annotated Seminole agency census of 1957 as independent Seminoles. Also, they could not be members of any other federally recognized Indian tribe. Second, the act designated exactly how the funds awarded to the Florida Indians would be divided among the three groups: 77.2 percent to the Seminole Tribe of Florida, 18.6 percent to the Miccosukee Tribe of Indians, and 4.64 percent to the independent Seminole Indians of Florida as a group. Third, the secretary was directed to pay its share of the funds held in escrow directly to the Seminole Tribe of Florida, "to be allocated or invested as the tribal governing body determines to be in the economic or social interests of the tribe"[34] The funds for the Miccosukees and independent Seminoles were to be held in trust by the federal government pending approval of specific plans for distribution. Also, a provision was inserted which protected the independent Seminoles' rights and claims to lands and natural resources in Florida. The Senate version prevailed and Public Law 101-277 was passed on 30 April 1990.

After forty years of litigation and negotiation the Florida Seminoles had finally received redress for those "clearly unconscionable" land payments made by the United States government in the midnineteenth century. The issue which had shaped economic expectations for two generations of Seminoles had come to an end—ironically, at a time when the Seminole tribe was enjoying unprecedented prosperity. Although the final percentage distribution was still not considered equitable from the Florida Seminole perspective, it was probably the best they could have hoped for. Congress was clearly conditioned to make awards based on comparative figures, and numbers were against them if the 1906–14 tribal rolls were accepted. Moreover, consideration of a division based on contemporary tribal enrollments such as the Oklahoma Seminoles originally requested would have yielded even more lopsided results. The Florida Seminoles' contention that they had not received federal assistance commensurate with that afforded the Oklahoma group was effectively rebutted, especially for the period since the 1930s. Also, the relative affluence of the Florida reservations and thriving tribal ventures into bingo and tax-exempt cigarette sales were well known—in a sense, Florida Seminoles were victims of their own success. With the voluntary and seemingly magnanimous inclusion of the Seminole Freedmen in the award, the weight of congressional sympathies definitely swung to the Oklahoma tribe's position.

On the positive side, the astronomical increase in funds available to all groups was an unanticipated outcome of the fourteen-year delay between the Indian Claims Commission award and final distribution. Assuming that the Florida Indians collectively shared in 24.596 percent of approximately $50 million—close to $12.3 million—the Seminole Tribe of Florida received 77.2 percent of that amount, or about $9.5 million. The exact figure of the final distribution is difficult to determine because the funds were held in multiple accounts administered by the Bureau of Indian Affairs. One of the attorneys representing the Florida Seminoles believes that the final amount ultimately disbursed to both groups will exceed $51 million. This infusion of capital provided a valuable boost to expanding tribal business interests in Florida and helped them secure a sound long-term financial base.

Perhaps equally important, the tribe had won a significant concession on the issue of autonomy. Although stringent controls were imposed on the Seminole Nation of Oklahoma's ability to invest or distribute its award without secretarial approval, the Seminole Tribe of Florida retained control of its funds and the council could direct their use. Funds designated for the Miccosukee tribe and the independent Seminoles were placed in federal trust accounts where they still remain. Therefore the outcome of the land claims case can be hailed as a signal victory for the Seminoles in defense of tribal sovereignty.

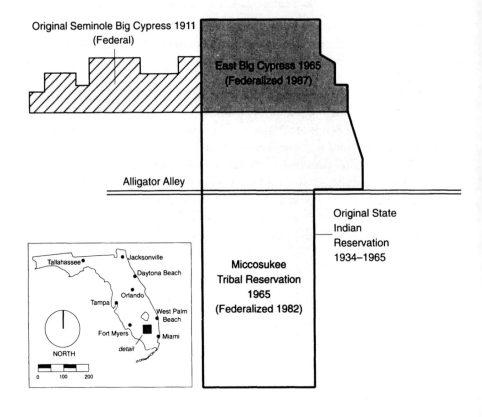

Original Seminole Big Cypress 1911
(Federal)

East Big Cypress 1965
(Federalized 1987)

Alligator Alley

Original State
Indian
Reservation
1934–1965

Miccosukee
Tribal Reservation
1965
(Federalized 1982)

Tallahassee
Jacksonville
Daytona Beach
Orlando
Tampa
West Palm
Beach
Fort Myers
Miami
detail
NORTH
0   100   200

2. Origins of the Seminole Big Cypress Reservation

CHAPTER 7

The East Big Cypress Case

T he second major struggle to secure Seminole rights became known as the East Big Cypress case.[1] This resulted in a thirty-nine-year political and legal conflict between the Seminoles and the state of Florida to determine jurisdiction in one of the state's most environmentally sensitive regions. The area identified as the East Big Cypress Reservation, a 28,000-acre tract lying in western Broward and Palm Beach counties, formed a rectangle measuring approximately six miles north to south and eight miles east to west. On the west the tract abutted the federal Big Cypress Indian Reservation that was acquired for the tribe in the 1890s, expanded by executive order in 1911, and named formally during the 1930s.[2] Approximately 16,000 acres of the East Big Cypress preserve was included within Conservation Area 3A, a sawgrass-covered vestige of the original Everglades flowage, controlled by a state water management agency. To the north were privately held agricultural lands, while the 76,000-acre Miccosukee Indian Reservation formed its southern boundary.

The Miccosukee Reservation and the Seminole East Big Cypress Reservation were created in 1917 by an act of the Florida legislature, which set aside 99,000 acres as the State Indian Reservation.[3] However, the land originally designated for this reservation had been located in Monroe County in what is presently Everglades National Park. Accordingly, when Congress established the park in 1934, it provided for relocation of the reservation.[4] In 1935 the state legislature authorized an exchange of the park lands for approximately equal acreage in western Broward and Palm Beach counties. When these land transfers were approved the following year by the Florida cabinet sitting as the Board of Commissioners of the Internal Improvement Trust Fund, the new reservation contained 104,800 acres—a net gain of some 5,000 acres for the Seminoles. The trustees conveyed this tract to the Board of Commissioners of State Institutions in 1937, and that body eventually granted a flowage easement for flood control and water management work within the reservation lands.[5]

Because all Florida Indians were previously considered to be Seminoles, the new Miccosukee tribe began its legal existence in 1962 without a land base. The three federal preserves existing in Florida at that time, as well as the State Indian Reservation, ostensibly belonged to the Seminole Tribe of Florida. However, in 1965 both tribes requested that the legislature address the status of the State Indian Reservation. The tract was then divided. The Miccosukees received the lower 76,000 acres and the Seminoles retained the 28,000 acres adjacent to their existing federal reservation.[6] Thereafter, the Seminole portion was referred to as the East Big Cypress Reservation to differentiate it from the adjacent tribal land held in federal trust status.

Legislation dividing the state reservation also permitted the tract to be placed in federal trust at such time as the tribes and the Bureau of Indian Affairs deemed it appropriate. Although the state approved the transfer in 1974, federal authorities would not accept the acreage. The Miccosukee tribe almost immediately initiated litigation and negotiations to have its holdings federalized and also to gain effective control over a much larger parcel of land in south Florida. These efforts were partially successful and led to passage of the Florida Indian Land Claims Settlement Act of 1982 — but at a price.[7] The Miccosukees agreed to a prohibition of commercial activities at variance with state laws within the limits of the reservations. Although it allowed some business activities, the law specifically proscribed the sale of tax-free cigarettes and the operation of bingo games that had become so lucrative for other tribes. Miccosukee leaders initially insisted that they had no interest in such activities and preferred to restore their traditional values and lifestyle on their own land.

The Seminole tribe, too, sought to have its part of the state reservation federalized as a protection against the vagaries of state politics. They saw the problem: if the state could shift Indian lands in 1935, what prevented them from doing so again? However, two roadblocks stood in the way of trust status. First, federal authorities balked at considering such action as long as the state claimed control over 16,000 acres for flowage easement within Conservation Area 3A. Secondly, the federal government refused to take any action while the tribe and the state were litigating the status of the land. Therefore, the federalization of the East Big Cypress Reservation was put on hold until these issues were resolved.

The question of control within the boundaries of the State Indian Reservation dated to 1948 when the Central and Southern Florida Flood Control District (FCD), forerunner of the South Florida Water Management District (WMD), began to plan a massive drainage project for the region. In December 1948 the superintendent of the Seminole agency, Kenneth Marmon, outlined to the commissioner of Indian affairs actions taken to ascertain the impact on the Seminole reservations of the flood control program proposed by the U.S. Army Corps of Engineers. He met with district engineer Col. W. E. Teale and his assistant, H. A. Scott, and they assured him that every effort would be made to comply with the recommendations as submitted by the Indian Service (synonym for BIA)[8] through the secretary of the interior. Marmon wrote:

> I indicated to both Colonel Teale and Mr. Scott, that our Indian Service was in favor of the proposal whereby flooding would be reduced on the reservation lands, including the State Indian Reservation. I especially called their attention to our protest to the proposed construction of the canal and dyke [sic] running north and south along the Collier-Broward county line, which, if constructed and carried out according to present plans . . . would deprive the Indians of the use of the State Indian Reservation. The present proposed program would flood 104,800 acres of some of the best grazing lands now being used during the winter months by the Big Cypress Agricultural and Livestock Enterprise. This flooding would also deprive the Seminoles of the hunting area.[9]

Although Marmon represented the Indian Service views and concerns to the Corps of Engineers, he apparently never intended to carry the issue to the Seminoles. Early in 1950 he was notified that a new alignment had been selected for the canal which placed it three miles east of the Hendry-Broward county line.[10] Again there was no mention of consultation with the Indians nor their involvement in the final determination of the project. Evidently the Indian Service accepted the proposal by letter in March 1950, and the matter seemed settled as far as the Corps of Engineers was concerned.[11] Plans for the project were completed, and in August the Board of Commissioners of State Institutions dedicated a flowage easement in East Big Cypress to the FCD including "the right to permanently or intermittently flood" all or any part of the land.[12]

By 1953 Marmon's view on the location of Levee L28 changed, and he solicited the support of various officials to have the Corps of Engineers revise the plans. The board of governors of the FCD was confounded by this request. Its secretary, W. Turner Wallis, responding to an inquiry on the matter from Senator Spessard Holland, wrote, "We are not able to understand ... Mr. Marmon's present position.... The matter was long ago agreeably settled by the Corps of Engineers with the approval of Mr. Marmon's superior.... Mr. Marmon now wants to further realign the levee so as to establish it along the extreme east boundary of the Reservation some several miles east of the alignment that was amicably determined three years ago."[13]

Then a Seminole position was introduced into the decision making process concerning East Big Cypress. Wallis continued:

> The resolution which Mr. Marmon had the Seminoles adopt on January 7, 1953 ... does not appear to reflect the independent thinking, judgment or wishes of the Seminoles themselves. It speaks of the lands being "diverted from the trust imposed in flagrant violation of Acts creating this State Indian Reservation." Such statements not only do not bespeak the truth, but might well serve to inflame a proud tribe that has long debated the advisability of concluding a treaty of peace with the Government. What motivates such action at this time when the matter has long been amicably settled, we have not yet been able to determine. Further, ... Mr. Marmon knows that Levee L-28 is not even in the authorized first phase of the program, so that any actual threat of construction is years away.[14]

How Wallis could intimate that Marmon had coerced or convinced the Seminoles to adopt this resolution and that it failed to represent the wishes of the Indian people is unclear. One implication, however, was that the Seminoles were easily duped and did not truly know their own minds in the matter. The letter impugns Marmon's integrity and suggests a possible conflict of interest. That Marmon, himself an Indian, might have reassessed the situation and brought his views to the attention of the Seminole leaders is not considered.

The Seminole resolution noted that if the plan was implemented, more than half of their lands suitable for grazing cattle during the dry season and for hunting during the balance of the year would soon become part of a huge reservoir for surplus waters. Such an action, they held, would result in great loss and was a flagrant violation of the laws creating the State Indian Reservation. The document concluded:

> we, the Tribal Trustees, and we the Cattle Trustees, of the Seminole Indians of Florida, in meeting assembled, protest in all earnestness the discrimination against our people in the preparation of the said Flood Control Project and ... we call upon ... the Secretary of the Interior of our Federal Government and the Board of Commissioners of State Institutions of our State Government, to use every effort to bring about such revisions of the plans for said Project as will move that section of the Levee known as L-28, which as now proposed would run through the State Indian Reservation from north to south, easterly to become the eastern boundary of the said Reservation.[15]

Although Marmon or a non-Indian likely drafted the resolution, one element of the reservation-dwelling Seminoles, speaking through the only organizational structure available to them, had opposed an apparently illegal intrusion into the State Indian Reservation. No federally recognized Seminole tribal government as yet existed, and the presence of several groups with different names underscored the difficulty in identifying the true locus of Seminole political power. The cattle trustees selected by the people at Brighton and Big Cypress had functioned since 1939, while Marmon reportedly organized the tribal trustees in the late 1940s prior to filing the land claims case, but it was questionable whether any combination of these groups could legitimately speak for the entire tribe.

The Seminole Indian Association soon became involved in the dispute over Levee L28. In November 1954 Robert Mitchell and Bertram Scott brought together in Orlando some twenty-five persons representing the major governmental agencies engaged in the project, as well as six Seminole Indians, to consider the alignment of the levee and its impact on the state reservation. Oscar Rawls, assistant chief of the planning and reports branch, Corps of Engineers, was called upon to explain why the present alignment had been chosen and why it should not be moved to the eastern edge of the reservation. He explained that originally the alignment had been along the Hendry-Broward county line, knowing that some refinement would be necessary in later studies. Subsequent field reconnaissance and field studies, with maps and aerial photographs, were made and

> it was found that the edge of the Everglades virtually bisected the State Reservation from north to south. East of the line was the level sawgrass of the Everglades; West of the line was the sloping soils with maiden cane growth. The former was worthless as cattle feed; the latter quite good and water tolerant. [U.S. Soil Conservation Service] maps showed that this was the line of demarcation between worthless soils good only for conservation purposes to the east, and valuable soil suitable for agriculture on the west. Thus the choice of alignment was primarily dictated by soil characteristics. There were engineering reasons why eastward alignment would be undesirable.[16]

Testimony by BIA soil and cattle experts supported Rawls's argument, and apparently won the grudging support of Mitchell and Scott. As for the Seminoles, Rawls noted, "The Indians present spoke English poorly and apparently understood it in the same manner. They were not empowered to make individual decisions, having to refer all actions back to their tribal council. They stated certain platitudes such as: Land once given to the Indians should not be taken from them; that they had voted against having the alinements [sic] run through their reservation and wanted it moved to the eastern boundary; they said their council would never change this attitude. They apparently object to the trespassing of white men, including surveyors."[17] Although there was evidently little sympathy for the

Indian input, to avoid such resentments in the future the group suggested that Marmon be informed of intrusions into Indian land and that he explain to the Indians the purpose of the surveys.

Equally important, Rawls seems to have detected some ambivalence in Marmon's position on locating the levee: "Mr. Marmon, evidently in favor of the present alignment all along, appears to be unable to persuade the tribal council that this is best for them, since they look with misgivings on most actions of the white man. Messrs. Mitchell, Scott, and Marmon and all other Indian representatives are fully persuaded of the desirability of the present alinement [sic] and state that they will take this to the tribal council for full explanation and persuasion. They expressed confidence in the success of the outcome."[18] As a further inducement all parties agreed that the Seminoles would continue their previous use of the conservation area lands, including the grazing of cattle during the dry season.

Superintendent Marmon and Robert Mitchell eventually persuaded the directly affected Seminole community to change its position and accept the new L28 alignment.[19] In 1955 Marmon transmitted to the Flood Control District a resolution signed by the leaders of the Big Cypress Reservation approving the proposed location of Levee L28 approximately three miles east of the Hendry-Broward county line. The resolution, dated 30 November 1954, stated, "A meeting of all adults living on this reservation was called by Frank Billie, acting as tribal trustee, to discuss the proposed Flood Control Project ... on the State Reservation. A total of 96 residents attended. It was decided that the Flood Control Project could be built on the State Reservation land. The decision was approved by a show of hands. This approves the present proposed location of L28 (levee). The undersigned are authorized by the Seminole Indians living on the Big Cypress Reservation to represent their interests in this matter."[20] The resolution was signed by Frank Billie and Morgan Smith, trustees; Henry Cypress, representative; and Jimmie Osceola, secretary. The state of Florida later contended that this document constituted Seminole consent to granting a flowage easement in East Big Cypress. But a question remained as to whether the actions of a group from the Big Cypress Reservation was legally binding on the entire Seminole tribe since that group did not constitute a tribal government as defined by the Indian Reorganization Act.[21]

Despite lingering Seminole concerns about the alignment of Levee L28, the project was completed by the Corps of Engineers in 1965. The controversial work roughly bisected the preserve. Canals and levees were constructed through the tract for approximately eleven miles. These varied in width from 600 to 750 feet and covered an area of 900 acres. The western 12,000 acres of Seminole land ostensibly was "recovered" and made usable for agricultural purposes, primarily cattle grazing. The 16,000 acres lying east of Levee L28 remained wild as part of the water impoundment area.

During the 1970s the Seminole Tribe of Florida, headed by aggressive leaders and encouraged by the new national emphasis on Indian self-determination, moved to regain control of its lands in East Big Cypress. In 1974 a civil action was brought in the Broward County circuit court.[22] However, because of the nature of the case it soon was moved to the U.S. District Court for the Southern District of Florida.[23] The lawsuit was prepared with assistance from the Native American Rights Fund and was supported in part by a grant from the Ford Foundation. Tribal attorney Stephen Whilden argued that the action was brought "to establish the rights of the Seminole Tribe of Indians of the State of Florida in 16,000 acres of reservation land in the State of Florida, which are lands subject to the protection of the Indian Non-Intercourse Act [and state law]."[24]

This triggered thirteen years of litigation and negotiation between the Seminole tribe, the State of Florida, and the WMD. The Seminoles outlined three causes for action. First, the reservation land in East Big Cypress was subject to the protection of article 6, clause 2 of the U.S. Constitution as well as the Indian Non-Intercourse Act. The United States never had consented to or approved of any dedication of these lands to another party, and thus the Seminoles retained title and right of possession to the land. Second, the dedication of the land and construction upon and use of it by the state and its agencies constituted a taking of Indian land for public purposes without payment of just compensation in violation of article 10, section 6 of the Florida Constitution. And third, the state and its agencies, as trustees for the reservation lands, had breached their fiduciary duties to the

Seminoles by converting the property to their own use and profit. Specifically, the state had reserved and retained income from mineral leases on East Big Cypress that should have gone to the Seminoles.

The Seminoles asked the court to declare that they were the free and clear owners of the 16,000 acres and that the state had no right, title, or interest in the property, or, as an alternative, to award just compensation, including interest, for the wrongful taking of the land. They also requested the court to order the state to provide the tribe with an accurate accounting for East Big Cypress for the period 23 December 1936 to 19 March 1974. Third, damages were demanded for the wrongful receipt and retention of income by the state, as well as other reasonable and proper relief, including interest, costs, and attorneys' fees.

The state's defense rested primarily on a claim of immunity from suit under the Eleventh Amendment of the U.S. Constitution, which prohibits suit in federal courts against a state by citizens of another state or a foreign nation. If the Seminole tribe was held to be a sovereign nation, then the case would move from the federal court back to the state court. The Seminole case hinged on whether, at the time of the 1950 deed conveyance, East Big Cypress was Seminole tribal land within the meaning of the 1790 Non-Intercourse Act. If it was, even though the state held legal title to East Big Cypress, the tribe's right to full beneficial use of the land was unlimited. Furthermore, the tribe argued that the federal government had not consented to dedication of the land to the WMD. Although the Non-Intercourse Act argument was the tribe's strongest position, it temporarily was put aside in hopes of reaching a negotiated settlement with the state and water management district.

Despite acrimony between the attorneys representing the state and the Seminoles, negotiations were pursued from 1980 to 1983. They proved to be of no avail. One point of contention was the tribe's decision to grow sugar cane in Conservation Area 3A, where the WMD held sugar production to be an incompatible use of the land. The Seminoles also clashed with the state over who held jurisdiction on Indian lands in Florida. The tribe wanted to police the land without interference; the state insisted that it retain Public Law 280 civil and criminal jurisdiction in the state reservation area. The "Save

Our Everglades" program promoted by Gov. Bob Graham as part of his environmental protection project to restore Florida wetlands also became entangled in the negotiations. Pursuant to the program, Seminole lands in Palm Beach County (known as the Rotenberger tract) were to be used to reestablish a natural sheet flowage of water into the conservation area and, eventually, to Everglades National Park. A state-initiated land exchange proposal by which some 14,000 acres of land east of Levee L28 would be swapped for an equal amount of land outside the reservation boundaries was almost accepted by the Seminoles, but it foundered on the state's inability to devise a value-for-value exchange mechanism. Thus after almost eight years the issue remained stalemated.

On 30 March 1984 the state moved to dismiss the Seminole suit with prejudice on jurisdictional as well as substantive grounds.[25] The WMD filed a similar motion. However, by the early 1980s several landmark Indian rights cases before the U.S. Supreme Court would have great bearing on the Seminole suit; therefore, the attorneys representing the tribe sought to stay proceedings pending the outcome of those cases. As requested, federal judge Norman Rottenger Jr. issued the stay order in May 1984.[26]

Shortly after Judge Rottenger's action, the Supreme Court strengthened the Seminole position by finding that tribal lands could not be conveyed under the Indian Non-Intercourse Act. The court's 1985 decision in *County of Oneida, New York, et al. v Oneida Indian Nation (Oneida II)* affirmed an award to the Oneida tribe based on 1795 violations of its federal rights by the state of New York.[27] The court also held in a related case (*Oneida I*) for the Oneidas who had sued the state of New York for unlawfully obtaining possession of their large aboriginal territory in violation of the 1790 Non-Intercourse Act.[28]

In April 1985 the tribe's attorneys filed a memorandum opposing the defendant's motion to dismiss. Drawing on the recent Supreme Court precedents they argued that there was no "relevant legal basis" for holding that Indian claims against the states were barred by the Eleventh Amendment and that the Seminoles, like the Oneidas, had a valid claim under the Non-Intercourse Act. Seminole attorneys contended that the language of the modern act had been construed broadly to cover not only consensual transactions with Indian tribes, such as the attempted purchase considered in *Oneida II*, but also unilateral transactions designed to accomplish divestiture or alienation of tribal title. Therefore, they urged, "the inescapable meaning of this statutory scheme requires that the Non-Intercourse Act be applied."[29] They insisted that the federal court held jurisdiction over the plaintiff's related state law claims, since both the federal and state claims arose out of a common nucleus of operative facts.

The focus then shifted from establishing Seminole rights under federal law to an attack based on Florida state law. The tribe moved for a partial summary judgment on the state's occupation and control over approximately 16,000 acres of land in East Big Cypress.[30] The state countered, asserting that before the court could consider judgment on the state land-taking issue, the court first must find that it had jurisdiction to hear the claim and that the reservations contained in the 1937 deed were invalid. A federal court's assumption of jurisdiction, the state argued, precluded judgment for the plaintiff. Judge Rottenger withheld any decision, deadlocking the case, and a second round of negotiations ensued.[31]

The case now took a significant turn as the state split with the WMD over East Big Cypress.[32] The state, as trustee for the Seminoles and as the party holding title to the state reservation, threatened to file a cross claim against the WMD alleging that the agency had exceeded its authority for the use of Indian lands. Further, it contended that the WMD was limited to the terms of the 1950 dedication which conveyed rights for a flowage easement and an easement to construct and maintain canals, levees, and associated water control structures; the district had no authority to require the tribe to apply for permits to make any other use of these lands such as cattle grazing. The state demanded that the WMD acknowledge that it had a flowage easement only, provide grazing access to the tribe, and pay a fee for the rights it sought in Conservation Area 3A.

In response the WMD denied owing any money and insisted that cattle grazing or other agricultural use within the conservation area required water management systems contrary to the purposes of their project. According to the WMD argument, such use impeded the sheet flow of water and the purification of surface waters before they entered the ground and surface water systems. The district conceded that the Seminoles could use the conservation area as "natural range," but it would not allow planting of grasses or digging of drainage ditches. Nevertheless, the state held that the WMD could not deny the tribe access to the property in question. The district also questioned the state's representing the Seminoles who had their own counsel and claimed that this conflict damaged the interests of both parties. The WMD warned that the entire easement might be invalidated if the state pursued its argument that the district's interest in Indian land was in violation of the Non-Intercourse Act.

A judicial determination on the validity of the 1937 deed reservations, the subsequent 1950 easement, and any violation of the Non-Intercourse Act appeared necessary. The tribe wanted the issue decided by a federal court; the state and the WMD insisted that it be determined in state court. In the fall of 1985 a partial legal compromise was reached to avoid the state's cross claim against the WMD. The state and district then filed a document with the court which purported to clarify remaining tribal rights and access to East Big Cypress.

The Seminoles responded to this agreement by threatening to block implementation of the Modified Hendry County Plan. The WMD was preparing to initiate this $20 million project for flood control and drainage after years of planning and financial expenditures. The plan was of paramount concern to agricultural interests in south Florida. It would drain potential citrus lands to the west of the existing WMD drainage system and impound the excess water in Conservation Area 3A, so Seminole lands were crucial to its implementation. Much of the project was to be constructed on the Big Cypress Reservation in Hendry County and would bring additional runoff into the disputed conservation area. The tribe had protested the plan since the 1970s, but the district moved ahead with construction. Unaccountably the WMD had neglected to notify the Seminoles about public hearings on the matter as they had done with other area landowners. Therefore, the tribe requested a public hearing on the project, and all parties understood that Seminole objections—such as calling for an environmental impact study—could block progress indefinitely. This brought the WMD and state to the negotiating table. Jim Shore recalls, "I think the first time that we got their attention was when we more or less halted their first Hendry County Plan."[33]

The district was already seeking a resolution to the East Big Cypress impasse. In February 1986, $3 million had become available to settle the Seminole suit, but the state and the wmd failed to agree on how much each agency would pay, and the offer was withdrawn. The case appeared headed back to court, and the tribe still threatened to thwart the Modified Hendry County Plan. At that juncture, though, the district decided to negotiate directly with the Seminoles. A member of the district's board of governors, Timer Powers, took a leading role in resolving the issues. After working with the Seminoles for several months and gaining their respect, Powers contacted tribal counsel and requested a meeting. Seminole leaders, still suspicious of the wmd, expected more delaying tactics, but they accepted the overture. Although Shore remained highly skeptical, he maintained that the tribe had wanted to negotiate all along because it was the realistic thing to do.[34]

The first meeting, held in February 1986, began inauspiciously with a heated exchange between tribal chairman James Billie and the district's executive director, John Wodraska. Timer Powers quickly assumed the role of mediator and implored both sides to seek common ground; Jerry Straus, a Washington attorney representing the tribe, played a similar role on the Seminole side of the table. The first question raised was whether the wmd would pay for the six sections of Indian land in Palm Beach County considered an integral part of the governor's "Save Our Everglades" scheme. Wodraska said yes, but Billie was reluctant to commit the tribe to selling land without approval of the Tribal Council. The parties then explored the idea that under a permit system, both the district and Seminoles could use lands that were not wetlands. Both the tribe and wmd also expressed an interest in protecting environmentally sensitive land. As a result of this discussion, the negotiators began to develop a rapport, setting the stage for productive meetings in the future.

Throughout 1986 the wmd and the Seminole tribe continued to negotiate over the Modified Hendry County Plan, and the district decided that an operable weir, rather than a fixed facility, should be constructed to control water flow. The district refused, however, to divulge its operating plan for the project. The tribal leaders' concerns about maintaining a sufficient flow of water to their lands in times of drought also persisted, and they requested a public hearing. Then, in July, the Seminoles outlined the terms of a settlement to Timer Powers.[35] The tribe offered to settle the federal suit, as well as the land claim, based on the presidential order of 1839 (Macomb Treaty) for the sum of $6.8 million. In 1976 the Indian Claims Commission had dismissed the Macomb claim, but the Seminoles continued to raise it as a negotiating ploy. While state negotiators balked, the WMD leadership appeared more sympathetic. Wodraska informed Florida's attorney general, Jim Smith, that only a monetary settlement for the Indians could acquire the six sections of the Rotenberger tract and keep the Modified Hendry County Plan from remaining stalled indefinitely. The attorney general, who was running for governor, saw advantage in inheriting the popular "Save Our Everglades" program and in support from agricultural interests. Governor Graham also wished to see a settlement before his term ended and while funds remained available. The attorney general ended his resistance.

On 5 September 1986 the parties achieved a final agreement at the state capital, in Tallahassee. Governor Graham facilitated this process by providing his conference rooms prior to a scheduled meeting of the cabinet. Approximately forty people including Wodraska, Powers, and representatives of other state agencies met in one room, while the Seminole contingent, including chairman Billie and the tribe's attorneys, conferred in another. After hours of negotiating they struck a deal. It called for $7 million in compensation for past projects in Conservation Area 3A and for purchase of Indian land. Specifically, the agreement provided that: the lawsuit would be dismissed with prejudice; the Seminoles would receive $4.5 million for the fee-simple title and easement in 14,720 acres of their land in Conservation Area 3A, and the WMD would release its easement in three sections of Indian land lying west of Levee L28 and contribute $500,000 of in-kind services toward the development of Seminole lands lying west of Levee L28 or at the Brighton Reservation; the tribe would sell its six sections in Palm Beach County (the Rotenberger tract) north of Conservation Area 3A to the state for $2 million; the tribe would waive any aboriginal right that it had to 5 million acres of land in Florida based on the presidential order of 1839 (Macomb Treaty); the Seminole tribe would formally withdraw its opposition to the Modified Hendry

County Plan; perhaps most significantly, a water rights compact between the state and the Seminole tribe, the details to be completed
later, would become part of the final settlement; and when all parties
were bound by that regulatory system, Florida committed to transfer remaining lands within the state reservation to the United States
to be held in trust for the tribe. The tribe further stipulated that it
would never use the transferred lands for bingo or tax-free cigarette
sales—the Seminoles failed to see this would be a loss due to the site's
isolated location. Three days later, according to a news report, "Gov.
Bob Graham and the Cabinet granted conceptual approval to what
Graham called a 'historic' agreement reached by the state and the
tribe and the South Florida Water Management District."[36]

All parties seemed pleased with the agreement. John Wodraska
insisted, "This will be a great savings for the taxpayers of Florida.
It is critical to important components of the Save Our Everglades
program."[37] Powers commented that it "will last into centuries to
come. It has the potential to do that."[38] Only Jim Shore expressed
some reluctance. "The tribe," he stated, "does not like giving up its
land base, no matter how big or small. The $7 million sounds good,
but the tribe would rather keep all the land that it has. Money comes
last."[39]

The months immediately following approval of the agreement
were spent in considering how the money was going to be obtained
and informing federal agencies about the impending water rights
compact. Although some objections were raised within the BIA and the
Department of the Interior, they ultimately concurred. In November the Seminole Tribal Council unanimously approved the general
terms and conditions of the settlement. A Tribal Council resolution
adopted 4 August 1987 ended the tribe's claims against the state of
Florida and the South Florida Water Management District.[40]

Following approval of the agreement, creation of a water rights
compact became the next concern. The compact entered into by the
state of Florida and the Seminole tribe represents a unique episode in
the history of Indian water resources negotiations. A recent study of
Indian water rights settlements summarized the Florida agreement as
one in which "the disputants negotiated a settlement of the land-use
and water-rights conflict. The tribe relinquished some of its land-title

claims and entered into a cooperative agreement for local management of riparian water rights in return for money compensation and a limited recognition of its water-rights claims."[41] But the settlement's importance was more far-reaching than this would imply; as the tribe's attorneys reported, "this was the first time federally protected Indian water rights were recognized in an eastern riparian state."[42]

To fully appreciate the significance of the compact it must be understood in the context of water rights doctrine in the United States. Eastern states with their abundant water resources have followed English common law on riparian water rights. This water right is created by ownership of land abutting a body of water. No riparian owner may diminish the natural flow of the water to the detriment of other riparian owners. Each riparian owner is entitled to withdraw an amount for reasonable use, limited only by the rights of other riparian owners. Riparian rights are permanent and cannot be lost through nonuse. In arid western states with limited water resources the prevailing doctrine became that of prior appropriation; water rights arise when water is taken and applied to a beneficial use. The first to appropriate water has priority over competing users of the same source. Under the prior appropriation doctrine water-use rights can be forfeited by nonuse. As state legislatures generally failed to consider Indian tribes when allocating valuable water resources, their only recourse was to pursue claims in federal court. Two Montana tribes brought suit to secure their water rights, and, when the court found for the tribes, the case was appealed to the Supreme Court. In *Winters v United States* (1908) the high court upheld the findings and reasoning of lower courts that Indians had reserved rights which assured an adequate flowage of water to their reservations.[43] The date a reservation was established became the date from which its water rights were reserved, making Indians senior users in many areas of the West. Moreover, Indian rights could not be extinguished through nonuse; neither could their water right be limited in quantity if it was used for reservation purposes.[44]

As an essential element in settling the East Big Cypress case the Seminole tribe moved to establish its legitimate water rights on the reservations. The Florida Water Resources Act of 1972 had established a state permit system in lieu of the prevailing riparian system, and the state assumed that the tribe was subject to its jurisdiction for the regulation of water use. In fact, the Seminole Tribe of Florida, Inc. operated with WMD permits for withdrawing canal waters to irrigate their cattle pastures and other agricultural enterprises. In dry periods, however, the tribe was often deprived of an adequate water supply; at other times neighboring landowners alternately flooded Indian lands or diverted their water without WMD regulation. Additionally, the impending expansion of citrus interests as a result of the Modified Hendry County Plan left the tribe fearing for its future groundwater supply. Tribal attorneys advised the Seminoles that their water rights on the reservations were entitled to protection under federal law and could be vindicated in federal court. Accordingly, the tribe denied the state's right to regulate water use on the reservations without tribal consent and congressional approval; it also asserted its federally protected water rights under the *Winters* doctrine. The tribe argued that even if *Winters* didn't apply, it had federal rights based on riparian and groundwater-use rights attached to reservation lands at the time they were acquired, and which were not subject to subsequent Florida laws. In short, the state lacked civil regulatory jurisdiction on the reservations. Florida authorities assumed that *Winters* applied only to western tribes, but no federal or state court had addressed the issue.

Although the tribe appeared to have a solid legal argument, its water rights remained undefined. Litigation would take years, and even if the tribe prevailed in court and established federal reserve water rights, they would be difficult to quantify. Also, the administration of these rights could result in years of conflict. The parties agreed that a negotiated solution was the desirable alternative to expensive and uncertain litigation. Consequently the compact was developed to solve problems never previously addressed through litigation or public policy. The tribe's attorneys soon found that negotiating the compact proved more difficult and complex than reaching an overall agreement on the case. However, all parties realized that it was the crucial element; if the compact negotiations failed, the entire agreement would unravel and the result would be litigation.

The compact brought the Seminoles state and federal recognition of substitute federal water rights in exchange for *Winters* rights. The final settlement approved by Congress in 1987 specified that the compact's provisions would have the force and effect of federal law. The compact recognized the special status of the Seminoles by acknowledging rights and obligations substantially different from those of other Florida citizens. The primary benefit received by the Seminole tribe was perpetual protection of its consumptive water use rights, that is, it received a preference or priority equal to that of any other party for the same use. This accorded the Seminoles parity with the largest agricultural interests in the region. The tribe later reached a settlement with adjoining landowners and agreed to limit its groundwater preference rights and exercise them subject to a reasonableness standard. The tribe obligated itself to comply with the essential terms and principles of Florida's water management system, but was left free of direct state and WMD control. It enacted a tribal water code and established a commission and professional water office to ensure that all reservation development projects remain in compliance with the compact. If the compact is violated the Seminole tribe can bring an action in federal court against the state or the WMD; conversely, if the tribe is deemed to be in violation of the compact, it can be taken to federal court, but otherwise it is free to act unilaterally.

Approval of the Water Rights Compact did not bring an end to controversies surrounding Seminole water usage, but it provided a legal framework for the cooperative resolution of future disputes. In the final analysis, as Shore and Straus stated,

> The Tribe's aim in pursuing the Compact was to preserve its sovereignty while securing clearly defined rights to water necessary to satisfy tribal needs and to allow orderly development of its lands. The Tribe also desired to protect tribal lands and waters from any activities of neighboring landowners that might violate its rights. Conversely, the State desired to bring the tribal lands under some measure of control or influence. Thus, the State sought to obtain an enforceable commitment from the Tribe to manage tribal lands and waters consistently with Florida water and environmental law. Both sides achieved their essential goals in the Compact.[45]

Early in 1987 a potential stumbling block to consummating

the compact appeared when Lykes Brothers, Inc., a major Florida agribusiness conglomerate with land holdings adjacent to the Brighton Reservation, became involved in the negotiations. The company challenged the compact under the assumption that the Seminoles received special water rights that threatened the firm's interests, and it unsuccessfully pushed for legislation that would have wrecked the carefully crafted agreement. Actually, Lykes Brothers was left with no choice but to negotiate. They had little chance of killing the Seminole settlement bill and then moving through the legislature because other agricultural interests, primarily the powerful Land Council, wanted the Modified Hendry County Plan approved. Also, it soon became clear that the Seminoles would abide by the same water management system as other landowners. In May 1987, following three months of negotiations, arrangements were reached with all parties, including adjacent landowners such as Lykes Brothers and United States Sugar Corporation.[46] The Florida legislature also acted, and on 4 July Gov. Bob Martinez signed the Seminole settlement bill into law.[47] A settlement agreement was filed with the U.S. District Court for the Southern District of Florida in October.[48] Only congressional action remained before the agreement with its Water Rights Compact became a reality.

Senators Bob Graham and Lawton Chiles introduced the legislation, entitled the Seminole Land Claims Settlement Act of 1987 (S. 1684); Rep. Tom Lewis sponsored a companion measure in the House. Hearings were held before the House Committee on Interior and Insular Affairs and the Senate Select Committee on Indian Affairs. In December a group of independent Seminoles, not affiliated with either the Seminoles or Miccosukees, objected to the compact fearing that it might jeopardize the aboriginal title that they claimed to Florida lands. A slight alteration in the wording of the bill settled their complaint. The legislation passed Congress and was signed into law by President Ronald Reagan on 31 December 1987.[49]

The agreement hammered out by the Seminole tribe, Governor (later Senator) Graham, the state cabinet, the legislature, and the South Florida Water Management District—and ultimately approved by the Congress—appears to be one of those rare instances in which all parties to the dispute came away to some degree winners, while the public interest was also served. The state gained control over vital wetlands and could move forward with its plans for water management and flood control while assuring an unrestricted flow of water to Everglades National Park. The public benefited from a stable environmental policy in the region. The settlement guaranteed the South Florida Water Management District control over a major source of fresh water for coastal populations and ended jurisdictional disputes over the use of Conservation Area 3A. The Seminole tribe gained $7 million in compensation for lands already taken by the state and for their acreage in Palm Beach County, plus a WMD commitment through the Water Rights Compact to provide sufficient water flow and flood control systems on their agricultural lands at the Brighton and Big Cypress Reservations. Also, the way had been opened to place the remaining Seminole lands in East Big Cypress under the protection of federal trust status. In return, the tribe dropped the federal court suit, renounced its aboriginal rights to five million acres of land in Florida under the Macomb claim, and cleared the way for the Modified Hendry County Plan to become a reality. Perhaps most importantly from an Indian prospect, the principle of Seminole tribal sovereignty had again been tested and reaffirmed.

CHAPTER 8

What Became of the Miccosukees?

L ate in the fall of 1953 a tourist couple from New York, driving
along the Tamiami Trail between Naples and Miami, happened upon a roadside sign that boldly announced: "Seminole
Indian Village—Live Alligators and Crafts." Intrigued, they pulled
over and entered the small palisade enclosure. The visitors found in-
side a few palm-thatched huts where Indian women worked at sewing
machines or offered their patchwork and basketry for sale. Entire
families lived there, and children constantly begged to have their
picture taken for pocket change. Across the compound a collection
of Everglades wildlife—including snakes and some lethargic alligators—were displayed in pens. All in all, the village typified Indian
family roadside enterprises of that era.

A little more than a decade later, in 1965, the same couple passed
that way and noticed the sign now read: "Miccosukee Indian Village." This time they did not stop. Later, the confused tourists pulled
into a service station and asked an attendant, "What happened to the
Seminoles? Who are those strange Indians?"[1]

The same people had lived there all along, the descendants of independent and traditional Indians who occupied the lower Everglades
for over a century. In the intervening decade, however, the process of
asserting their ethnic identity accelerated. The Miccosukees declared
themselves historically, culturally, and politically independent of the
Seminoles, and sought federal recognition as a separate tribe with its
own constitution and government. Accordingly, the late 1950s and
early 1960s witnessed the final stages in their transformation from
Trail Indians to the Miccosukee Tribe of Indians of Florida.

The emergence of the Miccosukees came as a surprise to longtime
Floridians and others who identified the state's Indian population as

Seminoles. To the casual observer there were no visible characteristics to differentiate Seminoles and Miccosukees—all exhibited Indian features, that is, they "looked Indian." Women from both tribes wore the same colorful beads and patchwork clothing, while many families still lived in the thatched-roof chikees. The men appeared to hunt, fish, and wrestle with alligators for tourists in the same way. Most Seminoles and Miccosukees even spoke the same language. To further confuse the issue, there were a number of families in which parents were members of one tribe while their children opted to join the other. So what really differentiated the two groups? Part of the answer is historical; the other is political.[2]

Historically, the Miccosukees claim unique cultural origins. A review of Indian migration and settlement in Florida during the eighteenth century reveals that an amalgam of Southeastern Indian peoples relocated to the peninsula. By far the largest element were Muskogean-speaking tribal groups from Georgia and Alabama, to whom English colonists affixed the synecdoche "Creeks" because they were first encountered at Ochese Creek in the late seventeenth century. Internally the Muskogeans were divided into Upper and Lower Creeks. The Upper Creeks, who lived in independent towns along the Coosa, Tallapoosa, and Alabama Rivers dominated the Lower Creek towns found on the Chattahoochee and Flint Rivers. They shared a common southeastern woodlands culture based on town social and political organization, a matrilineal clans and kinship system, as well as religious beliefs that were demonstrated in the annual busk ceremony known as the Green Corn Dance. They were, however, divided by language. Upper towns spoke Muskogee while many Lower towns retained Hitchiti as their primary language. Both Muskogee and Hitchiti are Muskogean languages but are mutually unintelligible. Even so, Muskogee became the lingua franca for diplomacy, trade, and religious ceremonies. In the southward migration of Lower Creeks during the 1700s, a town known as Miccosukee settled near present-day Tallahassee, and it is by that name that their descendants have been known. Ethnologists frequently use the spelling *Mikasuki* to differentiate their language from the modern tribal political organization.

The political divergence of Seminoles from Miccosukees—some

might say progressives from traditionalists—originated in the 1920s and 1930s when federal reservations opened at Dania, Brighton, and Big Cypress. A majority of the Florida Indians, both Muskogee and Miccosukee speakers, resettled there during the Depression years and underwent rapid acculturation. The reservation people found employment in New Deal relief programs, occupied government houses, sent their children to school, and began a beef cattle industry. Under the influence of missionaries many also converted to Christianity. John Collier, the Depression-era commissioner of Indian affairs, first suggested allowing the reservation Seminoles to form their own government; he also recognized that those Miccosukees living in lower Everglades camps near the Tamiami Trail were substantively different in philosophy and lifestyle from the reservation people. By the late 1950s about two-thirds of the Indians in the state were living on reservations and had organized themselves as the Seminole Tribe of Florida.

The Miccosukee's pursuit of land and tribal status resumed in the summer of 1957 when the State of Florida moved to grant them official recognition. Having failed in his mission to reconcile the reservation Seminoles with the Trail Indians, and understanding that federal acknowledgement of the Seminole tribe was imminent, Gov. LeRoy Collins accepted the recommendation of State Indian Commissioner Max Denton to recognize the Miccosukee Council's constitution. Denton also urged the cabinet to grant Miccosukees long-sought exclusive hunting and fishing rights in the western reaches of Conservation Area 3 that bordered the remaining Everglades. There no longer remained any possibility of uniting the two Indian groups, and Collins accepted that "we think we now see some possibility of getting all of these Indians into either the Trail group or the reservation."[3]

On 30 July 1957 the Florida cabinet met in Tallahassee with a delegation of ten Miccosukees headed by Buffalo Tiger, who claimed that 201 of the 355 Trail Indians had signed the constitution. Both Mike Osceola and attorney O. B. White were present and spoke against recognition for a group which did not represent all the Trail Indians. Ingraham Billie, who had broken with Buffalo Tiger and

Morton Silver a year earlier, did not attend the meeting.[4] Nevertheless, the cabinet members approved the Miccosukee constitution unanimously; afterward some eighteen delegates, including Indians and supporters from the contending factions, were invited to the executive mansion for tea.[5] In assessing the importance of state recognition for the Miccosukees, one historian has observed, "Actually, approval of this constitution did not mean very much for it involved neither authority nor use of funds."[6] Yet it firmly established that two tribal entities would coexist in Florida.

This still left the Miccosukees without lands of their own. In October 1957 their leaders made formal application for control of a tract of land in the conservation area which Denton had recommended, plus ten to twenty acres of state land along U.S. Highway 27 west of Miami on which they wanted to build a trading post. The latter would be purchased with part of the funds realized when the Seminoles eventually settled their land claims case — this assumed that part of the funds would be allocated to the Miccosukees. This plan hit a snag in May 1958 when Florida Attorney General Richard Erwin advised his fellow cabinet members and the governor against an agreement with the Trail Indians which might indicate that the state had any liability in the Seminoles' case pending before the Indian Claims Commission.

Commissioner Emmons expressed dismay that Florida officials would refuse to honor a land deal with the Miccosukees after recognizing their constitution. Earlier the issue had shifted back to Washington when on 6 January 1958 the Miccosukee Council requested federal recognition. Emmons responded that formal recognition was ordinarily extended only to tribal organizations with assets under the trusteeship of the federal government. The Miccosukees had no such assets, such as a reservation; therefore their request presented a unique situation. Even so, the commissioner understood that a substantial number of Florida Indians had not affiliated with the reservation Seminoles and received no services sponsored by the Bureau of Indian Affairs; also, the Florida cabinet had recognized the Miccosukee's organization, so Emmons wrote:

> I am, therefore, willing and glad to recognize your organization which you call the "Everglades Miccosukee Tribe of Seminole

Indians" as qualified to speak for and on behalf of those Indians who have affiliated with the organization by signing their names to the roll attached to the Constitution. More specifically, we are recognizing your organization as qualified to speak for its members on matters which are of concern to the Florida Seminoles as a whole (such as the pending claim against the United States) and in connection with any State lands where your organization may be given special jurisdiction by the State.[7]

The Miccosukees' attorneys seized upon this statement as conferring full federal recognition on the tribe rather than the very limited role ascribed by the commissioner. Time and time again the Miccosukees alluded to this letter whenever they made a claim of sovereignty, and especially in challenging the Seminole land claims case.[8] In 1961 the Department of the Interior's solicitor issued a legal opinion holding that Emmons's letter "was not intended to imply that the group was eligible for Bureau services or assistance on the basis of any status as a 'tribe.' "[9]

Stung by the rebuff from Florida's attorney general but encouraged by Emmons' letter, the Miccosukee Council and its lawyers resumed their aggressive campaign to gain federal recognition. The initial salvo was an article in the *Miami Herald* which voiced their threat to take the Indian's case to the World Court at The Hague.[10] The Miccosukee Council wrote to President Eisenhower twice during September making a "final compromise offer" to settle their dispute with the state and federal governments.[11] They also contacted Senator Smathers, imploring him to intervene on their behalf.[12] An exasperated Emmons wrote to Howard Osceola, leader of the council, reminding him that the United States had never officially recognized the Miccosukees as a sovereign nation, nor could the bureau be concerned with providing services to people merely because they possessed Indian blood quantum. The bureau's only responsibility in Florida was to serve as trustee for the lands on three Seminole reservations and provide services to the residents.[13]

Meanwhile the Miccosukees pressed their case in a national forum. In the fall of 1958 the tribe resorted to tactics that had gained widespread use among activists. According to one observer, "a group of Miccosukees traveled to Washington and took their grievances before the British, French and Spanish embassies. Early the next year they attracted even more attention in New York by publicly threatening to take their case to the United Nations. Several of the Indians even appeared on an NBC television talk show hosted by Dave Garroway. Emmons was a guest on the same program and tried to emphasize Florida's responsibility in the affair."[14] This publicity made Gov. LeRoy Collins very reluctant to deal with the Miccosukees.

Still, Emmons had not given up on persuading Florida to transfer jurisdiction over some 200,000 acres to the Miccosukees, so he convened a conference in Washington in November 1958 to pursue that issue.[15] The leading bureau functionaries attended, as well as Max Denton, Buffalo Tiger, and attorneys Morton Silver and George Miller. The Indian delegation reviewed their land claims, including the unratified Macomb Treaty of 1839, but they were willing to accept a compromise settlement. That was good news for the commissioner who needed something reasonable to propose to Florida officials. Denton then explained that Governor Collins, a well known civil rights advocate, had entered the picture only because he believed the state should assist minority citizens in improving their lives, but at no time did the governor or the cabinet assume responsibility for any claim the Indians might have. He also pointed out that rather than 200,000 acres, the area under discussion contained 153,000 acres more or less, because of private holdings within the region not controlled by the state. By the end of the day those present reached general agreement on the position Emmons and Denton would present to the Florida officials: simply put, the Miccosukees wanted as much land as possible placed in trust with no restrictions on the time limit of the trust.

Prior to the Washington meeting, Florida's cabinet had referred the Indian land question to a committee of five citizens—two newspaper editors, two judges, and an expert on Indian matters—to make a recommendation. Commissioner Emmons and Max Denton met with the committee in December but apparently their presentation was not persuasive. The committee report of 16 February 1959 identified the Seminoles as the only Indian tribe existing in Florida and its land claim was against the federal government, not the state. Thus the committee recommended that the state make no grants, gifts, or leases of land to the Trail Indians, and Governor Collins endorsed its findings.

The Association on American Indian Affairs, possibly the most effective Indian advocacy group in the country at that time, supported the Miccosukee efforts to secure lands of their own. Writing in their newsletter *Indian Affairs* the association's executive director, La Verne Madigan, reported that Florida's relations with the Miccosukees had become extremely strained. This could be traced to the Miccosukees' claim to a separate tribal identity and their intervention in the Seminole land claims case. "In the course of recent dealings between the Miccosukee and the state," she wrote, "a legal document has been presented which claims the land desired by the tribe in a way which requires Florida to admit her historical monetary debt to these Indians for much more than the acreage actually being sought."[16] In essence, state recognition of the Miccosukee position would oblige it to provide compensation for all the land ever lost by Indians in Florida. This sweeping provision greatly concerned Attorney General Erwin, so it remained unlikely that state authorities would agree to such a settlement. Despite this obstacle Madigan and the AAIA continued to lobby state officials to set aside specific lands for the Miccosukees.

The Trail Indians were infuriated by the actions of the citizen's committee and Governor Collins; they considered it another breach of faith by whites and moved to take more drastic action. Learning that the Tuscarora, one of the Six Nations of the Iroquois, had thwarted the efforts of the New York Power Authority to acquire part of their reservation for a reservoir, the Miccosukees made contact with Tuscarora leader Wallace "Mad Bear" Anderson and involved him in their struggle for recognition.[17] There were, however, serious questions about Mad Bear's status as an Iroquois leader. According to historian Laurence Hauptman, "Despite the news stories to the contrary, Anderson was not at the time of the protests a political leader on the reservation. His role in the events of 1958–60 are much exaggerated, largely perpetuated by ... skillful manipulation of the media."[18] As intimated, Mad Bear represented a new generation of militant Indian leaders who understood the media's power and manipulated it for their ends. In March the opportunistic Anderson and the Miccosukee Council hosted a meeting of thirty-six spokesmen from eight tribes; they hoped to form a united Indian nation to pursue their grievances against the federal government, and ultimately to apply for membership in the United Nations.[19] Delegates claiming to represent some 180,000 Indians met at a Miccosukee camp west of Miami and signed four buckskins indicating their approval of the plan. Two of the buckskins were taken back to western and northern tribes, and a third remained with the Miccosukees. Mad Bear then proposed that a "buckskin of recognition" be sent to acknowledge the revolutionary government of Fidel Castro in Cuba.[20] As a result, Castro invited an Indian delegation to visit his country in July 1959. This was a publicity bonanza for Mad Bear, who had his picture taken embracing Fidel and later wrote, "They rolled out the red carpet for us, including police escort in Cadillacs, bands and machete waving campisinos [sic]."[21] Rumors also circulated that Cuba might sponsor the Iroquois for membership in the United Nations.

The Miccosukee contingent, including Homer Osceola, Buffalo Tiger, and other members of the council, as well as Morton Silver, sought and received Castro's recognition as an independent nation. This drew a withering blast from the *Miami Herald*'s editorial page: "The silly season seems to be with us again. It blossomed in a bit of grandstanding by a dozen of Florida's Seminole Indians. They junketed to Cuba for the big doings in Havana last weekend. There they swapped documents with Premier Fidel Castro.... The Cuban gambit was the latest in a long series of headline-hunting antics by this ill-advised group, which must embarrass most of the 1,000 Seminoles in Florida. We'd blush, too, if we took such foolishness seriously, which we don't."[22] The reservation Seminoles voiced their displeasure with the Miccosukees and moved to distance themselves from the action. "These people don't speak for us," said Mike Osceola. "If we have differences with the U.S. we believe in settling them over the conference table—not with our tomahawks."[23] Florida's Indian commissioner was also disturbed by the visit to Cuba. When asked by a reporter if the reservation people also wanted an independent nation, Denton replied, "They are proud of their American citizenship and are doing all they can to work with the state and federal governments."[24] The full extent of Denton's displeasure soon became apparent.

Following some astute lobbying by Indian support groups such as AAIA, the 1959 Florida legislature authorized the trustees of the Internal Improvement Trust Fund (the state cabinet) to set aside lands for the use and benefit of Indians.[25] When the cabinet voted to set aside 143,620 acres in south Florida for use by the Seminole Indians, Governor Collins emphasized that the land was not being turned over as an obligation to any claim but would be held in trust for use by all Indians subject to state laws and regulations of state agencies. Denton informed the governor that 754 of the 1,045 Indians in Florida belonged to the Seminole tribe while the Miccosukees represented a minority of about thirty-five individuals, and recommended that the reservation Indians be given authority to administer the land—which would have effectively undercut Miccosukee aspirations. But Collins demurred, saying, "I am afraid we might start a civil war if we turned it over to the reservation tribal council."[26] Back in Miami a testy Buffalo Tiger responded, "We live on this land now and would never permit the reservation Indians to administer this land or run our affairs."[27] He also blasted Denton's statement that his tribe represented only thirty-five adults: "If he ever visited the Everglades and talked to our people he would know that we represent over 300 Indians who choose to be left alone on this land which we have occupied for over 100 years."[28] Denton knew that the Miccosukee Council represented more than thirty-five individuals, so perhaps he remained irritated at the tactics employed by Morton Silver and the Miccosukee leadership, especially the trip to Cuba. In any case, the cabinet took no action to resolve the matter.

Commissioner Glenn Emmons, who did not want to see this opportunity to secure lands for the Miccosukees slip away, revived the negotiations. He brokered a settlement in which the Miccosukees retained administrative control of the 143,620-acre tract but which opened the land for use by all Florida Indians. The Seminoles accepted, but with a major stipulation: if the Miccosukees failed in administering the area, it automatically reverted to their government. The commissioner hosted a meeting at a Miami hotel on 15

November 1959 where the Miccosukee and Seminole representatives formally agreed to this arrangement, although Ingraham Billie later denounced it.[29] More important, Governor Collins refused to go along and again referred the matter back to the citizens committee. Part of the problem, according to the AAIA, was the state's insistence on guarantees from the federal government that it would recognize a responsibility to the Miccosukees comparable to its responsibility to other tribes. Florida was unwilling to incur legal or financial responsibility for the Miccosukees. But short of federal acknowledgement of the tribe it is difficult to see how such guarantees could have been given. Robert Mitchell of the Seminole Indian Association always believed part of Collins's reluctance to grant Miccosukees control over the land stemmed from their visiting Cuba and negotiating with Castro, for which he held Silver responsible. By late 1959 public opinion in the United States regarding Castro's revolution had begun to turn negative as he swung into the Soviet sphere of influence. It rapidly became a political liability to be identified with the Castro regime, and no doubt the very conservative members of the cabinet and legislature kept this issue alive in Tallahassee. The Cuba venture became a pivotal issue in negotiations with the bureau. Years later Buffalo Tiger recalled, "When Castro took over Cuba, he wanted us to come over as his guests. We went and were treated OK. When we got back the United States said 'OK, don't go back. Promise you won't, and you will be Miccosukees.' We needed our own power, and we had to go to Cuba to get it."[30]

With land negotiations entering their second year, Glenn Emmons stepped down as commissioner in March 1960, when the Kennedy administration came to office. The new commissioner of Indian affairs, Philleo Nash, would be equally supportive of the Miccosukee cause. The bureau, abetted by the Association on American Indian Affairs, continued to press Florida officials, and in the spring of 1960 they achieved a settlement by which Miccosukees received a land lease. Apparently any misgivings about the Miccosukees having dealt with a Communist dictator were subordinated to the necessity for a resolution to the land issue. Early in April the Florida cabinet voted to add the acreage utilized by the Miccosukees to the 108,000 acre State Indian Reservation already held in state trust. On 13 July following a massive letter-writing campaign by the AAIA membership, the Department of the Interior acknowledged that the Miccosukees had a legal relationship to the United States—though its exact nature was not specified. Finally in August the cabinet voted to have the entire tract of land placed in federal trust; the bureau accepted this in principle on 5 October 1960. Only the details remained to be worked out and La Verne Madigan was ecstatic; *Indian Affairs* heralded the AAIA's role in achieving the settlement and declared, "All Americans are indebted to Governor Collins and his cabinet for placing our national honor above the now academic question, 'Was it Florida or the United States that deprived the Miccosukees of security on their homeland long ago?'"[31]

Her rejoicing proved to be premature. The Florida lands did not immediately pass into federal trust and eventually became the subject of protracted litigation. The Miccosukees did gain conditional use of 143,620 acres, but the lease which the cabinet granted had a limited duration and severely restricted use of the land. Buffalo Tiger summarized the tenuousness of this arrangement during an appearance before a Senate committee: "In 1960 the state granted us a license to most of this area. The license meant that we could stay as long as the State did not change its mind. In 1975 the State Attorney General questioned the lawfulness of the license.... In January 1979 we filed suit against the State because there seemed no other way to bring the negotiations to a conclusion."[32]

By 1961 Buffalo Tiger had decided on an independent course of action. The only way to assure Miccosukee security in the future would be through federal acknowledgement; he hoped to follow up on a tentative federal commitment made the preceding fall and was encouraged in this by Robert Mitchell and La Verne Madigan. Tiger moved to sever his relationship with Morton Silver, whose extreme positions often provoked or alienated federal and state officials. From that point forward Silver allied himself with Homer Osceola, William McKinley Osceola, and a few older individuals who resented the rise of the younger Tiger. They continued to call themselves an executive council, held meetings in Hialeah, published a newsletter, and created a diversion while the main body of Miccosukees moved toward creating their tribal government.

Commissioner Nash sent experienced BIA tribal affairs specialist Reginald Miller, a Menominee Indian, as an "economic development officer" to work with the Miccosukees. That title seemed necessary to deflect the concerns of powerful individuals, such as Congressman James Haley, who might oppose having a second federally recognized tribe in Florida. Miller met with the Trail Indians to determine if they were ready to draft a federal constitution and charter; simultaneously he worked to have a portion of the state-owned Indian lands placed in perpetual trust status. When Miller reported that a majority of the Miccosukees headed by Buffalo Tiger were definitely in favor of organizing, the bureau once again dispatched its leading expert in this field, Rex Quinn, to Florida. As he recalled it, "I was asked to come down to the Trail and help the Miccosukee Indians organize, and I did. . . . As a matter of fact, we wrote the constitution out there in Jimmie Tiger's camp. All of the leaders were there, the clan leaders, all of them were there. Everything, of course, had to be done on a purely unanimous basis. Some of those minor decisions took two or three days, because they didn't get a unanimous decision on them."[33] Quinn did not look forward to a repeat of his earlier confrontations with Morton Silver during the period when the reservation people were organizing. Subsequently he learned with pleasure that "in the intervening period between 1957 and 1962 . . . they had developed a great animosity toward Morton Silver."[34]

The constitution and bylaws adopted by the Miccosukees represented the tribe's values and lifestyle as they had evolved to midcentury. Being a small, homogeneous, and very conservative community in which face-to-face decision making remained possible, and because they had no existing corporate enterprise or vested interests (such as cattlemen, who had to be dealt with separately), the Miccosukees opted for a single constitution and governing document rather than two like the Seminoles. The preamble, in addition to the usual statements about promoting the general welfare, assuring the blessings of freedom, and the like emphasized the necessity to "conserve and develop our lands and resources" as a paramount goal.[35] This is understandable in light of the long struggle to gain access to precious Everglades land. The article dealing with tribal territory spoke vaguely of reservation land set aside for their use and occupancy and any that might be added by state or federal law. In fact, the Miccosu-kees had no permanent reservation to call their own. They held the large tract in Conservation Area 3 under a restricted-use lease from the state and shared use of the State Indian Reservation with the Seminoles. Even their homes and tribal headquarters were located on land leased from the National Park Service.

The membership article decreed that only those adults and chil-dren of one-half degree Miccosukee blood could automatically be admitted to membership. Those with lesser blood degrees would have to be approved by the Miccosukee General Council. Within six months of adopting their constitution the General Council was required to adopt an ordinance governing membership, loss of mem-bership, and the adoption of members into the tribe; Miccosukee Ordinance 1, adopted on 17 June 1962, confirmed the one-half degree of Miccosukee blood requirement for automatic membership.

The document vested primary tribal authority in a Miccosukee General Council composed of all members eighteen years of age or over. The Council would meet four times each year and twenty-five members constituted a quorum, provided at least three clans were present. No business could be conducted unless they maintained a quorum at all times. This institutionalized a balance of power among the clans and assured that all points of view on an issue would be represented. Originally the Council meetings were set for the first Sunday in November, February, June, and August, but this was later changed to the first Saturday—perhaps a sign of growing Christian or other outside social influences shaping the community.

The constitution identified five tribal officers: chairman, assistant chairman, secretary, treasurer, and lawmaker. At first the officers held their positions for three years, but later this was changed to four-year terms.[36] A person had to be twenty-three years of age and a member of the tribe for three years (except at the initial election) to seek office; however, no one qualified to hold office who had been convicted of a felony within the preceding three years, served as a BIA employee, or had been found guilty of misconduct by the Council. This sec-tion reflected an early aversion to the federal government, but after the Miccosukee tribe began to accept bureau-funded programs, they amended it to eliminate federal employment as a disqualification for office.[37]

The five elected officers also served as the Miccosukee Business Council, which met monthly to conduct the affairs of the tribe when the General Council was not in session. This provided continuity in day-to-day business dealings with the world outside the reservation. The bylaws initially required a three-member quorum with at least three clans represented for the Business Council to function, but this proved impractical and the clan requirement was soon dropped.[38] The chairman became the most powerful figure although he was constrained from acting on matters binding the tribe until either the General Council or the Business Council had deliberated and enacted an appropriate resolution. Oddly, the chairman could not vote in either the General Council or the Business Council except in the case of a tie. Echoing a traditional Indian leadership pattern, this emphasized the necessity for a chairman to build a consensus on significant issues.

The articles dealing with powers of the General Council and Business Council revealed an interesting division of budgetary control. The General Council reserved unto itself the right to approve an annual budget and all expenditures, yet the Business Council could modify that budget up to an aggregate of twenty-five percent. This left overall control over expenditures with the polity, but the Business Council retained flexibility to adapt to changes. Members of the Business Council exercised broad powers to conduct tribal business affairs, including the right to lease, manage, permit, or otherwise deal with tribal lands. It could perform contracts and agreements of all descriptions to a limit of $3,000 subject to approval by the secretary of the interior (the cap and secretarial approval were subsequently removed). Also, with the approval of the secretary it could employ legal counsel (a requirement under the Indian Reorganization Act). After 1976 the Business Council would also be authorized under Florida statutes "to pass ordinances governing the conduct of its members and providing for the maintenance of law and order and the administration of justice within lands set apart for the occupancy of the tribe."[39]

A bill of rights guaranteed equal political rights and economic opportunities to all members of the tribe, as well as freedom of conscience, speech, association, or assembly, and due process of law with the right to petition for redress of grievances. A desire to perpetuate traditional ways is evident in the statement, "The members of the tribe shall continue undisturbed in their religious beliefs and nothing in this constitution and bylaws will authorize either the General Council or the Business Council to interfere with these traditional religious practices according to their custom."[40]

The *Constitution and Bylaws of the Miccosukee Tribe of Indians of Florida* was submitted for ratification on 17 December 1961. According to the certification of adoption signed by Buffalo Tiger as chairman of the constitutional committee and committee member Sonny Billie, with the BIA officer Reginald Miller as witness, the tribe adopted the document by a vote of forty-one in favor and none opposed in an election in which at least thirty percent of the eligible voters cast their ballots. Thus at its founding the Miccosukee tribe counted a membership which probably did not exceeded 140 adult Indians. Furthermore, it seems improbable that balloting was actually necessary; more likely, as Quinn has suggested, the Miccosukees achieved a consensus of opinion concerning their new government. Upon the recommendation of Commissioner Philleo Nash, Assistant Secretary of the Interior John Carver Jr. approved the constitution on 11 January 1962.[41] The Trail Indians had gained full federal acknowledgment.

The Miccosukee General Council held its first meeting on 28 January 1962, and Buffalo Tiger was elected chairman with Sonny Billie assistant chairman. Other officers were John Poole, treasurer; John Willie, secretary; and George Osceola, lawmaker. The Bureau of Indian Affairs assigned Reginald Miller as superintendent of the Miccosukee agency with headquarters located in the town of Homestead, some forty miles from the Miccosukee settlement along the Tamiami Trail. It seems fitting that the tribe selected Buffalo Tiger as its official leader; early on he emerged as their most prominent spokesman in negotiations with federal and state authorities. Tiger served as chairman for twenty-three years and during that tenure became a significant figure in national Indian affairs, particularly through his work in the National Tribal Chairmen's Association. Under his leadership the Miccosukees were instrumental in the founding of United

Southeastern Tribes (USET) as an advocacy organization for federally recognized tribes east of the Mississippi River.

As its first order of business the new tribe sought permission from the National Park Service to remain on the land they occupied at Forty Mile Bend on the Tamiami Trail. The park service issued a temporary permit for a strip of land five miles long and five hundred feet wide bordering the northern boundary of Everglades National Park. In 1961 the Corps of Engineers relocated a canal which necessitated moving U.S. Highway 41 northward, but the Miccosukee community along the old roadway remained intact. The tribe opened a school there in December 1962 using a portable classroom building provided by the Dade County School Board. This school began by offering two grades of instruction with a teacher and materials provided by the bureau. Two years later the park service issued a fifty-year restricted-use lease on the property which stipulated that it could only be used for Indian housing, educational, and administrative facilities, and as a place to make and sell handicrafts.[42] No dredging or filling could be carried on which interfered with the free flow of water through or over the park lands. It also required removal of the temporary school building within five years, and administrative buildings built for the tribe were to be designed in harmony with the scenic values of the park. The BIA responded in 1965 by erecting a rustic stone and wood school building with two classrooms, a kitchen, and an office suite. For a time the Miccosukee school also served as the location for community meetings.

The Miccosukee economy developed very slowly. Through the early 1960s the Business Council worked primarily with income from grazing leases on the State Indian Reservation, Flood Control District payments, and loans from the Bureau of Indian Affairs. During this period the tribal budget rarely exceeded $20,000 and the chairman became its only paid officer with an annual salary of $6,500. Most employed Indians derived their income from tourism-related enterprises such as handicrafts and airboat rides; they lived well below the poverty level. The Miccosukee leaders found it imperative to develop revenue-producing enterprises providing employment for members as well as to underwrite tribal operations. On 19 December 1964 the Miccosukee Tribal Enterprise—consisting of a restaurant and service station/grocery store located on the north side of Tamiami Trail—opened with fifteen Indian and four non-Indian employees. These facilities, perched on a narrow strip of land provided by the state, were built with part of a $150,000 loan from the bureau. The enterprises provided only a modest boost for tribal employment and income; the payroll for fiscal year 1965 amounted to $23,200, with $15,200 paid to Indians.[43]

Another source of Indian employment was the BIA itself. A few Indians worked for the Miccosukee agency headquarters in Homestead or at the tribal school, but these were low-paying nonprofessional jobs. After a time federal authorities announced plans to pave some seventeen miles of roadway through the State Indian Reservation from the Big Cypress Reservation to connect with the cross-state toll highway known as Alligator Alley. Since part of the road passed through the Miccosukee land, the bureau expected many Miccosukees to be employed on the construction project, and Buffalo Tiger urged his people to apply for the relatively well-paying government jobs. Because the tribe's constitution barred any BIA employee from holding a tribal office, they amended the document to accommodate this economic opportunity.

The Miccosukee population grew to the point that the tribe enrolled 262 members by 1969. It also administered various forms of health and social services to 450 individuals, many of them nonenrolled independent Seminoles who lived along the Tamiami Trail. Like other tribes, Miccosukees benefited from the Great Society programs of the 1960s. A Community Action Agency approved for the Miccosukees tribe employed eight Indians, primarily in the Head Start program. In addition, a Neighborhood Youth Corps (NYC) provided jobs for school-age youths during the summer. Although these programs were intended to provide Indian employment, the director, J. W. Rehbein, was not an Indian. He prepared an economic development plan for the tribe which sought funds from the Economic Development Agency (EDA) for technical and training assistance, as well as to build a multipurpose tribal headquarters building. This failed to receive federal approval because the Miccosukees did not own the land on which they lived. The Miccosukees needed a reservation, and their advocates persuaded the 1965 Florida legislature to divide the State Indian Reservation into two parts, one to be administered by the Seminole tribe and the other by the Miccosukees. The trustees of the Internal Improvement Trust Fund then assigned the oil and mineral lease rights within the tract to the tribes, which presented a potential for new revenue; legal control over the state reservation still resided with the State of Florida. Accordingly, acquiring a clear title to their lands and placing them in federal trust status became a paramount Miccosukee goal.

Following tribal organization a number of dramatic changes occurred in Miccosukee living conditions which demonstrated the flexibility and adaptability of these people. For example, in 1966 the tribe took title to twenty-five modern frame houses with electricity and plumbing—yet retaining many style features of the traditional chikee—which formed the nucleus of a new community. The tribe had initially sought EDA funds for construction but was turned down when the agency learned that the houses would be placed on land leased from the park service. The BIA then provided Housing Improvement Program monies; still, Miccosukees put a great deal of their own effort into the construction. While the new housing initially benefited only a minority of the population, their willingness to accept governmental assistance represented a significant shift in attitude.

Frustrated by their lack of economic progress and making no headway in securing more land from the state government, the Miccosukees pursued a bold course of action in the 1970s. Taking a lead from President Nixon's recently announced commitment to a policy of Indian self-determination, the Miccosukees proposed contracting all of their services directly from the federal government. They complained that the BIA system of administration, especially having the Miccosukee agency located forty miles from the tribal headquarters and housing area, remained inadequate. Tribal leaders charged the agency superintendent at that time—their third in nine years—with being insensitive to Indian needs; he supposedly visited them infrequently, appeared to be more concerned with budgetary matters and smoothness of operation than serving the people, and rarely sought Indian input into decisions affecting them directly. They were also displeased with perceived inequities in pay between tribal and BIA employees.

The Business Council expressed its opinion that the quality of services delivered to Indian people could be substantially improved if the tribe took control of the BIA facilities and programs. Specifically, it promised to reflect the needs of the tribe in reservation projects and school curriculum; improve the quality of training given Miccosukee personnel for teaching, maintenance, and other professions; implement new educational concepts and methods while minimizing dropouts; and improve the operation of the school and eliminate bureaucratic duplications. The tribe proposed to close the Homestead agency, eliminate the superintendent's position, and relocate all programs to the tribal headquarters on the Tamiami Trail. In 1971 the Miccosukees became the first Indian tribe to contract with the federal government for all services to its people. The Miccosukee's success with contracting impressed Congress, which passed the Indian Self-Determination Act of 1975 extending similar opportunities to other tribes.

The Miccosukees contracted their educational program from the bureau with funds sent directly to the tribal government. It hired teachers and support personnel, authorized the development of instructional materials, and retained accountability at the local level. The Miccosukee school developed a community-centered curriculum that, in addition to standard subjects, made extensive use of tribal elders to teach youngsters traditional values and folkways. The tribe implemented cultural studies in special Everglades camps set up just for this purpose. Additionally, the school initiated a federally funded Title 7 bilingual education program to develop both English and Miccosukee language skills. Although there was no evidence initially to prove that the bilingual program enhanced academic achievement, a study by Harriet Lefley found that Miccosukee children displayed greater self-esteem than their Seminole counterparts who attended a bureau-run school on a nearby reservation.[44] Since 1976 the Miccosukees have operated an accredited educational system through the high-school level.

Prior to receiving federal recognition the Miccosukees had access to federal health services only by journeying to one of the Seminole reservations. Consequently, most Indian people living near the Tamiami Trail suffered from a variety of ailments. In 1963 representatives of the Dade County Department of Public Health, the U.S. Public Health Service, the Bureau of Indian Affairs, and the University of Miami School of Medicine conducted a special health-screening program. It determined that "most of the Miccosukees were found to be infested with intestinal parasites; dental caries (decay) was widespread; 27 persons had possible heart abnormalities; five persons were found to have tumors which required further study; and the hemoglobins of a number of [Miccosukee] Seminoles were extremely low."[45] As a result, federal funds were provided for health services including outpatient and inpatient hospital care, health and nutrition education, and dental care for the children. During the 1970s the tribe contracted with the Indian Health Service to operate an out-patient clinic on the reservation.

The Miccosukee restaurant and service station operations remained an economic drain, and the principal on the $150,000 loan could not be significantly reduced during the 1960s. There were a number of reasons why these enterprises initially failed. First, the opening of Alligator Alley as a direct east-west toll road across the Everglades between Fort Lauderdale and Naples diverted a high percentage of the tourist traffic that formerly crossed on the Tamiami Trail. Also, it was difficult to find competent managers and enough dependable workers to keep the facilities staffed. Finally, because of the isolated location some thirty-five miles west of Miami and a lack of adequate law enforcement by the Dade County sheriff's office, the restaurant and service station/grocery were subjected to frequent burglaries and break-ins. This made tribal control of its own law enforcement another high priority for the business council.

In 1974 the Florida Governor's Council on Criminal Justice studied the rising crime rate on Indian reservations and recommended establishing special improvement districts as a means of allowing Indian tribes to provide adequate law enforcement with the use of federal funds. Both Seminole and Miccosukee leaders often complained of problems with non-Indians entering their lands. Buffalo Tiger reported that his nephew had been killed by a hit-and-run driver on the Tamiami Trail, and there were instances of motorists taking gun-shots at Indians from the highway. "The only serious problems we have are people coming from outside," Tiger said. "Being out in the Glades, it seems you have no law enforcement. It's open. Drug prob-lems, crime problems get to us quicker."[46] The Seminole chairman, Howard Tommie, announced that local officials ignored a lot of the crime on reservations; seven tribal deputies patrolled 100,000 acres but had no right to arrest rustlers or poachers. After the Florida legislature enacted enabling statutes, both tribes became eligible for Law Enforcement Assistance Administration (LEAA) and other federal grants. In 1976 the Miccosukees established a public safety depart-ment to provide police and fire protection on the reservation; they also initiated a tribal court to exercise jurisdiction over civil offenses committed on reservation lands.[47] Two judges preside over cases brought before this court, one assessing the case based on Miccosu-kee laws and customs and the other viewing it from the perspective of contemporary law. Most often sentences are meted out in accor-dance with traditional tribal punishment for such offenses. Criminal offenses are transferred to the appropriate non-Indian jurisdiction.

The final segment of the Miccosukee journey to self-sufficiency dates from their suit against the State of Florida in 1979. It began in response to the state attorney general impugning the legality of their 1960 lease in Conservation Area 3. The litigation rested upon the state's flooding of more than half of the State Indian Reservation and the alleged establishment of a five-million-acre "executive order" reservation by the Macomb Treaty in 1839, including the cities of Naples and Fort Myers. After several years of negotiations the Mic-cosukee tribe and the State of Florida reached a settlement stipulating that the tribe would receive $975,000 from the state in considera-tion for settling the suit and relinquishing their rights to all potential or unsettled claims based on aboriginal title and the 1839 "executive order" reservation created by the Macomb Treaty; the Miccosukee portion of the State Indian Reservation as well as three parcels along the Tamiami Trail would be taken into trust by the secretary of the interior for benefit of the Miccosukees; and the tribe was to receive approximately 189,000 acres of land in the Everglades under per-petual lease. The State of Florida retained Public Law 280 civil and criminal jurisdiction in the new Miccosukee reservation lands, and all state statutes relating to alcoholic beverages, gambling, and sale of cigarettes would be in force. Also, the state retained legal title to the leased area which would be treated as a federal Indian reservation for most purposes.[48] This legislation, known as the Florida Indian Land Claims Settlement Act of 1982, passed in Congress on 31 December 1982.[49]

With their lands secured in federal trust status and the availability of federal funds for development, the Miccosukee economy began to thrive. The tribe operates a service plaza on Interstate 75 (the old Alligator Alley right-of-way) within the reservation and has also expanded and upgraded the Miccosukee Cultural Center on the Tamiami Trail. The center, which includes a model Indian village where the public can view craftsmakers at work and other traditional activities, draws thousands of visitors annually. The tribe enjoys good relations with federal, state, and local governments. It provides law enforcement on U.S. Highway 41 (Tamiami Trail) under an agreement with Dade County and recently extended its policing effort to the Broward County reservation to assist tribal members and the general public using Interstate 75 while traveling between Naples and Fort Lauderdale.

Most promising, however, is the Miccosukee venture in high-stakes bingo—an activity they avoided for years despite the prosperity that it brought to the Seminole tribe. Likewise, until recently the Miccosukee tribe declined tax-free cigarette sales rather than possibly being considered a Seminole political satellite under the peculiar wording of state law.[50] In 1990 the tribe opened the Miccosukee Indian Bingo Center—which seats 2,000 players—on twenty-five acres at Tamiami Trail and Krome Avenue, just west of Miami. The site has been accepted in federal trust under the Gaming Regulatory Act of 1988 and now constitutes another reservation for the tribe. The bingo hall almost immediately began to yield enormous profits; this would provide the tribe with capital needed for future business expansion. It also involved them in controversy and litigation that one investigative reporter has called the Great Indian Bingo War.[51]

In 1993 the Miccosukees moved to disassociate themselves from

Tamiami Partners, Limited, a non-Indian investment group which bankrolled and managed the bingo operation. The tribe charged the investment-management group with failing to meet its financial obligations; also, it did not give preferential hiring to Indians. The Miccosukees were to receive $30,000 per month until construction costs were recovered; after that the tribe retained 60 percent of the profits and the investing partners, 40 percent—the maximum allowed to non-Indian investors by federal law. The tribe said the partners dipped into profits to make the monthly payment rather than using them to retire the construction debt. Furthermore, the Indians accused some individuals associated with the investment-management group of having connections with organized crime. The Miccosukee leadership then asked their tribal court to void the contract. For their part, Tamiami Partners responded that Miccosukee leaders had unduly interfered with the bingo management and breached their contract; it claimed that the tribe was trying to seize a multimillion-dollar asset and asked a federal judge to force the Indians into arbitration. The tribe countered by denying Tamiami Partners a license to operate bingo on their land as required by law, and the investors appealed to the federal court for relief. At that point the Miccosukees forcibly closed down the bingo hall and ignored the court's order to reopen and reinstate the partners. Despite a fine of $10,000 per day imposed by a federal judge in Miami (subsequently lifted by a federal appeals court) the Miccosukees refused to reopen the bingo hall, standing on their rights as a sovereign nation. The Bureau of Indian Affairs supported the Miccosukee position. While the courts decided the case the Miccosukee tribe continued to operate the bingo hall—and realized a profit estimated at $7 million a year. In 1994 the U.S. District Court for the Southern District of Florida issued its decision in the case *Tamiami Partners, Ltd. v Miccosukee Tribe,* dismissing the claims against the tribe, the tribal court, and the Tribal Gaming Agency on the grounds of sovereign immunity.[52] The tribe's attorney predicts that the case will be appealed and ultimately make its way to the U.S. Supreme Court.

The quality of tribal leadership became a key ingredient in the survival and progress of Florida's Indian people during the second half of

this century. Throughout most of their brief history as a federally recognized tribe the Miccosukees have been led by individuals steeped
in traditional culture. Buffalo Tiger, who served as chairman from
1961 to 1985, although reared in the Everglades became acculturated
and lived in Miami with a non-Indian wife; he developed into a force-
ful advocate for his people in both Washington and Tallahassee. And
yet he functioned within a tribal context that remained largely consensual and clan dominated. The Miccosukee polity still thought in
terms of living with the land rather than developing it, so in 1976 the
General Council voted to forego any part of the Seminole land claim
monies—even though they sorely needed those funds. Years later
Tiger still expressed the view, "The land belongs to God. Don't sell
it. Just use it."[53] The Miccosukee worldview often clashed with the
economic demands of survival in the twentieth century, and Buffalo
Tiger had to tread carefully between both worlds. Despite undeni-
able gains, many of his people became dissatisfied and believed the
Seminoles were better-off financially. Disgruntled forces eventually
unseated Tiger and replaced him briefly (1986–87) with Sonny Billie,
a medicine man who also worked as a construction contractor. In an
extremely close election Buffalo Tiger received sixty-three votes to
sixty-six for his opponent. A recount upheld the election result and a
brief period of relative instability followed because the Miccosukees
had known only one chairman for such a long time.

Today, leadership of the Miccosukee tribe has passed to a new generation of young tribal leaders. The current chairman, Billy Cypress,
is college educated and moves easily in both the Indian and non-
Indian worlds. He has little to say about the Miccosukee's reasons
for not wanting their share of the claim money. "It's the community's prerogative. That's what they decided. That's how democracy
works."[54] On the other hand, Cypress led the fight to take over the
bingo hall and oust its non-Indian managers, knowing that it offered
the key to future financial independence. One report had estimated
that "even if the 400-member tribe ends up having to pay Tamiami,
its share of the profits will mean an annual $10,000 for each man,
woman and child."[55] Such a dramatic increase in affluence can only
accelerate the pace of Miccosukee acculturation. So even without the
land-claim money, the pace of change has all but engulfed the Micco-

sukee world, and the young people face a far different life than their elders experienced. Cypress is sincerely committed to rapid economic development for his people while attempting to preserve traditional Miccosukee ways. That will not be easy in a rapidly evolving south Florida milieu.

CHAPTER 9

The New Seminole Polity

P hilologists classify the term *assumption* as a polysemic—a word having multiple definitions. One connotation for the verb *to assume* is something taken for granted; it is presumed to exist. In that sense the Seminoles of Florida always assumed that they possessed both *de facto* and *de jure* sovereignty as an Indian nation. A second definition of assumption implies the wresting or taking possession of sovereign rights—presumably by whatever means are at hand. Unlike their ancestors who tenaciously defended the Florida homeland through warfare, twentieth-century Seminoles effectively exercised sovereign rights through a combination of legislative and judicial means. In the process they experienced a fundamental social and political transformation that created a new polity, one in which tribal macroidentity supplanted the busk group, camp, and clan as the primary locus of individual allegiance. Historical examination of Indian sovereignty issues, as well as the means by which it was reformulated among tribes, informs the argument that a new Seminole polity had emerged by midcentury.

At the outset one question must be addressed: Why should an Indian tribe even assume that it possessed sovereignty? Given the massive demographic, economic, social, and political disasters that have befallen Native Americans over the last two centuries, it would seem naive bordering on delusional to make such a claim. Yet apparently Indian tribes have always possessed it to some degree. Ratification of the Constitution in 1789 established broad parameters for federal Indian policy. An authority on Indians and constitutional law reminds us that the Constitution mentions Indians specifically three times, the most important of these being in the commerce clause which authorized Congress "to regulate Commerce with foreign Nations, and the several States, and with the Indian Tribes."[1] This was complemented by two sections of article 6: the first reaffirmed previously negotiated treaties, most of which were with Indian tribes; the second was the supremacy clause, which makes federal treaties and statutes superior to state law. Thus the Constitution defined Indian tribes as sovereign entities recognized by the United States. Nevertheless, constitutional applications to Native American rights have been fluid and controversial.[2]

Beginning with the first Trade and Non-Intercourse Act in 1790, Congress affirmed that the federal government held an exclusive right to deal with Indian tribes. Drawing on both constitutional and statutory authority, George Washington and his secretary of war, Henry Knox, initiated a policy of "expansion with honor," which called for negotiation and treaties with Indian nations as the basis for acquiring tribal lands.[3] Abandoning the previous policy of military conquest, "the United States government thus treated with Indian tribes with legal procedures similar to those used with foreign nations, a practice that acknowledged some kind of autonomous nationhood of the Indian tribes."[4] Nevertheless, the limitation on Indian sovereignty was evident in American insistence on the right of preemption, the exclusive right to purchase tribal lands. Also, the new government had strengthened its military, and many subsequent treaties were coerced as a result of victories like that by Gen. Anthony Wayne at the Battle of Fallen Timbers in 1794; as a result, the Treaty of Greenville the following year opened up much of the Old Northwest for settlement. Eventually some four hundred treaties were concluded with various tribes until Congress ceased making treaties with Indians in 1871.

The most important Indian laws were the treaties, statutes, and executive orders establishing reservations. Therefore, because most Indian law and policy was geographically based and general in nature, the Court found it necessary to place it in a larger context of constitutional law and national policy. This began very early in the last century when the broad shape of Indian law was set in three opinions written by Chief Justice John Marshall, which collectively are known as the Marshall Trilogy.[5] In the first of these cases, *Johnson v McIntosh* (1823), the Court ruled that Indian tribes, because their possession predated European settlement, held an ownership interest in their aboriginal lands. However, the tribes could not transfer ownership to anyone but the United States. This stabilized and federalized frontier property law while implying that the tribes were not altogether sovereign within the American system.

The second case in the Marshall Trilogy, *Cherokee Nation v The State of Georgia*, was decided in 1831. At this point the existence of large, politically independent tribal enclaves east of the Mississippi River stood in the way of American expansion. The State of Georgia had denied the validity of Cherokee rights under its treaties with the United States and took action disestablishing the Cherokee courts and legislature while dividing Indian lands among five Georgia counties. The Cherokees, claiming to be a foreign nation, sued Georgia directly in the Supreme Court, which was empowered to hear cases between foreign nations and the states. The court dismissed the case, holding that it lacked jurisdiction because the Cherokees were not a foreign nation as defined by the Constitution. More important, though, Chief Justice Marshall spelled out the position of Indian tribes within the American system. He defined them as "domestic, dependent nations" with specified sovereign rights within their territory; however, the tribes were also deemed to be wards of the United States.

Worcester v The State of Georgia (1832) was the third case in the Marshall Trilogy. Samuel Worcester and a fellow Congregational missionary working among the Cherokees were arrested and imprisoned for failure to pay a license fee and refusing to acknowledge allegiance to Georgia. The Cherokee supporters among northern churches brought the case before the Supreme Court. By that time Marshall had formulated his position on tribal autonomy and held that the Cherokees' treaty rights prevailed. Writing for the Court he enjoined Georgia from enforcing its laws in Cherokee territory and ordered the release of the prisoners. Georgia refused to comply or even acknowledge the action of the Court while President Jackson held that he lacked legal authority to intervene. The highest court, even though lacking a mechanism to enforce its ruling, had reaffirmed the sovereign status of the Cherokees within their own lands. According to a recent study this presented an expansionist America with an even greater problem: "This recognized sovereignty of Native American groups was an obstacle in the sense that Congress or the courts had to extinguish that sovereignty or otherwise reduce it in order to legally assert control over Indian nations."[6]

Despite this victory in the courts, Indians began to lose control of their lands. One by one the Eastern tribes signed treaties ceding their lands, and in return accepted monetary compensation plus large tracts in the newly designated Indian Territory. Northern tribes such as the Potowatomi, Sac, and Fox were assigned land in present-day Kansas, while the Southern tribes were relocated in the region that became Oklahoma. Cherokees embarked on the Trail of Tears, where a quarter of their number perished, and the other tribes were subjected to equally dreadful conditions. The Seminoles of Florida were also victims of this great deportation of native peoples—except that they refused to go peacefully. War chiefs led by Osceola rejected the federal removal treaty and began an armed conflict to remain in Florida. The Second Seminole War (1835–42) was among the costliest Indian wars fought by the United States.[7] Although the Seminoles lacked a central tribal organization and fought more as independent bands, effective guerrilla resistance in the largely uninhabited Florida peninsula tied up a numerically superior government force; when the struggle ended, about 1,000 Indians remained in Florida. It was not until the conclusion of the Third Seminole War (1855–58) that all but a hundred or so Seminoles were finally removed to the Indian Territory.[8]

It is worth noting that the Seminoles in Indian Territory were one of the Five Nations which federal authorities dealt with for the remainder of the century. Under provisions of the removal treaty the Oklahoma Seminoles received monetary compensation for Florida lands, settled on a tract provided by federal authorities, and accepted health and education benefits. All subsequent treaties and allotments were negotiated with the tribal government which the western Seminoles established until the Five Nations were abolished by congressional action.[9]

During the decades bracketing the Civil War, tribes of the Great Plains and Southwest also came under pressure to reduce their land base as the nation continually expanded westward. By the late 1860s the balance of military power was decisively in favor of the U.S. Army.[10] As tribes were defeated, the federal government sought to relocate Indians on reservations where they could be kept apart from other Americans. The authorities were aided in this effort by a national Christian humanitarian reform movement, whose leadership coalesced at the annual Lake Mohonk (New York) conferences. By the late nineteenth century, mainstream Protestant churches and missionary groups had enormous influence in determining federal Indian policy.[11] The creation of reservations was in part an attempt to physically protect the Indians from the wrath of settlers, as well as to control the illegal trade in alcohol which was so destructive to their way of life. Soon the reformers changed both their goals and tactics: they attempted to detribalize Indians by breaking up their commonly held land base while simultaneously undermining traditional forms of tribal organization, governance, and religion. The new emphasis was on assimilating the Indian into the mainstream of American life, and the vehicle for accomplishing this was the General Allotment Act of 1887, commonly called the Dawes Act for its author Massachusetts Sen. Henry Dawes. This legislation called for breaking up the Indian reservations into family-sized allotments, converting the Indians into yeoman farmers, and granting U.S. citizenship to replace their tribal allegiances. Those reservation lands in excess of Indian needs were to be sold off to settlers; the process was slow and not all of the reservations were allotted, but before the practice was discontinued in 1934 some ninety million acres of native-owned land had been transferred to white ownership.

With the tribes relegated to reservations there was little more than lip service paid to Indian sovereignty—in reality they were captive peoples. The Supreme Court and Congress were the two agencies most responsible for dismantling the tribes' legal position which had been carefully formulated by John Marshall. Treaties severely limited the range of Indian action. Tribes were required to remain on prescribed lands and deal with outsiders only through the federal bureaucracy. Increasingly disheartened and disabled, few Indian tribes were willing or able to reorganize themselves to take advantage of the new system into which they were being forcibly integrated. Only the Five Nations in the Indian Territory near the end of the last century presented a challenge to overweening federal paternalism. But when the educated and sophisticated leaders of the Cherokee, Creek,

Choctaw, Chickasaw, and Seminole tribes developed legislative and legal institutions to protect their interests, they were thwarted by national political and economic forces. The Dawes Commission of 1893, in conjunction with the Curtis Act of 1898, broke up the Five Nations. Tribal lands were allotted, courts and governments dismantled, and the Indian Territory passed into history when the State of Oklahoma was created in 1907. Because they were so few in number and lacked large tracts of land coveted by white settlers, the Florida Seminoles, unlike their brethren in the Indian Territory, benefited from benign federal neglect throughout much of this era.

The attack on Indian sovereignty persisted through the early decades of the twentieth century. Indians were unable to make effective use of their allotments due to lack of capital and expertise; most Indian allotments were leased to white farmers or cattlemen while remaining tribal lands and resources often fell under the control of private companies with the approval of the Indian Office. Living conditions, health, and education on the reservations deteriorated while the tribes came under increasing pressure to discontinue traditional dancing and religious ceremonies. Even the citizenship which Indians ostensibly acquired via allotments remained in question until Congress passed the Citizenship Act of 1924. Despite these blows, Indian communities would not disappear; the tribes survived and resisted all efforts to "civilize" them. The efforts of the Mohonk conference reformers to totally assimilate the Indian into American life had failed, and a new day was dawning which would see the resurgence of Indian rights.[12]

A new breed of progressive reformers typified by John Collier now took the stage. American Indian cultural integrity and political sovereignty were in tatters, and it became the passion of reformers to make them whole again. Collier, for one, had long been committed to cultural survival, having served as a professional social worker among the immigrants of New York City and later living for a time among the Pueblo Indians at Taos, New Mexico. Rather than eradicating traditional Indian cultures and assimilating them into the American mainstream, Collier called for their regeneration and believed they could serve as a model for the rootless and materialistic post–World War I society. He articulated a program to preserve tribal life through economic development, political organization, and legal protection. He worked with the General Federation of Women's Clubs and other groups in 1922 to defeat the Bursum Bill, which would have affirmed non-Indian claims to Pueblo lands resulting in significant loss of Indian territory. The bill failed and Collier emerged as the leading Indian reform figure of his day.

Collier formed the Indian Defense Association in 1923 and served as its executive secretary for a decade. The association strongly advocated greater Indian involvement in the determination of federal policies, especially the leasing of their lands and mineral wealth; it also worked to protect tribal dancing and religious ceremonies from the attacks of bureaucrats and the Christian reformers. The IDA agenda to protect Indian cultures received backing from the General Federation of Women's Clubs with its nationwide network of Indian committees, as well as the Association on American Indian Affairs and numerous other smaller associations. In Florida, Ivy Stranahan, of Fort Lauderdale, served for many years as Indian affairs chairman for the State Federation of Women's Clubs; as such she consistently supported Collier's work and maintained a correspondence with him for nearly two decades.[13]

Well in advance of achieving suffrage, the women of Florida, speaking through their clubs and religious organizations, were a potent force at the state capital lobbying on behalf of the Seminoles.[14] Such leaders as May Mann Jennings, Ivy Stranahan, and Minnie Moore-Willson were relentless in their efforts to set aside a tract of land as a state reservation for the tribe. In 1917 the state legislature finally designated 99,000 acres in the lower Everglades as the State Indian Reservation, a preserve where the Seminoles could live, hunt, and fish. Unfortunately, it was located in a region which Seminoles rarely frequented and was also unsuitable for agriculture or cattle ranching. The tract would ultimately be incorporated into Everglades National Park, and the Seminoles received a comparable amount of land elsewhere as a state reservation.[15] On balance, Stranahan and the others were intent on securing land for the Seminoles and promoting their social well-being; in the process they did not come to grips with the potentially divisive issue of tribal political control within their limited domain.

When John Collier became commissioner of Indian affairs in 1933, one of his major goals was to revitalize tribal societies by investing them with a limited form of sovereignty. The vehicle for implementing these policies was the Wheeler-Howard Bill, which, in a severely attenuated form, became the Indian Reorganization Act of 1934. Once the act became law the tribes were given a year in which to vote on accepting its provisions. In essence this provided a singular window of opportunity for Indians to reorganize themselves along lines laid down by Congress. It offered only limited self-government, and they remained dependent on the federal government for economic support, but that appeared to be a vast improvement over the conditions which prevailed during the preceding half-century. When the IRA balloting was held, 181 tribes voted to accept it while 77 opted to reject it.[16]

Congress passed the Indian Reorganization Act with very little language revealing legislative intent as to implementation, and that opened the way for Collier and his associates to shape it administratively. Even for those tribes voting for inclusion under the IRA and for the exercise of limited self-rule, there remained many questions regarding the legal basis of their sovereignty. Collier's solicitor, Nathan Margold, and his assistant Felix Cohen, addressed this issue in a creative way by issuing an opinion which reaffirmed the concept of inherent tribal sovereignty first articulated by John Marshall.[17] Cohen, who remains the preeminent authority cited on American Indian law, later wrote, "From the earliest years of the Republic the Indian tribes have been recognized as 'distinct, independent, political communities,' and, as such, qualified to exercise powers of self-government, not by virtue of any delegation of powers from the Federal Government, but rather by reason of their original tribal sovereignty." Therefore, the most basic principle of all Indian law is, "*those powers which are lawfully vested in an Indian tribe are not, in general, delegated powers granted by express acts of Congress, but rather inherent powers of limited sovereignty which has never been extinguished.*"[18] True, Indian sovereignty had been reinstituted, but not without restrictions; obviously, in most spheres tribes remained subordinate to federal and state law. Almost before the ink was dry on the Indian Reorganization Act, many tribes had begun the long process of establishing the legal parameters of their authority.

There could be no question that the Seminoles possessed tribal sovereignty—but who would exercise it? At the close of the nineteenth century Florida's Seminoles remained one of the most isolated and reclusive Indian societies in the nation; few outsiders had visited the Everglades camps or understood their social and political organization. Moreover, the tribe's official relationship to the federal government was not altogether clear. Under old treaties dating from the removal era, federal authorities had always negotiated with the Seminoles in the Indian Territory until their government was disbanded; the Florida people were either ignored or subsumed under the larger group. Then, during the 1890s the federal government undertook a series of actions which created at the very least a de facto recognition of the tribe. In 1892 a physician who formerly operated the Women's National Indian Association's mission station at Immokalee, Dr. J. E. Brecht, was appointed federal agent for the Florida Seminoles and served until 1899. Foreseeing a time when the Seminoles could no longer roam freely in south Florida, the government also began to acquire scattered parcels which became the nucleus for federal reservations in Florida. The Bureau of Indian Affairs established a permanent Seminole agency in 1913. However, it was the Seminoles' acceptance of the Indian Reorganization Act which confirmed federal recognition of the group.

Despite the importuning by Collier and Secretary Harold Ickes during their 1935 visit, there was a less than overwhelming Seminole response to the Indian Reorganization Act, and only twenty-one of them cast ballots—all in favor.[19] This act proved to be very significant because it maintained the Seminole right to establish a federally recognized tribal government. But the Seminoles displayed no immediate desire to adopt a constitution and organize as a tribe. Even among the Indians who moved to federal reservations during the 1930s there was limited receptivity to government intervention in their lives; most Seminoles, especially those who remained in the Everglades, were independent people who wanted to be left alone. However, reservation families began to change their perspective after the cattle program was introduced and they became more prosperous. This division was highlighted in a study by the Indian Office's applied anthropology unit.[20] As a result, Commissioner Collier suggested that the Florida Indians should be considered as two separate tribes, thus allowing the acculturated reservation element to apply for a constitution and business charter while the traditionals could remain in their Everglades homes, but nothing came of his proposal. From that point forward, though, federal authorities no longer treated the Florida Indians as a unified tribal entity.

In the 1950s the Miccosukees experienced a cultural and political revitalization under the leadership of Buffalo Tiger, Ingraham Billie, and the Miccosukee General Council, and this presented a problem for the Bureau of Indian Affairs. It now had to contend with two groups—closely related through language, clan, and kinship, yet widely separated by a broad acculturation gap—seeking federal acknowledgment as sovereign tribes. During the darkest years of the termination era, Commissioner Glenn Emmons and other federal officials tried to work out an arrangement which would satisfy both groups while mollifying a Congress intent on curtailing expenditures for Indians.

The threat of termination was a transforming experience for the reservation Seminoles. Indian families saw everything they had worked to build—homes, pasture lands, cattle herds—threatened, and moved to protect themselves by invoking their rights under the Indian Reorganization Act. When the Seminole leaders, severely shaken by their experience with the congressional hearings, opted for sovereignty and a tribal government in 1957, they were initiating a process of tribal definition. Although it is widely assumed that a small Seminole tribe had remained in Florida, in fact no such political entity existed. The Seminole camps were loosely associated through membership in one of several busk groups, that is, they attended the annual busk (fasting) ceremony known as the Green Corn Dance and followed the political dictates of its medicine men and council of elders.[21] By the 1950s this indigenous structure had begun to break down under the impact of two forces. Foremost was a demographic shift as the majority of Seminoles took up residence on federal reservations and continued the acculturation process that estranged them from their traditional kinsmen. Second was the growth of a Baptist Indian constituency and leaders who galvanized the reservation people to form their own tribal government and business enterprises.

A number of observers have depicted the ethos of this new reservation Seminole polity as it evolved between 1933 and 1953. Life on the reservations, although little changed from the depression and war years, still provided experiences which differentiated the residents from their relatives in the Everglades. At the Dania/Hollywood Reservation, most residents had for many years lived in housing provided by the bureau or local support groups, attended government and (later) public schools, sought employment within nearby communities, and generally interacted with the dominant society. On the rural Big Cypress and Brighton Reservations, social orientation remained primarily within the community setting. Initially there were no government housing programs on the outlying reservations, and a tribal housing program was not initiated until the 1960s. The people continued to live in chikee camps, planted their small gardens, and raised a few hogs in addition to cattle. Educational facilities for their children were restricted to reservation day schools.[22] At the Big Cypress Reservation most parents displayed an indifference toward formal education. In addition, poor roads leading from the reservation to towns, as well as the distances involved, limited the opportunity for Indian youngsters to continue their education beyond the elementary years. In contrast, in 1954 the Brighton Reservation people opted to close the day school which had operated there since 1938 so their children could attend public schools in nearby Okeechobee City. At both Big Cypress and Brighton most tribal members either worked with the cattle enterprise or were employed by the BIA in various land clearing and road maintenance operations; likewise, at both locations off-reservation employment opportunities for Indians were almost exclusively in agricultural pursuits.

What had emerged, therefore, was not a single Seminole polity but actually three social and political variants. This is seen in the way each reservation responded to Christianity and the rise of Baptist political influence. Almost from the time of its establishment in 1926 the small Dania/Hollywood Reservation became a fertile ground for Baptists. It was home to a concentration of transient families who came there seeking bureau assistance, and most were headed by females. The residents experienced prolonged and positive contacts with white church members from nearby towns and often attended their services. Importantly, there were no medicine men to conduct a Green Corn Dance ceremony or exert influence over the Dania residents. Following the schism which spawned the Independent Mekusukey Baptist Church, the older First Seminole Baptist Church retained the largest membership, but the congregations found themselves on opposite sides of many political issues affecting the tribe, as well as competing for converts on the Brighton and Big Cypress Reservations.

The families who settled on the Big Cypress Reservation during the 1930s were very conservative Miccosukees from the lower Everglades. They were accustomed to following the dictates of their medicine men, so when Josie Billie converted to Christianity in 1945, twenty-two of his followers and their families followed his lead. But there may have been motives involved other than merely following a traditional leader. Ethel Cutler Freeman believes that these Indians came to the reservation and converted "because they did not belong to clans which would inherit official positions or status. Status could no longer be gained by war and hunting prowess. The acceptance of Christianity gave these Seminoles prestige. Church positions became goals for the ambitious."[23] A Southern Baptist mission church was erected in 1948, and the Miccosukees now transferred their social and religious conservatism to a new venue. Soon church members were forbidden to attend the Green Corn Dance, and the ceremony was banned from the reservation. This completed the split with relatives on the Tamiami Trail, but it did not necessarily bring them closer to the Dania congregations. The Independent Big Cypress Mission was founded at the reservation in 1966, but the residents had already gained a reputation for being the most rock-ribbed conservative Baptist constituency among the Seminoles.

By comparison, a Christian church was not allowed on the Brighton Reservation until 1951, largely because up to that point the people retained loyalty to their medicine man Frank Shore and a council of elders. Then both the Southern Baptists and the Independent Baptists erected churches. Within a few years a dramatic acculturational shift had taken place on the Brighton Reservation; even members of the medicine man's family had converted to Christianity. These reservation Baptists, like the congregations at Dania/Hollywood and Big Cypress, essentially followed their own agendas and did not vote in concert. Nevertheless, they were in fundamental agreement on a number of social issues and comprised a very significant and predictable voting bloc throughout the 1950s and beyond.

Long before a Seminole government materialized, the earliest political stirrings appear to have been dominated by the cattle interests.[24] The Seminoles' first halting effort to choose their cattle trustees through the elective process has been hailed as a preliminary adumbration of tribal self-government, but realistically the trustees were limited in their ability to make policy decisions due to governmental constraints. The agency superintendent and cattle manager, both non-Indians, were charged with making the Seminole cattle program function, and the trustees were expected to facilitate their efforts.[25] Even though the first leaders of tribal government were Baptists and cattlemen — two favored groups — the bureau's paternalism would persist so long as the tribe was dependent on federal funding. It ended only after the Seminoles achieved economic sufficiency and demanded a greater voice in their affairs as a result of the Indian self-determination movement.

The tribal constitution adopted in 1957 was a document which reflected the changing makeup of the Seminole polity over time. For example, through the provision of at-large seats it recognized the existence of Seminoles who did not live on the three federal reservations. Within six years the document was amended in favor of a council and officers elected exclusively by reservation residents. This consolidation of power signaled a triumph for the acculturated Christian element on the reservations even though the constitution specifically recognized the civil and religious rights of all tribal members. Also, by that time the newly organized Miccosukee tribe provided an alternative forum for cultural traditionalists. But even with power vested exclusively in the hands of reservation Seminoles, there remained the problem of bringing the three communities together for unified decision making. This was addressed through the device of having the chairman and president elected on an at-large basis by the voters on all three reservations. That ostensibly produced leaders who could transcend the parochial interests of the individual constituencies, and to a degree it succeeded. Yet by continuing to elect the council and board members from each reservation, the potential for division persisted. As an illustration, for many years the Tribal Council stalled on contracting the Big Cypress day school from the bureau, fearing it might not be self-supporting and would absorb tribal funds meant to benefit the other reservations. It would take very strong leadership from the chairman and president to persuade the reservation representatives to set aside policy differences—and in some cases personal animosities—for the common good.

More often than not the council and board members defended the interests of their reservations at a time when the Seminoles were trying to make do with very limited financial resources, prior to the existence of tax-exempt cigarettes and bingo. In some situations there were long-standing family and clan disputes which crossed reservation lines and made it difficult for individuals to get along. Certainly the early stages of Seminole tribal government were marked by numerous instances where the chairman or president came under personal attack—recall, for instance, Mike Osceola's accusations against Bill Osceola or the efforts to oust Joe Dan Osceola—and even a strong figure such as Howard Tommie, who typified Indian self-determination efforts in the 1970s, counted his inability to get the tribal councilmen to always work together as one of his administration's major shortcomings.

Nor could all of the resistance be laid merely on reservation parochialism. Several special interests had emerged within the tribe. The cattlemen's association, for one, remained a potent political force which commanded the lion's share of tribal economic resources.[26] Also, certain revenue-producing proposals, such as the sale of liquor, encountered vigorous resistance from the Baptists on all reservations and were dropped as options. Nevertheless, by the late 1970s there was already a process emerging by which special religious, economic, and reservation interests began to be subordinated to tribal interests. Council and board members were still keenly aware of their obligation to constituents, but they also took a broader perspective on policy issues affecting the entire tribe. All three reservations united in support of the land claims and water rights cases which took decades to resolve.

Perhaps the most striking reordering of social and political relationships in this Seminole polity was the new status accorded women. Historically, Seminole women filled traditional gender roles which assigned them a great degree of informal power. Emulating the old Creek-style matrilineal/matrilocal society, women perpetuated the clan lineage and owned the home, livestock, and other property. Many women also became respected for their knowledge of herbal medicine and were often engaged as curers. The men always consulted the women when major decisions were made in council, but they were never afforded positions of formal leadership—this, too, seems to have been a holdover from Creek cultural origins.[27] During the transition period in the early twentieth century when most Seminoles shifted from a hunting-trapping subsistence economy toward reservation life, it was the women who led the way by adapting to agricultural wage labor in south Florida. They also became quite entrepreneurial. In addition to selling berries, venison, and other food items to local residents, they sewed patchwork garments, made basketry, and produced other items for the tourist trade. Once the families moved to reservations, the women generally accepted government schools and healthcare for their children. Seminole women were also the first to accept Christianity and became the staunchest supporters of the Baptist churches.[28]

During the struggle to avoid termination it was the educated young women who served as interpreters for the Seminole delegation appearing before congressional committees in Washington and Florida to protest termination. Later they assisted bureau officials and Indian leaders in explaining the constitution that had been written for the tribe. The new government afforded Seminole women an opportunity to assume formal leadership positions. At the first election, women were chosen for seats on both the Tribal Council and Board of Directors, while Laura Mae Osceola was appointed to the influential position of secretary-treasurer.[29] This trend toward gender parity within the new polity reached its zenith in 1967 with the election of Betty Mae Jumper as chairman of the Seminole tribe.[30] She inherited the reins of government at a time when it first confronted a labyrinth of Great Society programs affecting Indian tribes. Her administration grappled with the rising expectations of the people and prepared the way for economic breakthroughs in the 1970s.

As individual Indians came to think of themselves as members of the Seminole tribe rather than primarily Hollywood, Brighton, or Big Cypress people, there were resultant psychological and social effects. The most important of these were increased self-esteem and ethnic identification. Even though most Florida Indian children are enrolled in public school, researchers have found that students attending the day schools of both Florida tribes tend to identify themselves positively as Indians. This is particularly true for Miccosukee youngsters whose school features a heavy cultural preservation component.[31] As another way of confirming ethnic identity, both the Seminoles and Miccosukees initiated annual powwows at which Indians from across the nation come together to share their music, dancing, and crafts with each other and with visitors to the reservations. The Florida tribes have cultivated pan-Indian contacts as a basis for broader economic and political action. Following World War II, Florida State University adopted the name "Seminoles" for its athletic teams, and both the institution and tribe have capitalized on that association. Tribal leaders attend functions at the Tallahassee school—Betty Mae Jumper was awarded an honorary doctorate in 1994—and an intensive summer educational program for Indian youngsters has been held on the campus since 1980.[32] A scholarship fund established by the state legislature provides financial assistance for members of the two tribes who pursue higher education.[33] Today Indians are involved in virtually every aspect of social and cultural life in south Florida; equally important, most Seminoles appear to be comfortable with both their ethnic identity and with wider society.

On another level, the emerging Seminole polity participated in a process which Stephen Cornell has identified as the creation of a "supratribal consciousness" among American Indians, the development of a self-conscious Indian identity that shapes the behavior and thought of individuals and groups.[34] Although the tribe remains the primary source of identification for most Indians, this new identity transcends tribal membership; nor is it coextensive with governmental or popular conceptions of who is an Indian. It is perhaps most strongly felt among urban American Indian communities which developed out of the massive demographic shifts resulting from World War II as well as BIA relocation and termination policies. Today a host of "American Indian" and "Native American" organizations join with the various tribal governments and in numerous cooperative political efforts on behalf of both tribal and supratribal interests. "Indeed, it is supratribalism that has made such politics possible. An Indian consciousness provides a distinctive basis for political action, and in the twentieth century it has transformed the politics of Indian-white relations."[35]

Achieving this sense of "Indianness" was not an easy process. The concept of "Indian" was a European taxonomic construct implying perceived similarities among the native peoples of the Americas. However, the natives of the New World did not have a concept of themselves as Indians. In fact, native societies were well aware of the differences that separated them from other groups and exhibited a powerful ethnocentrism. The tribe was the center of their universe and they often referred to themselves by names that meant "persons," "the people," or "human beings," and by implication others were something else. Since the seventeenth century there have been attempts to craft pan-Indian unity to resist European invaders. Some outstanding leaders such as King Philip, Pontiac, and Tecumseh briefly united disparate tribes, yet their movements failed. Early in this century the Society of American Indians, comprised heavily of acculturated individuals educated at the Hampton Institute and the Carlisle School, attempted to generate a national political movement, but it foundered as most Indians were still committed to tribal interests. The Indian New Deal under John Collier held out a promise for tribal regeneration, but did little to promote a national Indian identity. Only with the crisis of the 1950s when the Indian Reorganization Act faded, and termination threatened every Indian nation, did the traditional reservation and urban Indians unite. The National Congress of American Indians was founded in 1944 to articulate Indian concerns and help coordinate the efforts of tribal governments to resist federal policies. By the 1960s regional associations of tribes appeared, as did groups with more radical agendas, including the American Indian Movement and the National Indian Youth Council;

the latter was influenced by the rhetoric and tactics of the civil rights movement. Tribal and supratribal identities became linked. The survival of the tribe required an Indian consciousness and the ability to act as Indians and confront federal policy on its own terms. Federal Indian policy had turned tribal politics into Indian politics and greatly increased the tribes' political capacity.[36]

This dynamic movement was already under way by the late 1950s, but Florida Indians were initially far removed both physically and psychologically from it. Even after inaugurating their government in 1957, acculturated Seminoles living on the reservations remained socially and politically very conservative. Any cleavage over religious and cultural issues had been resolved following organization of the Miccosukee tribe, which provided an alternative for those hoping to keep the old ways, and there was much shifting of membership from one group to the other in the early years. As a result, little overt conflict occurred within the tribal government between traditionals and acculturateds such as existed on many western reservations. Those animosities often dated from the late nineteenth-century reservation experience when federal authorities and Christian reformers attempted to break down tribalism in a variety of ways. Most often government agents accomplished this by appointing acculturated mixed-bloods to positions of importance, or initiating tribal courts and police which undercut authority of the old chiefs. By contrast, in Florida the first elected Seminole leaders were full-bloods; they were also English-speaking Baptist ministers and cattle owners accustomed to working closely with agency bureaucrats and local agribusiness interests. The relationship between the Bureau of Indians Affairs and the Seminoles, while not perfect, had at least been one of tolerant support, and the tribal leaders were not anxious to abjure such an arrangement.

Relatively few Seminoles had ever lived anywhere except in the Everglades or on the reservations; thus they did not identify with the urban Indian experience or empathize with the extreme ideology of such groups as AIM and NIYC. Nonetheless, Seminoles were not oblivious to the winds of change sweeping the land during the 1960s and 1970s. They were aware of the seizure of Alcatraz, the sacking of the BIA building in Washington, and the clash between the FBI and Indians at Wounded Knee. They were not unsympathetic, they simply avoided direct confrontation—especially if it threatened violence. By the second decade of tribal organization the Seminoles had developed more subtle strategies for achieving their ends. One observer, assessing tribal leadership during this period, found that "they've learned to play the game and rather successfully.... They've pretty much made Red Power into Green Power."[37] In the long run, Seminole realization of economic success paved the way for political power; it enabled the tribe to gain leverage through forming its own political action committee to support candidates at the state and local levels.

In 1968 the Seminole Tribe of Florida ventured into the supratribal realm on a limited scale when it joined with three other federally recognized groups in the Southeast—the Eastern Band of Cherokee Indians, the Mississippi Band of Choctaw Indians, and the Miccosukee Tribe of Indians of Florida—to form an intertribal council. The following year United Southeastern Tribes, Inc. was created as a nonprofit corporation.[38] A board of directors is composed of the chairmen from each tribe plus one other member selected by the respective tribal councils. The board elects its president, vice president, secretary, and treasurer for two-year terms. In the first decade this organization grew rapidly and its name was changed in 1979 to United South and Eastern Tribes, reflecting increased membership that included several tribes from the northeastern region of the country.

A number of state and regional Indian organizations were created in the 1960s to increase the tribes' capacity to deal with the federal and state governments, but few had a discernible impact. USET remains one of the most successful efforts of this period, and its significance was captured by an anthropologist and former tribal planner for the Mississippi Choctaws: "The quarterly meetings of USET resulted in tribal chairmen or chiefs and members of their tribal councils sharing ideas and exchanging views. While quite different problems existed on the major southeastern reservations, there was a general sense of movement toward greater tribal self-government among all the tribes. Furthermore, the existence of USET promoted exchange between the growing technical staffs working for the tribal governments on each of the reservations."[39] The USET leaders realized that individually their tribes were small in population and lacked the political strength to have an effect upon the quality of services provided to them by the federal government. As a unified group, though, they could lobby more effectively in Washington, and their first successful effort was to improve health services for the tribes. Because of their geographical separation from "Indian Country," USET complained that tribes in the southeastern United States were inadequately served by the Indian Health Service Area Office in Oklahoma City, and in 1971 an IHS Program Office was established for USET members. Since 1975 the offices of both organizations have been located in Nashville, Tennessee, and USET membership has expanded to include numerous tribes.

The Seminoles provided significant leadership for several national organizations during their formative years; these brought together Indian leaders from across the country, thereby fostering the development of supratribal identity throughout the 1960s and 1970s. Betty Mae Jumper gained a great deal of attention as the first woman elected to the tribal chairmanship and became identified with the changing status of Indian women nationally. In addition to representing the tribe in negotiations with the federal bureaucracy, she also served on the National Council on Indian Opportunities. In 1970 Jumper was named one of the "Top Indian Women" of the year, and attended the National Seminar for American Indian Women, in Colorado.[40] And it was her administration that helped get USET organized; later, Seminoles including Joe Dan Osceola, Michael Tiger, and Howard Tommie served as early presidents of the organization. After the Seminole government stabilized and its economic status improved, Howard Tommie became active in the National Tribal Chairmen's Association and served on the NCAI litigation committee; he also chaired the National Indian Health Board. He appeared frequently before congressional committees giving testimony of a range of issues affecting Indian tribes, and was outspoken in support of Public Law 93-638, the Indian Self-Determination Act of 1975.[41] On the state level, the physically imposing and socially engaging Tommie—always a striking figure in his Seminole patchwork jacket—emerged as the prototype for a new style of articulate, politically savvy Indian representation in Tallahassee.

Governor Reubin Askew, by an executive order in 1974, created the Florida Governor's Council on Indian Affairs to advise his office on issues of concern to the tribes.[42] The council is cochaired by the leaders of the two federally recognized tribes, while its fifteen-member board is comprised of both Indian and non-Indian appointees. With a permanent staff and small budget, the council mounts an effective lobbying effort with both the executive and legislative branches of state government, and provides an Indian perspective on issues ranging from university scholarships for Indian youths and minority contracting to control of development impacting environmentally sensitive tribal lands. The council also acts as a conduit agency for several federal employment and training grant programs for Indian citizens who are not members of Florida's two federally recognized tribes. This function has occasionally led to friction between the Seminole and Miccosukee members and nonrecognized Indian groups in the state, often with the council staff caught in the crossfire.[43] On balance, though, the governor's council is recognized as a significant effort to provide all Indian citizens of Florida a greater voice at the state capital.

By the end of the 1970s the Seminole Tribe of Florida had emerged as both an exemplar of tribal autonomy and a major factor in developing the new supratribal Indian identity nationally. Through participation in pan-Indian associations such as NCAI and NTCA, it helped to heighten the awareness of tribal issues and shaped the national political agenda concerning Indian policy. The Seminoles— and the Miccosukees as well—also exercised initiative in helping found USET, reputedly the most significant regional Indian association in the nation today. Within Florida the Seminoles have established a new cultural, economic, and political identity. Gone are the days when they were considered merely exotic primitives who lived in thatched-roof chikees, created colorful patchwork garments, and wrestled alligators for the tourists. Their past remains a central element in their ethnic awareness, but the Seminoles are also moving toward the twenty-first century. Thanks to the establishment of a solid economic base, as well as the aggressive assertion of tribal legal rights and sovereignty during the first quarter-century following organization, today's Seminole and Miccosukee tribes face the future with certainty about their identity as a people. Their land and water rights are unquestioned; their ability to pursue viable, if occasionally unorthodox, avenues of economic development through bingo and tax-free cigarette sales is assured; and they have an opportunity to play a significant role in the future of their state and nation. Seminole assumption of sovereignty has at long last been realized.

Epilogue

nd so my trilogy concludes. It chronicles a century-long cycle of transformation which began with the Seminoles ranging freely across the Everglades, witnessed them surviving both the Great Depression and congressional termination, and ultimately emerging as a federally recognized tribe endowed with legal and political sovereignty. Logically the story should end at this point, but only rarely does a historian willingly invoke cloture on such a rich field of inquiry; the end of one phase can be the epiphany of another. Thus it is appropriate to consider the direction which future research might take.

A useful course has been suggested by Frederick Hoxie, who remarked, "Conceptually, historians of native communities would benefit from thinking of Indian history as an aspect of American social history. As such, Indian history can be understood as the study of a particular group's institutions and ideas about itself, as well as its relationships with other groups within the larger society. If this theme were pursued, Indian historians could address both the distinctiveness of the native experience and the relationship between native history and the development of national and regional cultures."[1]

Although the writing of tribal history necessarily involves relationships between Indian people and the larger society, certain timespans lend themselves more readily to such analysis—for example, periods of prolonged and intensive contact. Accordingly, nothing would be more germane to Hoxie's admonition than examining contemporary Seminoles in the context of an emerging multicultural American society as we enter the twenty-first century. In recent decades south Florida has evolved into a volatile mixture of races and nationalities, and the Seminoles comprise a small but significant component of this mix. Under the aggressive leadership of Chairman James Billie—presently serving his fifth term—the tribe's deliberate strivings for political and economic empowerment, as well as social equity, have certainly paralleled those of other racial and ethnic minorities throughout the region and nation. To adequately assess how Seminoles fit into this social synergy, at least four major themes should be explored.

The first theme is that of cultural and social regeneration within the Indian community. Despite their sudden economic resurgence, the Seminole people still suffer many of the social ills which afflict the larger society—drugs, alcohol, educational underachievement of youth, family violence, and underemployment, to name only a few. And like other minorities, they still feel a degree of alienation from the larger society, although the discrimination experienced by Seminoles is neither as pervasive nor as virulent as that encountered by some Indians elsewhere in the nation. Building upon programs established by the Great Society, the tribe expends a large portion of its revenues to offer a range of services for members including drug and alcohol rehabilitation, family and elderly services, and community recreational and educational opportunities. Thus tribal government has created an integrated family/community-improvement policy akin to that advocated by the federal government. As such, the Seminoles might serve as a model for similar national and local initiatives.

A second theme is continued economic development which allows Indians to control their own destiny. Utilizing cash flows generated primarily from cigarettes and bingo, the Seminole tribe has expanded into a broad spectrum of investments ranging from ownership of a Sheraton Hotel and various rental properties to development of reservation lands. At one time the Seminoles also underwrote bingo for several western tribes. Additionally, the older tribal enterprises, such as commercial leases, cattle, and citrus, remain profitable. So long as revenues from these interests remain high, tribal government will be able to absorb the costs of social services which the federal bureaucracy no longer provides, distribute dividends to its members, and invest for the future. Any radical alteration in economic prospects would have a concomitant social and political impact.

This leads to consideration of a third crucial theme: the constant testing of Indian legal and political rights, especially as they reduce tax revenues to various state and local governments. Although Seminole sovereignty within their lands has been well established through both statute and case law, tribal leaders exhibit concern that federal and state governments will seek to reign in expansion of bingo by enforcing the 1988 Indian Gaming Act. This is an outgrowth of rising Indian fears nationally that the federal judiciary, and especially the Rehnquist Court, can no longer be considered the greatest defender of tribal sovereignty—although in early 1994 a federal appeals court decision affirmed Indian rights to conduct casino gambling on the reservations free of state interference. This decision, if not overturned, could translate into many additional millions of dollars for the tribe and further confirm its sovereignty.

A final and still somewhat ill-defined theme, but one which is growing in significance, is the relationship of Seminoles and other American Indian tribes to the global issue of sovereignty for native peoples. The demand for self-determination has become a universal political theme, ranging from competing tribal entities in postapartheid South Africa and other nations of that continent, to the Maoris of New Zealand and aborigines of Australia, and even to the Hawaiian independence movement. In each of these instances there is a proclivity to compare local situations to that of American Indian tribes which have achieved a high degree of economic and political autonomy within a broader constitutional system. There is a high probability that American Indian tribes will become more involved in this movement; they are already acknowledged internationally as models of self-government, and the Seminoles, because of their high visibility and record of business success, could be one of the groups most widely emulated. It will be instructive to see how future scholarship synthesizes tribalism and nationalism, two seemingly antithetical forces which have emerged as major determinative factors for much of the world in our time.

Notes

1. WHY THE SEMINOLES?

1. Frederick E. Hoxie, "The Curious Story of Reformers and the American Indian," in *Indians in American History*, ed. Hoxie (Arlington Heights IL: Harlan Davidson, 1988), 219.

2. Francis Paul Prucha, *American Indian Policy in Crisis: Christian Reformers and the Indian, 1865–1900* (Norman: University of Oklahoma Press, 1976), 57.

3. Vine Deloria Jr. and Clifford Lytle, *The Nations Within: The Past and Future of American Indian Sovereignty* (New York: Pantheon Books, 1984), 140–53.

4. D. E. Murphy, "Final Report of the Indian Emergency Conservation Work and Civilian Conservation Corps–Indian Division Program, 1933–1942," typescript.

5. Alison R. Bernstein, *American Indians and World War II: Toward a New Era in Indian Affairs* (Norman: University of Oklahoma Press, 1991), 67–68.

6. U.S. Selective Service System, *Special Groups*, Special Monograph Series no. 10, vol. 1 (Washington DC: Government Printing Office, 1953), 8.

7. Deloria and Lytle, *The Nations Within*, 190–91.

8. Senate, *Survey of Conditions of Indian Affairs, Partial Report*, rept. no. 310, 78th Cong., 2d sess., 1943.

9. Senate, *Hearings on S. 1218, Repealing the So-Called Wheeler-Howard Act*, 78th Cong., 2d sess., 1944.

10. *U.S. Statutes at Large* 60 (1947): 1049.

11. Lyman S. Tyler, *A History of Indian Policy* (Washington DC: Bureau of Indian Affairs, 1973), 164.

12. James E. Officer, "Termination as Federal Policy: An Overview," in *Indian Self-Rule: First-Hand Accounts of Indian-White Relations from Roosevelt to Reagan*, ed. Kenneth R. Philp (Salt Lake City: Howe Brothers, 1986), 120.

13. Sol Tax, "Federal Indian Policy, 1945–1960," in *Indian Self-Rule*, ed. Philp 133.

14. Richard Drinnon, *Keeper of the Concentration Camps: Dillon S. Myer and American Racism* (Berkeley: University of California Press, 1987), 8–10.

15. *U.S. Statutes at Large* 67 (1953): 588.

16. House, *House Concurrent Resolution 108, Expressing the Sense of Congress That Certain Tribes of Indians Should Be Freed from Federal Supervision*, 83d Cong., 1st sess., 1953; hereafter abbreviated HCR 108.

17. Officer, "Termination as Federal Policy," 114.

18. Deloria and Lytle, *The Nations Within*, 191.

19. Donald L. Fixico, *Termination and Relocation: Federal Indian Policy, 1945–1960* (Albuquerque: University of New Mexico Press, 1986), 16.

20. Larry W. Burt, *Tribalism in Crisis: Federal Indian Policy, 1953–1961* (Albuquerque: University of New Mexico Press, 1982), 9–18; Fixico, *Termination and Relocation*, 180–82.

21. File 11100-1946-Seminole-224, BIACF, RG75, NA.

22. Donald S. Parman, "The Indian and the Civilian Conservation Corps," in *The American Indian: Essays from Pacific Historical Review*, ed. Norris Hundley (Santa Barbara CA: Clio Books, 1974), 127–45.

23. Harry A. Kersey Jr., *The Florida Seminoles and the New Deal, 1933–1942* (Gainesville: University Presses of Florida, 1989), 164–67.

24. James W. Covington, "The Seminoles and Selective Service in World War II," *Florida Anthropologist* 32 (June 1979): 46–51.

25. Harry A. Kersey Jr., "A 'New Red Atlantis': John Collier's Encounter with the

Florida Seminoles in 1935," *Florida Historical Quarterly* 66 (October 1987): 131–51.

26. Seminole Tribe of Florida, Inc., *Seminole Tribe of Florida Twentieth Anniversary of Tribal Organization, Saturday August 20, 1977*, mimeographed (Hollywood FL, 1977), 21.

27. James O. Buswell III, "Florida Seminole Religious Ritual: Resistance and Change" (Ph.D. diss., St. Louis University, 1972), 261–62.

28. First Seminole Indian Baptist Church, "Souvenir Brochure, Dedicatory Service, First Seminole Indian Baptist Church (Four Miles west of Dania) Dania, Florida, May 29, 1949," 2–3.

29. Ethel Cutler Freeman, "Cultural Stability and Change Among the Seminoles of Florida" in *Men and Cultures: Selected Papers*, ed. Anthony F. C. Wallace (Philadelphia: University of Pennsylvania Press, 1960), 251.

30. Robert T. King, "Clan Affiliation and Leadership among the Twentieth Century Florida Indians," *Florida Historical Quarterly* 55 (October 1976): 143–45.

31. James W. Covington, "Trail Indians of Florida," *Florida Historical Quarterly* 58 (July 1979): 37–57.

32. Kersey, *Florida Seminoles and the New Deal*, 106–7.

33. Officer, "Termination as Federal Policy," 115.

34. Tyler, *History of Indian Policy*, 164.

35. Tyler, *History of Indian Policy*, 70.

2. TERMINATION AND TURMOIL

1. Deloria and Lytle, *The Nations Within*, 195; Clayton R. Koppes, "From New Deal to Termination: Liberalism and Indian Policy, 1933–1953," *Pacific Historical Review* 46 (November 1977): 543–66.

2. Arthur V. Watkins, "Termination of Federal Supervision: The Removal of Restrictions over Indian Property and Person," *Annals of the American Academy of Political and Social Science* 311 (May 1957): 55.

3. Fixico, *Termination and Relocation*, 105–6.

4. Burt, *Tribalism in Crisis*, 39.

5. Interview with George A. Smathers, 6 November 1992, SEM 201A, UFOHA, 4.

6. Henry Ringling North and John Alden Hatch, *The Circus King* (New York: Doubleday, 1960), 321–31.

7. Deloria and Lytle, *The Nations Within*, 196–97.

8. Paul G. Rogers, interview 23 March 1988, SEM 197A, UFOHA, 4.

9. Fixico, *Termination and Relocation*, 103.

10. Library of Congress, Legislative Reference Service, *Digest of Public General Bills With Index*, 83d Cong., 2d sess., no. 7, final issue 1954, 7321.

11. U.S. Congress, *Termination of Federal Supervision Over Certain Tribes of Indians, Joint Hearings Before the Subcommittees of the Committee of Interior and Insular Affairs, Congress of the United States, Eighty-third Congress, Second Session on s. 2747 and h.r. 7321, Part 8 Seminole Indians, Florida, March 1 and 2, 1954, 1030.

12. U.S. Congress, *Termination of Federal Supervision*, 1027.

13. U.S. Congress, *Termination of Federal Supervision*, 1037.

14. U.S. Congress, *Termination of Federal Supervision*, 1053.

15. U.S. Congress, *Termination of Federal Supervision*, 1053.

16. U.S. Congress, *Termination of Federal Supervision*, 1054.

17. U.S. Congress, *Termination of Federal Supervision*, 1058.

18. U.S. Congress, *Termination of Federal Supervision*, 1059.

19. U.S. Congress, *Termination of Federal Supervision*, 1038.

20. U.S. Congress, *Termination of Federal Supervision*, 1039.

21. U.S. Congress, *Termination of Federal Supervision*, 1119

22. U.S. Congress, *Termination of Federal Supervision*, 1122.

23. Harry A. Kersey Jr. and Rochelle Kushin, "Ivy Stranahan and the 'Friends of the Seminoles,' 1899–1971," *Broward Legacy* 1 (October 1976): 6–11.

24. U.S. Congress, *Termination of Federal Supervision*, 1131.

25. Glenn L. Emmons to Ivy Stranahan, 17 December 1953, box 8, file 1, Indian Federal Agencies 1915–1951; Smathers to Stranahan, 13 December 1953, box 8, file 4, Indian Legislation 1951–1957, scfhs.

26. U.S. Congress, *Termination of Federal Supervision*, 1132–33.

27. U.S. Congress, *Termination of Federal Supervision*, 1137.

28. U.S. Congress, *Termination of Federal Supervision*, 1108.

29. U.S. Congress, *Termination of Federal Supervision*, 1108.

30. H. P. Davis to Commissioner of Indian Affairs, 11 March 1953, file 163-1955-Seminole-050, biacf, rg75, na.

31. U.S. Congress, *Termination of Federal Supervision*, 1135.

32. U.S. Congress, *Termination of Federal Supervision*, 1078.

33. U.S. Congress, *Termination of Federal Supervision*, 1085.

34. U.S. Congress, *Termination of Federal Supervision*, 1087.

35. U.S. Congress, *Termination of Federal Supervision*, 1088.

36. U.S. Congress, *Termination of Federal Supervision*, 1089.

37. U.S. Congress, *Termination of Federal Supervision*, 1093.

38. Spessard L. Holland to Stranahan, 24 October 1954, box 8, file 4, scfhs.

39. "Should the American Indian Be Given Full Citizenship Responsibility?" debate between Sen. George Smathers and Sen. Arthur Watkins, 22 April 1954, Dumont Television Station, Washington DC, quoted in Fixico, *Termination and Relocation*, 105–6.

40. Smathers interview, 5–6.

41. U.S. Congress, *Termination of Federal Supervision*, 1079–80.

42. Morrill M. Tozier, "Report on the Florida Seminoles, December, 1954," 2, file 17148-1952-Seminole-077, part I-A, BIACF, RG75, NA.

43. Tozier, "Report on the Florida Seminoles," 14.

44. Tozier, "Report on the Florida Seminoles," 19.

45. Tozier, "Report on the Florida Seminoles," 21.

46. Tozier, "Report on the Florida Seminoles," 22.

47. Emmons to Morton H. Silver, 5 April 1955, file 163-1955-Seminole-050, BIACF, RG75, NA.

48. House, *Hearings Before the Subcommittee on Indian Affairs of the Committee on Interior and Insular Affairs, Seminole Indians, Florida*, pursuant to H. Res. 30, 6–7 April 1955 serial, no. 8, 84th Cong., 2.

49. *U.S. Statutes at Large* 67 (1953): 588.

50. Richard M. Scammon, ed., *American Votes: A Handbook of Contemporary American Election Statistics* (New York: Macmillan, 1956), 54.

51. House, *Hearings Before the Subcommittee on Indian Affairs*, 3.

52. House, *Hearings Before the Subcommittee on Indian Affairs*, 18.

53. House, *Hearings Before the Subcommittee on Indian Affairs*, 7.

54. House, *Hearings Before the Subcommittee on Indian Affairs*, 27.

55. House, *Hearings Before the Subcommittee on Indian Affairs*, 26.

56. House, *Hearings Before the Subcommittee on Indian Affairs*, 26.

57. House, *Hearings Before the Subcommittee on Indian Affairs*, 45.

58. House, *Hearings Before the Subcommittee on Indian Affairs*, 74.

59. House, *Hearings Before the Subcommittee on Indian Affairs*, 37.

60. Bertram D. Scott to Emmons, 20 April 1955, file 163-1955-Seminole-050, BIACF, RG75, NA.

61. Haley to Scott, 22 April 1955, HP.

62. Francis E. Walter to Haley, 15 April 1955, HP.

63. *U.S. Statutes at Large* 70 (1956): 581.

64. 1954 Report of Congressional Committee of Friends of the Seminoles of Florida, file 163-1955-Seminole-050, part 1, BIACF, RG75, NA.

65. Smathers interview, 4.

66. Oliver La Farge, "Termination of Federal Supervision: Disintegration and

the American Indians," *Annals of the American Academy of Political and Social Science* 311 (May 1957): 44.

3. ORGANIZING A TRIBAL GOVERNMENT

1. *U.S. Statutes at Large* 48 (1934): 984.
2. Peru Farver to Emmons, 6 June 1955, file 17148-1952-Seminole-077, part I-A, BIACF, RG75, NA.
3. J. E. Davis to Emmons, 9 August 1955, file 17148-1952-Seminole-077, BIACF, RG75, NA.
4. Robert D. Mitchell to Buffalo Tiger, 12 April 1955, file 10905-1955-Seminole-260, BIACF, RG75, NA.
5. Scott to Emmons, 18 March 1955, file 163-1955-Seminole-050, BIACF, RG75, NA.
6. O. B. White to Emmons, 21 March 1955, file 163-1955-Seminole-050, BIACF, RG75, NA.
7. Emmons to Ingraham Billie, 6 May 1955, file 18394-1955-Seminole-053.3, BIACF, RG75, NA.
8. Dante B. Fascell to Emmons, 23 May 1955, file 163-1955-Seminole-050, BIACF, RG75, NA.
9. Emmons to Fascell, 27 May 1955, file 163-1955-Seminole-050, BIACF, RG75, NA.
10. Emmons to Stranahan, 2 November 1955, file 10530-1955-Seminole-070, BIACF, RG75, NA.
11. Burt, *Tribalism in Crisis*, 72.
12. Burt, *Tribalism in Crisis*, 120–21.
13. Covington, "Trail Indians of Florida," 48.
14. Mikasuki General Council to LeRoy Collins, 25 October 1956, file 10530-1955-Seminole-070, BIACF, RG75, NA.
15. *Tampa Sunday Tribune*, 10 April 1955, 1A, 14A.
16. Emmons to Stranahan, 10 April 1956, file 10530-1955-Seminole-070, BIACF, RG75, NA.
17. Scott to Emmons, 17 November 1956, file 163-1955-Seminole-050, BIACF, RG75, NA.
18. Freeman to Emmons, 10, 20 November and 13 December 1956, file 163-1955-Seminole-050, part III, BIACF, RG75, NA.
19. King, "The Florida Seminole Polity, 1858–1978" (Ph.D. diss., University of Florida, 1978), 163; interview with Reginald W. Quinn, 13 December 1973, SEM 99AB, UFOHA.

20. Quinn to Homer Jenkins, 26 March 1957, file 13671-1957-Seminole-055, BIACF, RG75, NA; cited hereafter as the Quinn Report.

21. Quinn interview, 7–8.

22. Quinn Report, 4.

23. King, "Florida Seminole Polity," 164; King, "Clan Affiliation," 138–52.

24. Covington, *The Seminoles of Florida* (Gainesville: University Presses of Florida, 1993), 239.

25. Seminole Tribe, *Twentieth Anniversary*, 11.

26. U.S. Department of the Interior, Bureau of Indian Affairs, *Indian Affairs Manual 83-1, Tribal Government* (Washington DC: Government Printing Office, 1959).

27. Quinn interview, 1.

28. Quinn interview, 2.

29. Quinn interview, 2.

30. Interviews with Bill Osceola, SEM 207; Jackie Willie, SEM 208; Jim O'Toole Osceola, SEM 203; and Laura Mae Osceola, SEM 209, 18 May 1992, UFOHA.

31. Brian W. Pietrzak, "Seminole Tribal Government: The Formative Years, 1957–1982" (master's thesis, Florida Atlantic University, 1988), 67.

32. Bureau of Indian Affairs, *Constitution and Bylaws of the Seminole Tribe of Florida, ratified August 21, 1957* (Washington DC: Government Printing Office, 1958), 1.

33. Bureau of Indian Affairs, *Constitution and Bylaws*, 2.

34. Bureau of Indian Affairs, *Constitution and Bylaws*, 3.

35. Laurence M. Hauptman, "Africa View: John Collier, the British Colonial Service and American Indian Policy, 1933–1945," *The Historian* 48 (May 1986): 369–70.

36. Bureau of Indian Affairs, *Constitution and Bylaws*, 5.

37. Bureau of Indian Affairs, *Constitution and Bylaws*, 5.

38. Bureau of Indian Affairs, *Constitution and Bylaws*, 5.

39. Bureau of Indian Affairs, *Constitution and Bylaws*, 5.

40. Pietrzak, "Seminole Tribal Government," 70.

41. Bureau of Indian Affairs, *Constitution and Bylaws*, 7.

42. Bureau of Indian Affairs, *Corporate Charter of the Seminole Tribe of Florida, ratified August 21, 1957* (Washington DC: Government Printing Office, 1958), 1.

43. Bureau of Indian Affairs, *Corporate Charter*, 3.

44. Quinn Report, 7.

45. *Miami Daily News*, 24 July 1957, 6A; *Fort Lauderdale News*, 3 March 1957, 5A; *Miami Herald*, 6 March 1957, 6A.

46. Quinn Report, 15.

47. Quinn Report, 16.

48. Quinn Report, 17.

49. *Miami Herald*, 14 July 1957, 2A.

50. Mike Osceola to Smathers, 9 July 1957, box 11, file 11G-1957, GASP.

51. *Orlando Evening Star*, 15 July 1957, 7A.

52. *Miami Daily News*, 15 July 1957, 5A.

53. *Jacksonville Journal*, 14 July 1957, 7A.

54. Emmons to Stranahan, 1 May 1957, file 163-1955-Seminole-050, BIACF, RG75, NA.

55. Mitchell to Emmons, 7 June 1957, file 8542-1957-Seminole-224, BIACF, RG75, NA.

56. William Zimmerman Jr. to Fred A. Seaton, 17 July 1957; Roger Ernst to Zimmerman, 30 August 1957, file 884-1957-Seminole-349, BIACF, RG75, NA.

57. Mitchell to Smathers, 10 June 1957; Rex Lee to Smathers, 17 July 1957; Smathers to Mitchell, 19 July 1957, GASP; Lee to James A. Haley, 16 June 1957, file 8542-1957-Seminole-349, BIACF, RG75, NA.

58. Emmons to Mitchell, 25 July 1957, file 8542-1957-Seminole-224, BIACF, RG75, NA.

59. U.S. Department of the Interior Press Release, file 12058-1957-Seminole-077, BIACF, RG75, NA.

60. Bureau of Indians Affairs, *Constitution and Bylaws*, 11.

61. Bureau of Indians Affairs, *Corporate Charter*, 11.

62. Seminole Tribe, *Twentieth Anniversary*, 11.

4. THE LEAN YEARS, 1957–1971

1. Kenneth A. Marmon to Emmons, 24 September 1957, file 13671-1957-Seminole-055, BIACF, RG75, NA.

2. Quinn to Jenkins, 11 October 1957, file 14043-1957-Seminole-0543, BIACF, RG75, NA.

3. Council Resolution no. C-1-57, 30 September 1957, file 14671-1957-Seminole-101.1, BIACF, RG75, NA.

4. King, "Clan Affiliation," 145.

5. Quinn interview, 9.

6. Buswell, "Florida Seminole Religious Ritual," 383–84.

7. King, "Clan Affiliation," 139.

8. Charles Hudson, *The Southeastern Indians* (Knoxville: University of Tennessee Press, 1989), 184–201.

9. Kathryn E. Holland Braund, "Guardians of Tradition and Handmaidens to

Change: Women's Roles in Creek Economic and Social Life During the Eighteenth Century," *American Indian Quarterly* 14 (summer 1990): 243.

10. Virgil N. Harrington to Thomas M. Reid, 15 September 1959, file 13671-1957-Seminole-055, BIACF, RG75, NA.

11. Council Resolution no. C-39-59, 9 January 1959, file 00-1957-Seminole-054, BIACF, RG75, NA.

12. Council Resolution no. C-91-60, 6 May 1960, file 00-1957-Seminole-054, BIACF, RG75, NA.

13. Interview with Billy Osceola, 1 May 1973, SEM 89A, UFOHA, 12.

14. Council Resolution no. C-14-60, 6 July 1959, file 00-1957-Seminole-054, BIACF, RG75, NA.

15. Council Resolution no. C-26-62, 6 November 1962, file 3182-1962-054, part I, BIACF, RG75, WNRC.

16. Council Resolution no. C-55-59, 2 March 1959, file 00-1957-Seminole-054, BIACF, RG75, NA.

17. Tribal Council minutes, 2 July 1962, file 3182-1962-054, part I, BIACF, RG75, WNRC.

18. Pietrzak, "Seminole Tribal Government," 77–87.

19. Seminole Tribe, *Amended Constitution and Bylaws of the Seminole Tribe of Florida*, mimeographed (May 1991), amend. I, 1.

20. Seminole Tribe, *Amended Constitution and Bylaws*, amend., XIII.

21. Seminole Tribe, *Amended Corporate Charter of the Seminole Tribe of Florida*, mimeographed (May 1991), amends. I, III, V, VIII, 2, 5, 9.

22. Seminole Tribe, *Amended Corporate Charter*, amend. XII, 2.

23. Seminole Tribe, *Amended Corporate Charter*, amend. XII, 2.

24. Pietrzak, "Seminole Tribal Government," 81.

25. Seminole Tribe, *Amended Constitution and Bylaws*, amend. IX, 8.

26. Seminole Tribe, *Amended Constitution and Bylaws*, amend. IX, 8.

27. Seminole Tribe, *Amended Corporate Charter*, amend. V, 2.

28. Seminole Tribe, *Twentieth Anniversary*, 20.

29. Board Resolution no. BD-54-64, 13 December 1963, file 7333-1964-Seminole-054, BIACF, RG75, WNRC.

30. Council Resolution no. C-42-61, 6 March 1961, file 00-1957-Seminole-054, part 3, BIACF, RG75, NA.

31. Deloria and Lytle, *The Nations Within*, 196–97.

32. Seminole Tribe Annual Credit Report, 24 July 1967, file 291-1966-Seminole-031, BIACF, RG75, WNRC.

33. Bureau of Indian Affairs News Release, 15 March 1967, file 3306-1967-Seminole-259, BIACF, RG75, WNRC.

34. Bureau of Indian Affairs News Release, 15 March 1967.

35. Bureau of Indian Affairs Report, Amphenol Co., file 2180-1967-Seminole-920, BIACF, RG75, WNRC.
36. Kersey, "Economic Prospects of Florida's Seminole Indians," *Florida Planning and Development* 20 (December 1969): 2.
37. E. W. Barrett to U.S. Senate Subcommittee on Indian Education, 21 January 1969, quoted in Kersey, "Economic Prospects," 2.
38. Quinn interview, 24–26.
39. Quinn interview, 24–26.
40. Quinn interview, 24–26.
41. Merwyn S. Garbarino, *Big Cypress: A Changing Seminole Community* (New York: Holt, Rinehart and Winston, 1972), 114–25.
42. Garbarino, *Big Cypress*, 121.
43. Quinn interview, 6.
44. Garbarino, *Big Cypress*, 116.
45. Kersey, "Economic Prospects," 2.
46. Council Resolution no. c-36-60, 5 October 1959, file 00-1957-Seminole-054, BIACF, RG75, NA.
47. Council Resolution no. c-23-66, 21 March 1966, file 10045-1962-Seminole-054.3, BIACF, RG75, WNRC.
48. Tribal Council minutes, 6 August 1962, file 3182 — 1962-Seminole-054, part 1, BIACF, RG75, WNRC.
49. Quinn interview, 12–13.
50. *U.S. Statutes at Large* 82 (1968): 77.
51. *Florida Statutes Annotated* (1991), sect. 285.18.
52. Interview with Joe Dan Osceola, 4 October 1972, SEM 67A, UFOHA, 3.
53. Joe Dan Osceola interview, 4.
54. Deloria and Lytle, *The Nations Within*, 197.
55. Deloria and Lytle, *The Nations Within*, 197–98.

5. HOWARD TOMMIE'S LEGACY

1. August Burghard, *Watchie-Esta/Hutrie (Little White Mother)* (Fort Lauderdale FL: privately published, 1968), 48.
2. William C. Sturtevant, "A Seminole Personal Document," *Tequesta* 16 (1956): 58.
3. Harry A. Kersey Jr., "The Tony Tommie Letter, 1916: A Transitional Seminole Document," *Florida Historical Quarterly* 64 (April 1986): 301–14.
4. *St. Petersburg Daily News*, 15 February 1927, 5; Patsy West, "The Miami Indian Tourist Attractions: A History and Analysis of a Transitional Mikasuki Indian Environment," *Florida Anthropologist* 34 (December 1981): 200–224.

5. Seminole Tribe, *Twentieth Anniversary*, 16.

6. Philip S. Deloria, "The Era of Indian Self-Determination: An Overview," in *Indian Self-Rule*, ed. Philp, 202.

7. Deloria, "The Era of Indian Self-Determination," 197.

8. *U.S. Statutes at Large* 88 (1975): 2204.

9. Deloria and Lytle, *The Nations Within*, 220.

10. *Miami Herald*, 13 May 1975, 1BW.

11. *Miami Herald*, 13 May 1975, 1BW.

12. Council Resolution no. c-66-75, 14 March 1975, STF.

13. *Florida Statutes Annotated* (1991), sect. 285.17–18.

14. Council Resolution no. c-39-71, 13 November 1970, STF.

15. Seminole Tribe, *Twentieth Anniversary*, 18.

16. Minutes of Special Joint Council and Board Meeting, 7 June 1971 (Installation of Officers), STF.

17. Seminole Tribe of Florida and Seminole Tribe of Florida, Inc., budget FY-1971, STF.

18. Interview with Howard E. Tommie, 14 January 1988, SEM 60A, UFOHA, 1–2.

19. Tommie interview, 3.

20. Tommie interview, 3.

21. Tommie interview, 3–4.

22. Tommie interview, 3.

23. *Miami Herald*, 13 May 1975, 1BW.

24. *Miami Herald*, 13 May 1975, 1BW.

25. *Miami Herald*, 13 May 1975, 1BW.

26. *Palm Beach Post*, 15 May 1975, c3.

27. *Miami Herald*, 8 April 1979, 11–17.

28. *Vending Unlimited v State of Florida*, 364 So. 2d 5480 (1978).

29. *Confederated Tribes of Colville v State of Washington*, 446 F. Supp. 1339 (1978).

30. *Florida Statutes Annotated* (1985), sect. 210.05.

31. Minutes of Special Meeting of the Tribal Council, 16 October 1975, STF.

32. Council Resolution no. c-38-76, 16 October 1975, STF.

33. *Miami Herald*, 8 April 1979, 12.

34. *Miami Herald*, 8 April 1979, 13.

35. Council Resolution no. c-60-74, 11 January 1974, STF.

36. *Miami Herald*, 8 April 1979, 12.

37. *Miami Herald*, 8 April 1979, 12.

38. *Miami Herald*, 8 April 1979, 13–14.

39. Council Resolution no. c-82-79, 3 January 1979, STF.

40. Council Resolution no. c-84-79, 3 January 1979, STF.

41. Council Resolution no. c-81-79, 3 January 1979, STF.

42. *Miami Herald*, 8 April 1979, 14.

43. Council Resolution no. c-142-78 and Board Resolution BD-117-78, 6 June 1978, STF.

44. Tommie interview, 7–8.

45. Tommie interview, 8–9.

46. *Palm Beach Post*, 1 March 1982, 1–2; Council Resolution no. c-21-80, 24 August 1979, STF.

47. "Bingo is the Best Revenge," *Time*, 7 July 1980, 8.

48. Dale L. McDonnell, "Federal and State Regulation of Gambling and Liquor Sales Within Indian Country," *Hamline Law Review* 8 (October 1985): 606–7.

49. *Seminole Tribe of Florida v Robert Butterworth*, 491 F.Supp. 1020 (1980).

50. *Seminole Tribe of Florida v Robert Butterworth*, 658 F. 2d 310 (1981).

51. John Taylor, "Florida's Seminoles Have Only Just Begun to Fight," *Florida Trend* 28 (January 1986): 111.

52. Bureau of Indian Affairs, Seminole Tribe of Florida Revolving Credit Loan Retirement Plan, July 1979; typed copy available at the Seminole agency, Hollywood FL.

53. Tommie interview, 8.

54. Tommie interview, 10.

55. Tommie interview, 11.

56. Tommie interview, 11.

57. Tommie interview, 5–6.

6. THE SEMINOLE LAND CLAIMS CASE

1. *U.S. Statutes at Large* 104 (1990): 143; Kersey, "The Florida Seminole Land Claims Case, 1950–1990," *Florida Historical Quarterly* 62 (January 1993): 35–55.

2. *U.S. Statutes at Large* 101 (1987): 1556; Kersey, "The East Big Cypress Case, 1948–1987: Environmental Politics, Law and Florida Seminole Tribal Sovereignty," *Florida Historical Quarterly* 69 (April 1991): 457–77; Jim Shore and Jerry C. Straus, "The Seminole Water Rights Compact and the Seminole Indian Land Claims Settlement Act of 1987," *Journal of Land Use and Environmental Law* 6 (winter 1990): 1–24.

3. *U.S. Statutes at Large*, 60 (1946):1049.

4. Nancy Oestreich Lurie, "The Indian Claims Commission Act," *Annals of the American Academy of Political and Social Science* 311 (May 1957): 56–70; Margaret Hunter Pierce, "The Work of the Indian Claims Commission," *American Bar Association Journal* 63 (February 1977): 227–32.

5. Roger J. Waybright to Marmon, 20 January 1955, file 163-1955-Seminole-050, BIACF, RG75, NA.

6. Interview with Waybright, 25 September 1978, SEM 177A, UFOHA, 4.

7. Marmon to Commissioner of Indian Affairs, 26 July 1949, quoted in Senate Select Committee on Indian Affairs, *Distribution of Seminole Judgment Funds*, 95th Cong., 2d sess., 206; cited hereafter as *Distribution*.

8. Waybright to Marmon, 20 January 1955, file 163-1955-Seminole-050, BIACF, RG75, NA.

9. Waybright to Marmon, 28 February 1955, file 163-1955-Seminole-050, BIACF, RG75, NA.

10. *Distribution*, 243–47.

11. Waybright to Marmon, 7 December 1956, file 163-1955-Seminole-050, BIACF, RG75, NA.

12. Covington, "Trail Indians of Florida," 48–49.

13. Waybright interview, 13.

14. Waybright interview, 13.

15. Interview with Effie Knowles, 21 March 1978, SEM 75A, UFOHA; interview with Roy L. Struble, 18 August 1972, SEM 180A, UFOHA.

16. *Seminole Indians of the State of Florida v United States of America*, 23 Ind. Cl. Comm. 108 (1970).

17. *Seminole Nation of Oklahoma v United States of America*, 24 Ind. Cl. Comm. 1 (1970).

18. *Seminole Indians of the State of Florida v United States*, 455 F. 2d 539 (1972).

19. *Seminole Indians of the State of Florida and the Seminole Nation of Oklahoma v United States of America*, 38 Ind. Cl. Comm. 62 (1976).

20. *Seminole Indians of the State of Florida v United States*, 40 Ind. Cl. Comm. 107, 125 (1977).

21. *Seminole Indians of the State of Florida and the Seminole Nation of Oklahoma v United States of America*, 39 Ind. Cl. Comm. 167 (1976).

22. *Distribution*, 1–63.

23. Robert T. Coulter, "Seminole Land Rights in Florida and the Award of the Indian Claims Commission," in *Distribution*, 64–511.

24. *Seminole Tribe of Florida v Andrus*, no. 79-0994-Civ., U.S. District Court for the District of Columbia, 9 July 1979.

25. *Seminole Tribe of Florida v Andrus*, no. 78-0994-Civ., U.S. Court of Appeals for the District of Columbia, 9 July 1980.

26. *Congressional Record*, 100th Cong., 2d sess., 4 March 1988, 2048.

27. Senate, *A Bill to Provide for the Use and Distribution of Funds Awarded the Seminole Indians in Dockets 73, 151, and 73-A of the Indian Claims Commission*, 101st Cong., 1st sess., S. 1096 (1989).

28. James E. Billie to Sen. Daniel Inouye, 25 April 1988, HSDW.

29. Typed transcripts of testimony, HSDW.

30. "Statement of Mr. James Billie, Chairman, Tribal Council of the Seminole Tribe of Florida Before the House Committee on Interior and Insular Affairs on H.R. 2838 and H.R. 2650," typed manuscript, HSDW.

31. Senate, *Providing for the Use and Distribution of Funds Awarded the Seminole Indians in Dockets 73, 151, and 73-A of the Indian Claims Commission*, 101st Cong., 2d sess., S. Rpt. 101-212 (1990).

32. House, *Providing for the Use and Distribution of Funds Awarded the Seminole Indians in Dockets 73, 151, and 73-A of the Indian Claims Commission*, 101st Cong., 2d sess., H. Rpt. 101-399 (1990).

33. House, *Conference Report Providing for Use and Distribution of Seminole Award*, 101st Cong., 2d sess., H. Rpt. 101–439 (1990).

34. *U.S. Statutes at Large* 104 (1990):143.

7. THE EAST BIG CYPRESS CASE

1. Kersey, "The East Big Cypress Case," 457–77.

2. Executive Order no. 1379, 28 June 1911; Kersey, *Florida Seminoles and the New Deal*, 96.

3. *Florida Statutes Annotated* (1985), sect. 285.01, 205.02.

4. *U.S. Statutes at Large*, 48 (1934):816.

5. *Florida Statutes Annotated* (1985), sect. 285.06.

6. *Florida Statutes Annotated* (1985), sect. 285.061.

7. *U.S. Statutes at Large* 96 (1982):2012.

8. Prucha, *The Great Father*, vol. 2 (Lincoln: University of Nebraska Press, 1984), 1128–29.

9. Marmon to Commissioner of Indian Affairs, 28 December 1948, HSDW.

10. R. W. Pearson to Marmon, 16 February 1950, HSDW.

11. W. Turner Wallis to Holland, 30 January 1953; H. W. Schull to Smathers, 27 January 1953, HSDW.

12. Broward County Deed Records, book 704, 457.

13. Wallis to Holland, 30 January 1953, HSDW.

14. Wallis to Holland, 30 January 1953, HSDW.

15. Leland Black, Bureau of Indian Affairs, Seminole Tribe, "History of Involvement with the Central and South Florida Project," 4 February 1976, typescript, HSDW.

16. Oscar D. Rawls, "Meeting with Seminole Indian Association, Orlando, Fla., 24 November 54," 29 November 1954, typescript, HSDW.

17. Rawls, "Meeting with Seminole Indian Association."

18. Rawls, "Meeting with Seminole Indian Association."
19. Mitchell interview, 7.
20. Marmon to Wallis, 19 January 1955, HSDW.
21. *U.S. Statutes at Large* 48 (1934): 816.
22. *Seminole Tribe of Indians of Florida v State of Florida et al.*, complaint, case no. 74-4430, Circuit Court of the Seventeenth Judicial Circuit, Broward County, Florida, 1974.
23. *Seminole Tribe of Indians of Florida v State of Florida et al.*, complaint, case no. 78-6116-Civ-NCR, U.S. District Court for the Southern District of Florida (abbreviated hereafter as SDF), 17 March 1978.
24. Amended complaint, case no. 78-6116-Civ-NCR, SDF, 11 July 1978.
25. "Memorandum of Law in Support of Motion to Dismiss of State of Florida, Florida Board of Commissioners of State Institutions, Florida Board of Trustees of the Internal Improvement Trust Fund, and Florida Department of Natural Resources, Division of State Lands," case no. 78-6116-Civ-NCR, SDF, 30 March 1984.
26. Stay order, case no. 78-6116-Civ-NCR, SDF, 30 May 1984.
27. 53 *United States Law Week* 4225, 4 March 1985.
28. *Oneida Indian Nation of New York v State of New York*, 69 F. 2d 1070 (2d Cir. 1982).
29. "Plaintiff's Memorandum in Opposition to Defendant's Motions to Dismiss," case no. 78-6116-Civ-NCR, SDF, 5 April 1985, 5.
30. "Plaintiff's Memorandum of Law in Support of Motion for Partial Summary Judgment," case no. 78-6616-Civ-NCR, SDF, 4 April 1985, 19–20.
31. Gay M. Biery-Hamilton, "Draft Study of the 1987 Seminole Settlement" (1989), typescript, HSDW.
32. Telephone interview with Straus, 1 November 1990.
33. Interview with Shore, 20 November 1990, SEM 199A, UFOHA, 3.
34. Interview with Shore, 3.
35. Shore to Timer Powers, 29 July 1986, HSDW.
36. *Palm Beach Post*, 8 October 1986, 1C.
37. *Fort Lauderdale Sun Sentinel*, 11 September 1986, 1B.
38. *Palm Beach Post*, 6 October 1986, 1C.
39. *Palm Beach Post*, 6 October 1986, 1C.
40. Council Resolution no. C-01-88, 4 August 1987, STF.
41. Lloyd Burton, *American Indian Water Rights and the Limits of Law* (Lawrence: University Press of Kansas, 1991), 79–80.
42. Shore and Straus, "Seminole Water Rights Compact," 2.
43. 207 U.S. *Reports* 565, 573, 575–77.
44. Burton, *American Indian Water Rights*, 18–21.

45. Shore and Straus, "Seminole Water Rights Compact," 11–12.

46. "Water Rights Compact among the Seminole Tribe of Florida, the State of Florida, and the South Florida Water Management District," in *Seminole Land Claims Settlement Act; Hearings on S. 1684 before the Senate Select Committee on Indian Affairs, November 5, 1987*, 100th Cong., 1st sess. (1988), 83–122.

47. *Laws of Florida* (1987), chap. 87-292.

48. Settlement agreement, case no. 78-6116, Civ-NCR, SDF, 29 October 1987. The federal district court issued its approval order on 21 July 1988.

49. *U.S. Statutes at Large* 101 (1987):1556.

8. WHAT BECAME OF THE MICCOSUKEES?

1. Kersey, "The Miccosukees: Florida's Oldest 'New Tribe,'" *Forum: The Magazine of the Florida Humanities Council* (fall 1992): 18–24.

2. Harry A. Kersey Jr., "Seminoles and Miccosukees: A Century in Retrospective," in *Indians of the Southeastern United States in the Late 20th Century*, ed. J. Anthony Paredes (Tuscaloosa: University of Alabama Press, 1992), 102–19.

3. *Miami Daily News*, 24 July 1957, 6A.

4. Mikasuki General Council to Collins, 25 October 1956, file 10530-1955-Seminole-070, BIACF, RG75, NA; GASP, box 11, file 11G, 1957.

5. *Miami Herald*, 31 July 1957, 5A.

6. Covington, "Trail Indians of Florida," 49.

7. Emmons to Executive Council, Everglades Miccosukee Tribe of Indians, 27 January 1958, in 38 Ind. Cl. Comm. 94–95.

8. 19 Ind. Cl. Comm. 440.

9. Ed Williams, Deputy Solicitor, U.S. Department of the Interior, to Silver, 19 June 1961; *Distribution*, 413–14; GASP, box 30, file 11G, 1961.

10. *Miami Herald*, 31 July 1958, 6A.

11. *Distribution*, 406–7.

12. George J. Miller to Smathers, 26 October 1958, GASP, box 15, file 11G, 1958.

13. Emmons to Howard Osceola, 17 October 1958, GASP, box 15, file 11G, 1958.

14. Burt, *Tribalism in Crisis*, 122.

15. "Resume of notes taken at meeting held in Washington, D.C., November 17, 1958," file 2058-1957-Seminole-077, BIACF, RG75, NA.

16. La Verne Madigan, "A Most Independent People—A Field Report on Indians in Florida," *Indian Affairs* 37 (April 1959): 5.

17. Edmund Wilson, *Apologies to the Iroquois* (New York: Octagon Books, 1978), 270–72.

18. Hauptman, *The Iroquois Struggle for Survival: World War II to Red Power* (Syracuse NY: Syracuse University Press, 1986), 163.

19. *New York Times*, 12 April 1959, 25L.

20. Wilson, *Apologies*, 272.

21. Wilson, *Apologies*, 272.

22. *Miami Herald*, 29 July 1959, 6A.

23. *Miami Herald*, 4 August 1959, 5C.

24. *Miami Herald*, 4 August 1959, 5C.

25. *Florida Statutes Annotated* (1985), sec. 285. 14–15.

26. *Miami Herald*, 12 August 1959, 16A.

27. *Miami Herald*, 12 August 1959, 16A.

28. *Miami Herald*, 12 August 1959, 16A.

29. Ingraham Billie to Emmons, 19 December 1959, file 163-1955-Seminole-050, BIACF, RG75, NA.

30. "A Tale of Two Tribes," *Florida Times Union*, 3 June 1986, special supplement, 15.

31. Madigan, "U.S. and Florida Act on Miccosukee Lands," *Indian Affairs* 38 (October 1960): 1–2.

32. Senate Select Committee on Indian Affairs, *Hearings on S. 2893 to Settle Certain Land Claims within the State of Florida, and for Other Purposes*, 97th Cong., 2d sess. (1983), 92.

33. Quinn interview, 20.

34. Quinn interview, 20.

35. Bureau of Indian Affairs, *Constitution and Bylaws of the Miccosukee Tribe of Indians of Florida, Ratified December 17, 1961 with Amendments Adopted 1964 through 1977*, photocopy, 1.

36. Bureau of Indian Affairs, *Constitution and Bylaws of the Miccosukee Tribe*, 3.

37. Bureau of Indian Affairs, *Constitution and Bylaws of the Miccosukee Tribe*, 2.

38. Bureau of Indian Affairs, *Constitution and Bylaws of the Miccosukee Tribe*, 1.

39. Bureau of Indian Affairs, *Constitution and Bylaws of the Miccosukee Tribe*, 6.

40. Bureau of Indian Affairs, *Constitution and Bylaws of the Miccosukee Tribe*, 6.

41. John C. Carver to Reginald C. Miller, 11 January 1962, file 4374-1962-Micc.-054.3, BIACF, RG75, WNRC.

42. Use permit signed by Philleo Nash, Stuart Udall, and Director of the National Park Service, 24 January 1964, file 9435-1964-Micc.-980, BIACF, RG75, WNRC.

43. Reginald C. Miller to Commissioner of Indian Affairs, 10 January 1966, file 9157-1966-Micc.-905, BIACF, RG75, WNRC.

44. Harriet P. Lefley, "Effects of a Cultural Heritage Program on the Self-concept of Miccosukee Indian Children," *Journal of Educational Research* 67 (July–August 1974): 462–66.

45. Florida State Board of Health, "Health of Florida's Indians," *Florida Health Notes* 56 (December 1964): 216–17.

46. *Palm Beach Post-Times*, 8 December 1974, 4B.

47. *Florida Statutes Annotated* (1991), sec. 285. 17–18.

48. *Hearings on S. 2893*, 89.

49. *U.S. Statutes at Large* 96 (1982):2012.

50. *Florida Statutes Annotated* (1985), sec. 210.05.

51. John Dorschner, "The Great Indian Bingo War," *Miami Herald Tropic*, 31 October 1993, 12–21, 27.

52. *Tamiami Partners, Ltd. v Miccosukee Tribe*, no. 92-0489-Civ (SDF 1994).

53. *Broward Review*, 23 May 1988, 14.

54. *Broward Review*, 23 May 1988, 14.

55. Dorschner, "Bingo War," 27.

9. THE NEW SEMINOLE POLITY

1. Charles F. Wilkinson, "Indian Tribes and the American Constitution," in *Indians in American History*, ed. Hoxie, 119–21.

2. Wilkinson, *American Indians, Time, and the Law: Native Societies in a Modern Constitutional Democracy* (New Haven CT: Yale University Press, 1987), 54–55.

3. Prucha, *American Indian Policy in the Formative Years* (Lincoln: University of Nebraska Press, 1970), 43–44.

4. Prucha, *The Great Father*, 21–22.

5. Wilkinson, "Indian Tribes," 120.

6. Stephen Cornell, *The Return of the Native: American Indian Political Resurgence* (New York: Oxford University Press, 1988), 46.

7. John K. Mahon, *The Second Seminole War, 1835–1842* (Gainesville: University Presses of Florida, 1992), 325–26.

8. Covington, *The Seminoles of Florida*, 143; Covington, *The Billy Bowlegs War, 1855–1858: The Final Stand of the Seminoles Against the Whites* (Chuluota FL: Mickler House, 1981).

9. Arrell Morgan Gibson, "To Kill a Nation: Liquidation of the Five Indian Republics," in *The American Indian Experience, A Profile: 1524 to the Present*, ed. Philip Weeks (Arlington Heights IL: Forum Press, 1988), 189–203.

10. Robert M. Utley, "Wars of the Peace Policy, 1869–1886," in *Major Problems in American Indian History*, ed. Albert L. Hurtado and Peter Iverson (Lexington MA: D. C. Heath, 1994), 355–67; Thomas W. Dunlay, "Fire and Sword:

Ambiguity and the Plains War," in *The American Indian Experience*, ed. Weeks, 135–52.

11. Prucha, *American Indian Policy in Crisis*, 132–68.

12. Hoxie, "The Curious Story of Reformers and the American Indian," in *Indians in American History*, ed. Hoxie, 219; Hoxie, *A Final Promise: The Campaign to Assimilate the Indians, 1880–1920* (New York: Cambridge University Press, 1989).

13. Kersey, *Florida Seminoles and the New Deal*, 56–73.

14. Kersey, "Private Societies and the Maintenance of Seminole Tribal Integrity, 1899–1957," *Florida Historical Quarterly* 56 (January 1978): 297–316.

15. Kersey, "The East Big Cypress Case," 457–77.

16. Deloria and Lytle, *The Nations Within*, 172; Graham D. Taylor, *The New Deal and American Indian Tribalism* (Lincoln: University of Nebraska Press, 1980), 30–38.

17. Deloria and Lytle, *The Nations Within*, 158–59.

18. Felix S. Cohen, *Handbook of Federal Indian Law* (Albuquerque: University of New Mexico Press, 1971), 122.

19. Kersey, "A New Red Atlantis," 131–51.

20. Gene Stirling, U.S. Department of the Interior, Office of Indian Affairs, Applied Anthropology Unit, *Report on the Seminole Indians of Florida*, mimeographed doc. 126567 (1936).

21. Sturtevant, "The Medicine Bundles and Busks of the Florida Seminole," *Florida Anthropologist* 7 (May 1954): 30–71; Louis Capron, "The Medicine Bundles of the Florida Seminole and the Green Corn Dance," *Bureau of American Ethnology Bulletin* 151 (December 1953): 155–210.

22. Kersey, *Florida Seminoles and the New Deal*, 131–51; see also Kersey, "Educating the Seminole Indians of Florida, 1879–1970," *Florida Historical Quarterly* 49 (July 1970): 16–35; Kersey, "The Ahfachkee Day School," *Teachers College Record* 77 (September 1970): 93–104.

23. Freeman, "Culture Stability and Change," 251.

24. Garbarino, *Big Cypress*, 105–11.

25. King, "Clan Affiliation," 146.

26. Garbarino, *Big Cypress*, 66.

27. Braund, "Guardians of Tradition," 242; Brent Richards Weisman, *Like Beads on a String: A Culture History of the Seminole Indians in North Peninsular Florida* (Tuscaloosa: University of Alabama Press, 1989), 36–38.

28. Harry A. Kersey Jr. and Helen M. Bannan, "Patchwork and Politics: The Evolving Roles of Florida Seminole Women in the Twentieth Century," in *Negotiators of Change: Historical Perspectives on Native American Women*, ed. Nancy Shoemaker (New York: Routledge, 1995), 193–212.

29. Harry A. Kersey Jr., "Laura Mae Osceola," in *Native American Women: A Biographical Dictionary*, ed. Gretchen M. Bataille (New York: Garland, 1993), 191–92.

30. Kersey, "Betty Mae Jumper," in *Native American Women*, ed. Bataille, 131–32.

31. Lefley, "Acculturation, Child Rearing, and Self-Esteem in Two North American Indian Tribes," *Ethos* 4 (1976): 385–401; Lefley, "Effects of a Cultural Heritage Program," 462–66.

32. Florida Governor's Council on Indian Affairs, Inc., *Annual Report, 1991–1992* (Tallahassee, 1992), 12.

33. Florida Governor's Council, *Annual Report*, 5.

34. Cornell, *The Return of the Native*, 106–27.

35. Cornell, *The Return of the Native*, 107.

36. Cornell, *The Return of the Native*, 126.

37. Dorschner, "Bury My Heart on Custer Street," *Miami Herald Tropic*, 8 April 1979, 11.

38. Information on United South and Eastern Tribes, Inc., provided in correspondence with Michael D. Tiger, Deputy Director of Nashville Area Indian Health Service, 30 June 1993.

39. John H. Peterson Jr., "Choctaw Self-Determination in the 1980s," in *Indians of the Southeastern United States*, ed. Paredes, 144.

40. Kersey, "Betty Mae Jumper," 131–32.

41. Seminole Tribe, *Twentieth Anniversary*, 15–17.

42. State of Florida, executive order 74-23, 10 April 1974.

43. Personal observation of the author, who served as a member of the Florida Governor's Council on Indian Affairs during the period 1978–88.

EPILOGUE

1. Hoxie, "The Problems of Indian History," in *Major Problems in American Indian History*, ed. Hurtado and Iverson, 41.

Bibliographical Essay

Recent major interpretations of the American Indian experience during World War II and the immediate postwar period include Alison R. Bernstein, *American Indians and World War II: Toward a New Era in Indian Affairs* (Norman OK, 1991); Larry W. Burt, *Tribalism in Crisis: Federal Indian Policy, 1953–1961* (Albuquerque NM, 1982); Vine Deloria Jr. and Clifford Lytle, *The Nations Within, The Past and Future of American Indian Sovereignty* (New York, 1984); Richard Drinnon, *Keeper of the Concentration Camps: Dillon S. Myer and American Racism* (Berkeley CA, 1987); Donald L. Fixico, *Termination and Relocation: Federal Indian Policy, 1945–1960* (Albuquerque NM, 1986); Laurence M. Hauptman, *The Iroquois Struggle for Survival: World War II to Red Power* (Syracuse NY, 1986); Kenneth R. Philp, ed., *Indian Self-Rule: First-Hand Accounts of Indian-White Relations from Roosevelt to Reagan* (Salt Lake City, 1986); and Lyman S. Tyler, *A History of Indian Policy* (Washington DC, 1973). A special issue of *The Annals of the American Academy of Political and Social Science*, (no. 311, May 1957) contains articles by leading figures on both sides of the termination issue. The changing liberal views on Indian policy during the Truman administration are the subject of Clayton R. Koppes, "From New Deal to Termination: Liberalism and Indian Policy, 1933–1953," *Pacific Historical Review* 46 (November 1977).

Following the war years, conservatives in Congress moved swiftly to dismantle Indian policies formulated during the New Deal. To understand the broader implications of the Indian Reorganization Act for the formulation of Indian policy see Graham D. Taylor, *The New Deal and American Indian Tribalism* (Lincoln NE, 1980), and Kenneth R. Philp, *John Collier's Crusade for Indian Reform, 1920–1954* (Tucson AZ, 1977). Philp's is the definitive study of John Collier's work as both a reformer and as the Commissioner of Indian Affairs. A recap of the largest Indian New Deal program for the reservations is found in D. E. Murphy, "Final Report of the Indian Emergency Conservation Work and Civilian Conservation Corps-Indian Division Program, 1933–1942," typescript (Chicago, 1942). Three useful works that demonstrate the great variability in tribal responses to the Indian New Deal are Donald L. Parman, *The Navajos and the New Deal* (New Haven CT, 1976); Laurence M. Hauptman, *The Iroquois and the New Deal* (Syracuse NY, 1981); and Harry A. Kersey Jr., *The Seminoles and the New Deal, 1933–1942* (Gainesville FL, 1989).

A small number of scholars has explored the history of political organization among the twentieth-century Florida Seminoles. This group includes two unpublished studies: Brian W. Pietrzak, "Seminole Tribal Government: The Formative Years, 1957–1982" (master's thesis, Florida Atlantic University, 1982); and Robert T. King, "The Florida Seminole Polity, 1858–1978 (Ph.D. diss., University of Florida, 1978). An intriguing argument for tribal political leadership based on clan membership is presented in Robert T. King, "Clan Affiliation and Leadership Among the Twentieth-Century Florida Indians," *Florida Historical Quarterly* 55 (October 1976). Merwyn S. Garbarino, *Big Cypress: A Changing Seminole Community* (New York, 1972) examines the relationship between the emergence of a tribal cattle program and the development of political leadership during the 1960s. A more general description of Seminole and Miccosukee tribal governments is found in James W. Covington, *The Seminoles of Florida* (Gainesville FL, 1993).

Tightly focused studies of Seminole social organization have been provided by ethnologists who worked in Florida during the 1940s and 1950s. These include Ethel Cutler Freeman, "Cultural Stability and Change Among the Seminoles of Florida" in *Men and Cultures: Selected Papers*, ed. Anthony F. C. Wallace (Philadelphia, 1960); William C. Sturtevant, "The Medicine Bundles and Busks of the Florida Seminole," *Florida Anthropologist* 7 (May 1954); and Louis Capron, "The Medicine Bundles of the Florida Seminole and the Green Corn Dance," *Bureau of American Ethnology Bulletin* 151 (December 1953). James O. Buswell III, "Florida Seminole Religious Ritual: Resistance and Change," (Ph.D. diss., St. Louis University, 1972) offers a comprehensive analysis of changing Seminole religious practices and their impact on tribal sociopolitical structure at midcentury.

The emergence of modern tribal government provided new opportunities for Seminole women to engage in politics and assume formal leadership positions. This was not consistent with the historical gender roles of women in the Creek culture as described by Charles Hudson, *The Southeastern Indians* (Knoxville TN, 1989), and Kathryn E. Holland Braund, "Guardians of Tradition and Handmaidens to Change: Women's Roles in Creek Economic and Social Life During the Eighteenth Century," *American Indian Quarterly* 14 (summer 1990). Creek cultural continuity among Seminole women is also explored in Brent Richards Weisman, *Like Beads on a String: A Culture History of the Seminole Indians in North Peninsular Florida* (Tuscaloosa AL, 1989). A glimpse of the informal leadership roles played by Seminole women in the period prior to tribal organization is the subject of Ethel Cutler Freeman, "The Seminole Woman of the Big Cypress and Her Influence in Modern Life," *American Indigena* 5 (1944); and Patsy West, "The Miami Indian Tourist Attractions: A History and Analysis of a Transitional Mikasuki Indian Environment," *Florida Anthropologist* 34 (December 1981). The most comprehensive treatment of gender roles among contemporary Seminole women is found in Harry A. Kersey Jr. and Helen M. Bannan, "Patchwork and Politics: The Evolving Roles of Florida Seminole Women in the Twentieth Century," in *Negotiators of Change: Historical Perspectives on Native American Women*, ed. Nancy Shoemaker (New York, 1995). Sketches of individual Seminole female leaders are available in Harry A. Kersey Jr., "Laura Mae Osceola" and "Betty Mae Jumper," in *Native American Women: A Biographical Dictionary*, ed. Gretchen M. Bataille (New York, 1993). Former tribal chairman Betty Mae Jumper has published her own memoir, *. . . and with the Wagon Came God's Word* (Hollywood FL, 1988).

Non-Indian individuals and organizations played a major role in helping the Seminoles fend off termination and lent support to their new tribal government. The contributions of Ivy Stranahan are highlighted in Harry A. Kersey Jr. and Rochelle Kushin, "Ivy Stranahan and the 'Friends of the Seminoles,' 1899–1971," *Broward Legacy* 1

(October 1976), while the activities of Robert Mitchell and the Seminole Indian Association is featured in Kersey, "Private Societies and the Maintenance of Tribal Integrity, 1899–1957," *Florida Historical Quarterly* 56 (January 1978). Personal correspondence and records contain valuable data on this period. The most accessible are the Stranahan Collection, at the Fort Lauderdale Historical Society, the George A. Smathers Papers, at the University of Florida, and the James A. Haley Papers, at Florida Southern College. In addition, the University of Florida Oral History Archives contains interviews with many individuals mentioned in these collections.

There are a number of works dealing with the concept of American Indian political and legal sovereignty. The most relevant to this study were Lloyd Burton, *American Indian Water Rights and the Limits of Law* (Lawrence KS, 1991); Felix S. Cohen, *Handbook of Federal Indian Law* (Albuquerque NM, 1971); Charles F. Wilkinson, "Indian Tribes and the American Constitution," in *Indians in American History*, ed. Fred E. Hoxie (Arlington Heights IL, 1988); John R. Wunder *Retained by the People: A History of American Indians and the Bill of Rights* (New York, 1994); Francis Paul Prucha, *American Indian Policy in the Formative Years* (Lincoln NE, 1970); Prucha, *The Great Father: The United States Government and the American Indians* (Lincoln NE, 1984); Prucha, *American Indian Policy in Crisis: Christian Reformers and the Indian, 1865–1900* (Norman OK, 1976).

To place the Florida Seminoles in the context of modern tribalism at both the regional and national levels, the most useful sources are: J. Anthony Paredes, ed., *Indians of the Southeastern United States in the Late Twentieth Century* (Tuscaloosa AL, 1992); Walter L. Williams, ed., *Southeastern Indians Since the Removal Era* (Athens GA, 1979); Charles F. Wilkinson, *American Indians, Time, and the Law: Native Societies in a Modern Constitutional Democracy* (New Haven CT, 1987); and Stephen Cornell, *The Return of the Native: American Indian Political Resurgence* (New York, 1988).

Several studies have examined the exercise of Seminole tribal sovereignty in the context of their land claims and water rights cases. An extensive analysis of the Seminole case before the Indian Claims Commission is found in Harry A. Kersey Jr., "The Florida Seminole Land Claims Case, 1950–1990," *Florida Historical Quarterly*,

62 (January 1993). The history of efforts to secure Seminole water rights in Florida is set forth in Kersey, "The East Big Cypress Case, 1948–1987: Environmental Politics, Law and Florida Seminole Tribal Sovereignty," *Florida Historical Quarterly* 69 (April 1991). Seminole tribal attorneys provide a legal interpretation of the case and its broader implications for American Indian water policy in Jim Shore and Jerry C. Straus, "The Seminole Water Rights Compact and the Seminole Indian Land Claims Settlement Act of 1987," *Journal of Land Use and Environmental Law* 6 (winter 1990).

Few issues in modern Seminole life have generated more controversy than the introduction of state tax-free cigarette sales and unregulated high-stakes bingo games. Both have been challenged in federal courts and upheld as an affirmation of limited tribal sovereignty. For background on the gaming issue, see Allen C. Turner, "Evolution, Assimilation, and State Control of Gambling in Indian Country: Is *Cabazon v California* an Assimilationist Wolf in Preemption Clothing?" *Idaho Law Review* 24 (1987–88); and Dale C. McDonnell, "Federal and State Regulation of Gambling and Liquor Sales within Indian Country," *Hamline Law Review* 8 (October 1985). The court cases related to cigarette sales and bingo are discussed in Harry A. Kersey Jr., "Seminoles and Miccosukees: A Century in Retrospective," in *Indians of the Southeastern United States in the Late Twentieth Century*, ed. J. Anthony Paredes (Tuscaloosa AL, 1992). Two feature articles in the *Miami Herald* explore the impact of cigarette sales and bingo on Seminole and Miccosukee communities: John Dorschner, "The Great Indian Bingo War," *Miami Herald Tropic*, 31 October 1993; and Dorschner, "Bury My Heart on Custer Street," *Miami Herald Tropic*, 8 April 1979. A brief overview of Seminole business ventures during the Great Society era is found in Kersey, "Economic Prospects of Florida's Seminole Indians," *Florida Planning and Development* 20 (December 1969).

Several authors have dealt with the social and political evolution of the Miccosukee tribe. One of the first to do so was James W. Covington, in "Trail Indians of Florida," *Florida Historical Quarterly* 58 (July 1979). Covington expanded this work in his *The Florida Seminoles* (Gainesville FL, 1993). Another perspective on the Miccosukees is found in Harry A. Kersey Jr., "The Miccosukees: Florida's Oldest

'New Tribe,'" *Forum: The Magazine of the Florida Humanities Council* (fall 1992); and Kersey, "Seminoles and Miccosukees: A Century in Retrospective," in *Indians of the Southeastern United States in the Late Twentieth Century*, ed. J. Anthony Paredes (Tuscaloosa AL, 1992). The Association on American Indian Affairs became involved in Miccosukee political affairs during this period, primarily through its executive director, La Verne Madigan, and the Seminole Indian Association, which was an AAIA affiliate. Madigan made several trips to Florida and engaged in extensive correspondence with state and national officials, first pursuing the Miccosukee land claims, then pushing for federal recognition of the tribe. Reports on these activities are found in La Verne Madigan, "A Most Independent People — A Field Report on Indians in Florida," *Indian Affairs* 37 (April 1959); and "U. S. and Florida Act on Miccosukee Lands," *Indian Affairs* 38 (October 1960). Fidel Castro's recognition of the Miccosukees is documented in Edmund Wilson, *Apologies to the Iroquois* (New York, 1978).

There was little written about Seminole education and health issues prior to the 1970s, when a number of research studies appeared. Among the most useful are Harriet P. Lefley, "Acculturation, Child Rearing, and Self-Esteem in Two North American Indian Tribes," *Ethos* 4 (1976); and Lefley, "Effects of a Cultural Heritage Program on the Self-Concept of Miccosukee Indian Children," *Journal of Educational Research* 67 (July–August 1974); Harry A. Kersey Jr., "The Ahfachkee Day School," *Teachers College Record* 77 (September 1970); and Kersey, "Educating the Seminole Indians of Florida, 1879–1970," *Florida Historical Quarterly* 49 (July 1970). The only general assessment of Indian health problems in the 1960s is Florida State Board of Health, "Health of Florida's Indians," *Florida Health Notes* 56 (December 1964).

All government documents relating to the Seminole tribe are available through any library that is a U.S. Government Documents repository. The most extensively used archival resource was the Bureau of Indian Affairs Central Office files, record group 75. Florida Seminole files for the period 1945–61 are located at the National Archives, Washington DC, while Seminole and Miccosukee records from 1961–79 are located at the Washington National Records Center, in Suitland, Maryland. Since the 1970s both Seminole and

Miccosukee governments have retained copies of most files at the local level. The Seminole Tribal Council, by special resolution, allowed the author access to council and board of directors meetings minutes and resolutions which provide a day-by-day account of tribal government activities. Two essential documents provided by the tribe are Seminole Tribe of Florida, *Amended Constitution and Bylaws of the Seminole Tribe of Florida*, mimeographed (May 1991); and Seminole Tribe of Florida, *Amended Corporate Charter of the Seminole Tribe of Florida*, mimeographed (May 1991). These documents update the original 1957 constitution and corporate charter.

The research for this book is heavily grounded in oral history accounts provided by Seminole and Miccosukee tribal members, elected state and federal officials, government bureaucrats, and private citizens who supported the Seminole and Miccosukee tribes. All taped interviews utilized by the author are available for scholarly research at the University of Florida Oral History Archives, in Gainesville.

Index

Abbey, O. H., 32
adult education programs, 54–55, 113
Ahfachkee Day School, 113, 130–31
Alcatraz, seizure of, 218
Alligator Alley, 191, 194
Alpert, Leo, 43, 48
American Civil Liberties Union, 140
American Indian Defense Association, 2
American Indian Federation, 6
American Indian Movement (AIM), 107, 217
American Indians: and Christian reform movement, 205, 218; Eisenhower administration policies toward, 79; exodus from reservations, 4–5, 9; impact of World War II on, 5; and Marshall Trilogy, 202–4; rebuilding land base of, 2, 3–4; and relocation policies, 204–5; and U.S. Constitution, 201–2; U.S. government policy toward, before World War II, 2–3; U.S. government policy toward, during World War II, 1–6. See also assimilation policy; Collier, John; Florida Seminoles; Seminole self-government; Seminole tribal sovereignty; termination policy.
Amphenol Corporation, 96–97
Anderson, Clinton, 24
Anderson, Wallace "Mad Bear," 181–82
Antonucci, Joseph, 95
arts and crafts, 52–53, 98–99
Askew, Reubin, 221
assimilation policy, 2, 3, 6; and Christian

reformers, 205, 206; and Hoover Commission, 8; Myer's view of, 9. *See also* termination policy
Association on American Indian Affairs (AAIA), 34, 76; and Miccosukee land claim, 181, 184, 185
assumption, definitions of, 201

Bartlett, Dewey, 145
Bedell, Harriet, 73
Bellmon, Henry, 145
Berry, E. Y., 24, 27, 29, 31
Big Cypress Reservation, 14, 17, 31, 177; agricultural leases on, 93; Ahfachkee Day School on, 113, 130–31; arts and crafts factory on, 98; communal cattle enterprise on, 15; governing body of, 136; Miccosukee Baptists on, 212; as Miccosukee enclave, 19; oil and gas exploration on, 93, 96; origins of, 154; social orientation on, 211. *See also* East Big Cypress case
Billie, Frank, 51, 60, 81, 82–83, 161
Billie, Ingraham, 34, 47, 54, 177–78, 184, 210; applies for tribal membership, 103; and dismissal of Morton Silver, 57
Billie, James, 127, 149, 150, 167, 224; on government training programs, 123; and Seminole land claims case, 147, 148
Billie, Jimmie, 71
Billie, Josie, 137, 212
Billie, Sonny, 189, 198
Billy, Joseph, 30

255

In the *Indians of the Southeast* series

William Bartram
on the Southeastern Indians
Edited and annotated by
Gregory A. Waselkov and
Kathryn E. Holland Braund

Deerskins and Duffels:
The Creek Indian Trade with
Anglo-America, 1685–1815
By Kathryn E. Holland Braund

Cherokee Americans:
The Eastern Band of Cherokees
in the Twentieth Century
By John R. Finger

Choctaw Genesis 1500–1700
By Patricia Galloway

The Southeastern
Ceremonial Complex: Artifacts
and Analysis
The Cottonlandia Conference
Edited by Patricia Galloway
Exhibition catalog
by David H. Dye and
Camille Wharey

An Assumption of
Sovereignty: Social and Political
Transformation among the
Florida Seminoles, 1953–1979
By Harry A. Kersey Jr.

*The Cherokees: A Population
History*
By Russell Thornton

*Powhatan's Mantle:
Indians in the Colonial Southeast*
Edited by Peter H. Wood,
Gregory A. Waselkov,
and M. Thomas Hatley

*Creeks and Seminoles: The
Destruction and Regeneration
of the Muscogulge People*
By J. Leitch Wright Jr.